In this work Dr. Christopher Klofft displays for us a love story — that between God and humanity. With the deft strokes of an artist he paints the contours of this story in colors both warm and vivid. Klofft describes the basic parameters of the moral life as understood by the Catholic tradition and then moves easily into the vexing areas of life issues, sexuality, medicine, and of social and political ethics. Throughout this work Klofft never loses sight of the centrality of love in the tableaux of the Christian life. Written with a lucidity that makes it accessible to the beginner and yet the nuance that separates it from mere popularization, this is an attractive text for introductory courses in moral theology for both college-level and adult-ed courses.

John S. Grabowski, Ph.D.
Associate Professor and Director of Moral Theology/Ethics
School of Theology and Religious Studies
The Catholic University of America, Washington, DC

Christopher P. Klofft has provided those interested in the study of Catholic moral theology with a fine and complete introduction to the fundamental themes of this theological discipline. In a popular style, Klofft provides a presentation of Catholic morality that is reflective of the basic truth of Christianity that we are saved not by knowledge but by love. Professor Klofft rightly views the living out of morality that is, "new life in Christ," as a means of promoting the new evangelization. His emphasis that Catholic morality in the modern world receives its transformative power through the sacred liturgy is theologically and pastorally crucial. It is in and through the Eucharist that the moral agent personally encounters Jesus Christ who is the Way and the Truth and the Life. *Living the Love Story: Catholic Morality in the Modern World* is a most welcome addition to the growing contribution of Catholic lay theologians to the development of the Catholic moral tradition.

Most Reverend Robert J. McManus, STD
Bishop of Worcester

LIVING THE LOVE STORY

Living the Love Story

Catholic Morality in the Modern World

Christopher P. Klofft, STD

In accord with Canon 823 §1 of the Code of Canon Law, I hereby grant my approval to publish *Living the Love Story: Catholic Morality in the Modern World* by Christopher P. Klofft, STD

Most Revered Robert J. McManus, STD
Bishop of Worcester
Diocese of Worcester
May 22, 2008

Library of Congress Cataloging-in-Publication Data

Klofft, Christopher P.
Living the love story: Catholic morality in the modern world / Christopher P. Klofft.
p. cm.
ISBN-13: 978-0-8189-1263-4
ISBN-10: 0-8189-1263-4
1. Christian ethics—Catholic authors. 2. Love—Religious aspects—Catholic Church. I. Title.

BJ1249.K56 2008
241'.042—dc22

2007051834

Produced and designed in the United States of America by the Fathers and Brothers of the Society of St. Paul,
2187 Victory Boulevard, Staten Island, New York 10314-6603
as part of their communications apostolate.

ISBN-10: 0-8189-1263-4
ISBN-13: 978-0-8189-1263-4

Printing Information:

Current Printing - first digit	1	2	3	4	5	6	7	8	9	10

Year of Current Printing - first year shown

2008 2009 2010 2011 2012 2013 2014 2015 2016 2017

Dedicated to

Fr. Michael Bercik, OFM,

and to the members of St. Ann's Parish in Marlborough,

whose love of Christ and His Church

inspired the questions that led to this book.

Acknowledgments

I would like to extend my thanks to all those who helped with their prayers, support, and expertise in the writing of this project. Special thanks are due to Brother Antonio Antonucci, OSB, whose editorial support, theological acumen, and spiritual insight made this book far better than it would have been otherwise. I am also especially indebted to my wife Bridget, who constantly challenged me to make this text both more thorough and at the same time more accessible. Her love and support encourage me, not just in my writing, but in so many ways every day of my life. I have learned much about living the love story by living it with her. I must also thank my parents for all of their support throughout the years, and my family for their prayers and encouragement. Finally, I must thank the members of St. Ann's Parish, the members of the Jerusalem Covenant, and all those who have asked me questions along the way. I am deeply indebted to you all for your friendship and support.

Table of Contents

Introduction

Everybody loves a good love story. Maybe not everyone would admit to that, but there's something about the power of love to triumph over adversity and win the day that speaks to everyone on some level, even though we might not appreciate the excessively saccharine ways in which such stories are often presented. Based on life experiences, most people object to empty sentimentalism, romanticism that is merely in love with love itself, and idealistic characters that never really face difficulties. After all, some of us live in the real world.

But that doesn't minimize the power of the love story. In the best of such stories, protagonists triumph against truly horrific odds, braving even death in order to be with the beloved. Sometimes these stories end tragically. But even the happy endings are never easily won, and the sad final curtain still fosters a glimmer of hope that the struggle for love itself was worth the fight.

What is it about these kinds of stories that speak so effectively to the human psyche? Perhaps it's because people want to love and be loved. Perhaps it's because people know, or at least believe with all their hearts, that there are some things worth fighting for, some things even worth dying for. This struggle in the name of love seems to find its way into everyone's lives in one form or another.

When people experience love, love so strong that it transforms their lives such that they can never look at things the same way again, they inevitably wish to share their stories.

This is not to trumpet their own "success" at love, but simply to share the joy of that story, not only of love's power, but the ways in which love is made manifest in their lives, how every thing they do is different on account of that love. Their hearers may indeed come closer to experiencing the power of love in their own lives as well.

That brings us to this book. These reflections on love have everything to do with moral theology and evangelization. The Holy Spirit is the love that binds the Holy Trinity together in Christian understanding, so that Scripture says without hesitation, "God is love."[1]

That same mighty Spirit is vitally active in the life of the Church, in fact in every individual believer. The Holy Spirit is the love between the Father and the Son, the loving creative energy of all living things, the love of Christ for His Church, the love of God for His covenant people. The Author of the greatest love story is the Author of human life itself: the whole point of human existence is that we are called into a love relationship with God. The way that His love transforms our lives necessarily affects how we live. As our lives reflect God's love, we are called to share that love with others. This is the link between morality and evangelization, a connection made explicit by Pope John Paul II when he wrote, "*Evangelization... also involves the proclamation and presentation of morality...* the new evangelization will show its authenticity and unleash all its missionary force when it is carried out through the gift not only of the word proclaimed but also of the word lived."[2] Therefore, Catholic integrity demands that we concentrate not only on learning the truths of the faith, but also on living those truths out in our everyday lives.

Here, though, is where one encounters a problem. Over the past 40 years, the Church has wisely been concerned with the problem of atheism.[3] And, in the Western cultural climate of 40

---

[1] See 1 Jn 4:8. Of course, for an extended reflection on this, see also Pope Benedict XVI's *Deus Caritas Est.*

[2] *Veritatis Splendor* 107. Emphasis in original.

years ago, with the fear of the spread of atheistic communism and rapid changes in popular culture, atheism seemed to be on the rise. This problem remains in Europe. Despite the profound Christian cultural heritage of these countries, belief is under constant attack and so too fundamental moral values, in theory and lifestyle, have been undermined. The Church's serious concern for atheism in this part of the world wisely remains.

As we turn to the rest of the world, the picture is often much different. Expanding beyond the borders of the so-called "First World," one often finds extraordinary faith and devotion among the peoples of South America, Africa, and parts of Asia. Along with this faith is the corresponding moral perspective espoused by Christianity: the people live as they believe.[4] Then we come to the curious example of the United States of America. In the US, the majority of people do in fact profess some sort of belief in God. Most of these believers would even go so far as to profess some sort of belief in Christianity. While various cultural forces which negate these beliefs would protest, it is not inappropriate to label the United States as an avowedly "Christian nation." In this way, the United States stands apart from much of the developed West. Therefore, as a Christian nation, we should expect the moral lives of Americans to be evident on account of their Christian beliefs.

Obviously, we know this is not the case. America is a nation that is quick to defend some values while minimizing others, leading to a paradox between the values we profess and the values we express by our culture.[5] Some would claim that the export of America's popular culture is a form of "cultural impe-

---

[3] See *Gaudium et Spes* 19-21.

[4] This book concentrates, for the most part, on the developed West. For an extensive treatment of this phenomenon elsewhere in the world, and its possible meaning for the future of Christianity, see Philip Jenkins, *The Next Christendom: The Coming of Global Christianity* (Oxford: Oxford University Press, 2002).

[5] A detailed presentation of this experience specifically in terms of American Catholicism and Catholic sexual ethics can be found in John S. Grabowski, *Sex and Virtue: An Introduction to Sexual Ethics* (Washington, DC: The Catholic University of America Press, 2003), 1-22.

rialism" that ultimately has an adverse effect on the morality of other nations. Thus, we can arrive at the conclusion that many Americans, including many American Catholics, profess one set of beliefs, but do not generally live according to those beliefs. How can this be? How can a "Christian nation" not demonstrate consistent Christian values among its citizens?

The answer to these questions, indeed, lies in the disconnection between belief and lived action, but even more fundamentally by an impoverishment of the beliefs that are authentically Christian. After all, no one has a problem with the "happy" beliefs of Christianity. Everyone likes to imagine a joyous Jesus, with perfect hair, a well-trimmed beard on his soft, gentle face, laughing as he scoops up a child in his arms, with a rainbow in the background.[6] People like to make a distinction between the "angry, judgmental" God of the Old Testament, and the "loving, forgiving" God of the New Testament, as if Jews and Christians actually worshiped two different gods, or that the nature of God Himself somehow changed with Jesus. This dichotomy is as old as Christianity. Everybody wants to believe in Heaven and an eternal life of joy and happiness, but no one wants to believe in judgment or the prospect of Hell, with possible exceptions made for "really bad people," like Hitler or Stalin, but in any case, for "someone else, not me." People want to believe in a God that forgives all of our mistakes with a nod and a wink because, after all, "we're only human." The reader can certainly confirm these examples and cite countless others, but the point is clear: many, many people profess a belief in Christianity, but the state of our world and our society prove that they do not understand just what Christianity is.

This is not to say that Christianity is the dismal opposite of

[6] American Catholicism suffers from these images in large part due to an oversentimentalization of Christianity in the 1970s, as a misreading of the "spirit of Vatican II," equating it too readily with the spirit of the American '70s instead. Generations of CCD students from that time period forward have received this version of Catholicism as their catechesis.

this positive vision. Christianity *is* about joy; it *is* about an eternal life of happiness begun here on earth; it *is* about a loving, forgiving God. We *need* joy and happiness and love and forgiveness. Left to our own choices, we will *not* experience these things in their fullness, but only comfortable illusions mimicking them. God provides these experiences, but there is only one doorway to access them: Jesus Christ,[7] our way, truth, and life,[8] and His Cross. We experience joy and happiness in abundance because of Christ's Cross and His victory over sin and death, if we accept the responsibilities that the Cross demands of us. But at this point, I'm getting far ahead of myself.

For now, it is enough to agree that there needs to be a connection between what we believe and how we live. This is not necessary solely for our own personal, individual sincerity. Everyone wants to live in a better world. Most people believe that a better world is at least hypothetically possible. Christianity actually promises us a better world *and* gives us the way to "restore all things in Christ."[9] The connection between Christian belief and Christian morality will lead to nothing less than the transformation of the whole world. So what are we, as Catholic Christians, going to *do* to actually make that restoration take root?

No one would deny that this involves a change in behavior for most of us. We must stop imagining that our lackluster participation in the Mass and our generic effort to be "nice" to others (at least as long as they are "nice" to us) constitutes a vibrant, authentic Christianity. We must stop believing that our half-hearted attempt to remember rote prayers without deep introspection constitutes an actual relationship with God. We must stop acting according to the notion that as long as we are not serious criminals we are contributing to the building up of

---

[7] See Jn 10:7-10.

[8] See Jn 14:6.

[9] See Eph 1:10.

the Kingdom. We must start living like people who have been sanctified, who have been made right before God, who have become God's daughters and sons in Christ.

On the other hand, there is a reasonably good chance that, if you have read this far into the book already, you feel that you don't really fit the description that I have presented here. You go to Mass faithfully, you pray regularly and sincerely, and you strive to know the Church's teaching. This book will help you better articulate the reason for the truth of your beliefs. Or perhaps you do fit the description above, or you recognize that there are gaps in your knowledge, and you want to learn more. Perhaps you know "the rules," but you don't know the reason behind them, the bigger picture. This book is meant to present a vision of *how* Catholics think, because of Christ's covenant (reason), not to tell you *what* to think (rules). It attempts to wed both aspects of the Catholic person's identity, action and belief, in order to build up the Kingdom of God, to stress the importance of both faith and reason in the task of evangelization. If you are faithful in your everyday life, this book invites you to learn the Church's tradition more cogently so that you might answer questions about why you live the way that you do. If you know the Church's teaching well already, this book invites you to marry that intellectual tradition with the actions of your everyday life.

In order to accomplish this marriage of faith and reason, of lived experience and theological knowledge, I will be using certain key themes throughout the book. On the most basic level, many issues will be considered in terms of *action* and *character.* As an intellectual process, we will consider the rightness or wrongness of particular actions in light of the Gospel. Armed with this information, we are equipped to consider what kind of person performs such actions.

These basic terms make sense in the larger context of *relationship.* Morality is best understood in terms of relationships: relationships with other people, our relationship with our own sense of self, and our relationship with God. Our character and our actions necessarily have an effect on these relationships, so by knowing what kind of relationships we should foster, and why they are important at all, we can attain a better understanding of Catholic morality.

The reason for this emphasis on relationships is found in the love story referred to in the book's title. That is why I began with a reflection on love stories in general, because this book is about a love story. The story itself will be described in detail in Chapter Two. For now, it is sufficient to note that we are all participants in a particular relationship of divine and human dimensions. How we conduct ourselves in that one relationship quite simply determines the meaning of our lives. We are free to respond to this relationship as we wish, and there are definitely ramifications of our choice. Ultimately, happiness is to be found by those who choose to make the story in Chapter Two their own.

But before reading that story, a little background is necessary. Chapter One details the philosophical backdrop of the modern world. Examining certain currents of thought from the 16th century onwards, one can discern why the modern world seems so unclear about morality, why morality should be at all important, and why Catholicism in particular seems to have such a hard time making the Truth revealed by God known and understood. This chapter only provides a summary of these ideas, but the summary will be focused on the specific question of why Christian morality seems to make so little sense today to so many "modern people."

Chapter Two will introduce the fundamentals of Catholic moral theology. The chapter begins with a detailed presentation of the love story, the story of God's love for His people, beginning in the distant past and continuing into this very moment in the hearts of those who let Him in. This story provides the foundation for Catholic moral thought. This rich tradition is summarized in a consideration of the basic principles introduced above:

action, character, and relationship. The chapter also explains the importance of conscience and free will in the Church's thought. These concepts serve as the lens by which to focus all the issues of subsequent chapters.

While those chapters constitute a number of different issues surrounding specific themes, Chapter Three serves as an exception along the way. Rather than examining a variety of issues, this chapter focuses on the one issue of abortion. The reason for this focus is twofold. Few other issues are so readily identified with distinctly Catholic morality as the Church's teaching on abortion. This Catholic "tag" has been used to reduce this central issue to a sectarian squabble. However, the critical underlying principle of this issue is universal: the sanctity and value of human life. This truth has a fundamental impact on all other moral issues, and so a detailed consideration of it here serves as an additional foundational principle, elucidated in a specific context.

Chapter Four builds upon the sanctity of life by investigating the value of understanding the human person as both male and female. Our maleness and femaleness reveal our embodied nature. We are made in the Image of God, yet we are bodies as well. As this is part of God's design, we must discern what this means for us in both the vision and the details of the way that we live our lives. Like the value of human life, these conclusions will also affect subsequent chapters.

The following three chapters, the longest in the book, each investigate a specific area of Catholic moral thought. The first of these is sexual ethics, the subject of Chapter Five. The prominence of overt sexuality in our culture, from advertising, entertainment, and political and legal discourse, combined with a curiously strong (and misguided) set of secular presuppositions about Catholic teaching in regard to sexuality, requires a detailed comparison between several commonly held views of the modern world and the specific life-giving responses to them revealed by God in the teaching of the Church. This will be, for many readers, a happy revelation. The Church's teaching on sexuality is far richer than most uninformed secular moderns give it credit for; a better presentation of that vision in the words and actions of Catholics presents the possibility of serious cultural change.

The second specific area of Catholic moral theology is medical ethics, considered in Chapter Six. Within the category of medical ethics, there are two particularly important subcategories: beginning of life issues and end of life issues. These distinctions provide the structure of the chapter. These two subcategories do not exhaust the field of medical ethics; there are also issues regarding the patient-physician relationship and issues of justice in the availability and distribution of medical resources. However, concentrating on issues around the beginning and end of life does provide a focus on the issues that are most familiar to people outside the world of medicine, and therefore also become the more frequent topics of conversation, which afford opportunities for evangelization.

Chapter Seven develops the final broad category of issues within Catholic moral theology: social ethics. Social ethics encompasses the major issues that affect the direction of whole nations and peoples, such as morality in politics, war, and the actions of huge corporations. However, the issues considered under the heading of social ethics ultimately trickle down into the lives of people in their everyday circumstances: economic justice, the dignity due to other human persons, the value of the person when placed in comparison to economic or political gain. Social ethics even encompasses the subject matter of the previous chapters, as the decisions we make as individuals (in areas of sexuality and medicine) ultimately shape the course of society as a whole. Therefore, we need prudence to understand what the purpose of society should be in the mind of God and to grasp those principles in order to make that purpose into a reality. The task of evangelization has a special place here.

Finally, there is a meditation on the place of worship in

relation to morality. Its place as the final chapter is to highlight the vital importance of liturgy as the catalyst and summary of Christian practice. Liturgy is a face-to-face, heart-to-heart encounter with God, our Source, in Word and Sacrament. As such, it is an excellent way to integrate heart and mind, to provide unity to knowledge and experience, and to empower Christians to more fully engage the mission of evangelization. Armed with the wisdom of the Church, enlivened by the Holy Spirit, emboldened by the saints who have gone before us, God's love is incarnate and made visible to a world that desperately needs it. Liturgy is the source and summit of Christian life, the root and crown of living His life and building His Kingdom. God grant that this humble book empower us as we prepare ourselves to respond to this high calling!

Biblical Abbreviations

OLD TESTAMENT

Genesis	Gn	Nehemiah	Ne	Baruch	Ba
Exodus	Ex	Tobit	Tb	Ezekiel	Ezk
Leviticus	Lv	Judith	Jdt	Daniel	Dn
Numbers	Nb	Esther	Est	Hosea	Ho
Deuteronomy	Dt	1 Maccabees	1 M	Joel	Jl
Joshua	Jos	2 Maccabees	2 M	Amos	Am
Judges	Jg	Job	Jb	Obadiah	Ob
Ruth	Rt	Psalms	Ps	Jonah	Jon
1 Samuel	1 S	Proverbs	Pr	Micah	Mi
2 Samuel	2 S	Ecclesiastes	Ec	Nahum	Na
1 Kings	1 K	Song of Songs	Sg	Habakkuk	Hab
2 Kings	2 K	Wisdom	Ws	Zephaniah	Zp
1 Chronicles	1 Ch	Sirach	Si	Haggai	Hg
2 Chronicles	2 Ch	Isaiah	Is	Malachi	Ml
Ezra	Ezr	Jeremiah	Jr	Zechariah	Zc
		Lamentations	Lm		

NEW TESTAMENT

Matthew	Mt	Ephesians	Eph	Hebrews	Heb
Mark	Mk	Philippians	Ph	James	Jm
Luke	Lk	Colossians	Col	1 Peter	1 P
John	Jn	1 Thessalonians	1 Th	2 Peter	2 P
Acts	Ac	2 Thessalonians	2 Th	1 John	1 Jn
Romans	Rm	1 Timothy	1 Tm	2 John	2 Jn
1 Corinthians	1 Cor	2 Timothy	2 Tm	3 John	3 Jn
2 Corinthians	2 Cor	Titus	Tt	Jude	Jude
Galatians	Gal	Philemon	Phm	Revelation	Rv

Chapter One

The Culprit: The Legacy of the So-Called Enlightenment

The challenges that afflict evangelization today did not appear out of thin air. In the realm of morality, present-day confusion is the direct result of changes in fundamental patterns of thought. If one wishes to understand why morality is complicated and controversial for so many people today, one needs to understand these changes. So, before one can even begin to consider specific moral issues in the modern world, or even the theology that a Catholic would use to support Church teaching, one needs to understand how the world came to be the way it is now in the early 21st century. As Christians, it might be easy for us to say that we are reaping the inevitable consequences of our sins, and that would be correct. However, that summary statement fails to do justice to the much more complicated, and occasionally much more sordid, tale that explains our current plight. In this chapter, we will look at that story and the effects that it has had on Christianity as a result.[1] This historical rec-

[1] I must admit that this is a distinctly Western view of history, and it ignores historical events elsewhere in the world. While that may seem a little too restricted, the story of Christianity has been far more affected by events in Europe than anywhere else in the world. The roots of the modern problem I articulate in this chapter are also all exclusively European and, for better or worse, cultural imperialism has deposited these ideas throughout the rest of the world to a greater or lesser degree.

ollection will not take us all the way back to the beginning of human history. It is there that one can find the roots of human selfishness, but the specifically modern breed of selfishness can be traced back about 500 years. In the 16th century, the first steps were taken to lay the groundwork for what would come to be called "the modern age." The possibility of what was to come was made manifest ironically enough in the Protestant Reformation. This ultimately created a way of looking at the world that allowed reason to become more important than faith. While that view still exists for some, it has also been proven a failure to others. Rather than return to the faith that had guided humanity for so long, however, these thinkers just came up with new answers, all of which were equally flawed, though each was lacking in different ways. By the late 20th century, several new "third generation" ideas have provided a framework of looking at reality that seems internally consistent, but which conceals madness under the surface. Unbeknownst to many, the world has embraced this madness, this illusion, rather than face the comfort of the Truth. Let's start our investigation where the revolution began.

The First Shot in the Revolution: The Protestant Reformation

In looking at the Reformation in the 16th century as our starting point, this should not be understood as a broad statement about the differences between Catholics and Protestants, nor as a triumphant denouncement of Protestantism in the name of Catholicism. These approaches would miss the point that pertains to the issue at hand.[2] Regardless of the validity of the

[2] Of course, the division within Christianity *is* a scandal, and a restoration to unity is a goal that we must all constantly pray for and work towards.

Reformers' critiques of the Church or their methods in trying to bring about change, something critical happened in Western society: people discovered that it was acceptable to disagree with the Church, and if one was particularly unsatisfied, one could leave the Church and follow Christ in a similar but different way.

Another error immediately suggests itself here. This is not to say that the world was supposed to adopt an attitude of believing that "everything a leader in the Catholic Church does is always right" because that's what God supposedly "wants" of us humans.[3] Some of the prime actors in the Reformation were reacting against legitimate excesses of *some* or even *many* members of the Christian community. These were often local cases of questionable policy or practice. The real difficulty was not in the Reformers' just protest against these abuses, but the wholesale rejection of essentials of the Christian faith. In short, it revamped the very meaning of Christian identity in relation to the objective truth and gave each individual the apparent ability to formulate his or her own faith and practice. And *this* was the radically new idea: that if one could not find satisfaction within the Church, one could just leave. This opened a door to consequences that the Reformers could not have foreseen.

Light and Darkness are the Same to the Blind: The Enlightenment

By the 17th and 18th centuries, long after the splintering of Christianity into numerous sects, a new current of thought began to take more distinctive form. There had been an exaltation of the power of human reason since the cultural and scientific

[3] I am making a critical distinction here between "the Church" and "leaders in the Church," for the Church Herself *is* always right, as it is guided by the Holy Spirit. See *Lumen Gentium*.

breakthroughs of the Renaissance in the 15th century. But this was new — the power of reason was held up to be superior to faith; in fact, faith in God was sometimes even considered to be a superstition to be abolished. After all, it had already been demonstrated that one didn't have to accept any one group's view of God. It was an easy step to take to question why one should need God at all. And so it began to happen for some of these new thinkers.

This new approach took many different forms. In the realm of science, new breakthroughs were made, such as the birth of modern physics in Sir Isaac Newton. In the realm of politics, thinkers such as Hobbes and Locke, among others, introduced new ways of thinking about human government. In the realm of metaphysics, Descartes and Kant established new ways of looking at reality. This period of history has come to be known as the Enlightenment. This is the beginning of the Modern period of human history, and the attempt to put these new ideas into practice has become known as the modern project.

At the risk of over-generalization, Enlightenment thinkers trusted in the power of human reason to make the world a better place. As a result of this attitude, certain historical events occurred that *have* arguably made the world a better place. The revolutions in America and France opened the door for democratic forms of government, for instance. But at what cost did we have to pay for these benefits?

Take for example the revolution in France. Idealistic rebels thought that there was no need for King or Church, for human beings, using their reason and working together, could make a just society among themselves. The revolutionaries should have realized that their ideals were a bit hypocritical when they began to kill nobility and clergy in pursuit of this new "just society"! And even after that period of bloodshed was over, it was followed by a time known as "the Terror." Rather than work together for the common good, in the absence of the traditional authorities of God and King, humanity reverted to its most base impulses: rape and murder were the order of the day.[4] In fact, it was ultimately the stabilizing influence of a new absolute ruler, Napoleon, which moderated this civil bloodshed, and instead traded it for war.

Despite the noble intentions of many of the Enlightenment thinkers, some of whom did remain Christian, humanity is not able to create a just and equitable society apart from God. Human sinfulness, each person's well-ingrained selfishness, will always rise up in some individual or group to take advantage of another. It didn't take long before humankind was blinded to the Truth of who God had called us to be, and to the blind, light and darkness look the same. But what was the driving ideal behind all of this? According to many of the writers of this time, it was all about *freedom*. They sought a freedom apart from any ruler, but also, for many, apart from any distant God high in the sky, an abstract ruling judge. The next chapter will demonstrate how they may have formed that image of God.

But freedom is a good thing, right? Yes, it is; one of the greatest gifts that God has given to us. But what is it freedom *for*? Is it so that one can do whatever one feels like doing? Or is it so that a person can respond to God's loving call to us to be perfect? We are not made free to sin, but rather free to love. Sin always leads away from freedom to slavery, another concept that the Enlightenment thinkers protested against in their cries for liberty. While many of the Enlightenment thinkers rejected the idea that one is free to do whatever one wishes, that doesn't mean that they exactly embraced the concept of freedom as freedom to love. But at least on paper, the architects of the Enlightenment understood that freedom meant that each individual also had corresponding duties towards others. Society worked when people worked together. We need to keep this question of freedom in mind as we continue with the story.

---

[4] For plenty of details on the misguided ideals of the Enlightenment and the horrors that resulted, see the works of E. Michael Jones.

Dreamers and Madmen: The Romantic Movement

By the late 18th century, some thinkers had recognized that the modern project, the ideals of the Enlightenment put into motion, was not working. In analyzing why it was not working, some of them concluded that the foundational premises used to establish a just society were wrong. These new thinkers came to be known as the Romantics. Foremost among them was Jean-Jacques Rousseau. Instead of Enlightenment optimism, Rousseau and the other thinkers in the Romantic Movement recognized that society is a necessary evil at best; a construct that people must endure because they live together. One can never hope to actually have a perfectly just society, because people get in the way of one another. Romantic philosophers saw people as inherently good; it was society that brought out the worst in them. However, it was also recognized that everyone living a solitary life was a pleasant but unrealistic ideal. Therefore, society is structured according to a *social contract* that everyone agreed on. This idea was originally proposed by Thomas Hobbes in the 17th century, but it was revisited by the Romantic philosophers to address the perceived "problem" of society. The social contract delineated the rights and responsibilities of members of that society. So, for example, we realize that we have a right to life. Therefore, we also have the corresponding responsibility to not take the lives of others. The Romantic philosophers, however, modified the idea of the social contract by prioritizing the freedom of the individual to do what he wished, provided that it did not violate the terms of the social contract. In other words, the law prohibiting murder is not solely good because it respects everyone's rights. It is good because it allows one to live the way he wants to live without worrying about someone killing him. It was this latter component that was distinctly Romantic.

The connection between freedom and responsibility had been minimized. This greatly enhanced the notion that people are free to do whatever they want to do, but are moderated or hindered in their pursuits only by outside influences that wish to limit them, such as the law. This evolving (or perhaps more appropriately, devolving) view of freedom will continue to shape the events that lead to the present 21st century confusion.

But the Romantic Movement also had an unintentionally cynical effect on the understanding of who we are as human beings. By saying that the community of human persons is what ultimately generates selfish responses in people is a perversion of the doctrine of original sin. In truth, human persons are selfish because they prefer to choose themselves and their own illusions rather than face the love that God offers. Such a love demands transformation, change, growth, and foolishly, people resist this pull to be conformed to God's image and likeness because it is perceived as too difficult. And on our own, of course, it is indeed impossible! But it's not impossible when we accept God's invitation to relationship with Him. God also invited us to live in a community, to share life and love with one another. By contrast, the Romantics would have us believe that community is a problem for society: when a person's freedom to do as he or she wishes intersects with another person's freedom, the possibility for conflict ends up hindering both people's freedom to live as they wish. This demonstrates the inherent selfishness present in this approach. It would seem that the Romantic response to the Enlightenment exchanges one set of problems for a new one.

One thinker notably stands out at this point as a critic of all of these movements (including Christianity, if one would consider that a mere "movement"). That man was Friedrich Nietzsche, a late 19th century German philosopher. Nietzsche proves to be a fascinating figure: challenging in his observations, even as one may be repelled by his reasoning.

Nietzsche criticized the Enlightenment exultation of reason and the birth of democracy. He thought that these new social developments caused humankind to neglect the traditions of the past, which subsequently made us forget who we are. Furthermore, he complained that democracy was ultimately a weak political system, for it was a rule by the masses, the foolish and the ignorant.

He was also critical of certain aspects of Romantic thought. Nietzsche believed that the societies of the past were "heroic societies," and he could not imagine that these societies would generate weak or corrupt people. These old societies (and it must be noted that Nietzsche had an exceptionally biased view of history) created heroes among men; individuals of exceptionally strong character who could transform the world.

This last point seems to resonate to a certain degree with the aspirations of Christianity. However, Nietzsche instead reserved special venom for Christianity. He frequently criticized the faith as an offshoot of a "slave religion," whose followers worshiped a fool who didn't even have enough sense to avoid being killed. By the end of his life, Nietzsche proclaimed himself the Antichrist and strove to rise "beyond good and evil."[5] He insisted that the only reason people behaved morally was that they were afraid of an imaginary retribution from a non-existent cosmic tyrant. The true "superman" would create his own values.[6]

Two other key ideas of Nietzsche's must be considered. The first is perhaps his most famous: Nietzsche proclaimed that God is dead and that we have killed Him. Of course, Nietzsche didn't believe in God, so what does this phrase mean? It means that whatever value or benefit belief in God offered to civilization was now gone. Belief in God means nothing. In so many ways, a look around the world attests to the wisdom of Nietzsche's observation. However, it is critical to note that Nietzsche didn't see this as a bad thing. The death of God finally allowed those brave "supermen" to rise up to their rightful place in civi-

[5] By the end of his life, Nietzsche was also probably quite mad from syphilis.

[6] Another product of the Enlightenment that also corresponds with this idea of Nietzsche's is Darwin's theory of evolution. This relates to morality because of its concept, accepted by modern society, of "survival of the fittest." This phrase is often used to justify the behavior of individuals or groups, but the problem with it is that it fails to take into consideration individual rights or any objective value beyond the perception of the so-called "fittest" (however that is defined).

lization, to create values rather than be a slave to the values of Christianity.[7]

The necessary consequence of the death of God is the second key idea here. Nietzsche said that the inevitable result of democratic society would be a slide into *nihilism*, the disintegration of all values or meaning in life. According to Nietzsche, democracy produced a society of sheep, or what he called "the last man," the person who wants to just get along in life without having to really think. In the absence of the heroes of old, Nietzsche predicted that values would become meaningless because there would be no one to champion them (though keep in mind that he understood this problem in a much different way than a Christian would).

Nietzsche is important because he predicted the future of the modern project. While one might disagree about his solution to the problem, he is due credit for foreseeing the results that were wrought by his Enlightenment and Romantic forebears. In the 21st century, we have come to prize equality, choice, and freedom to such a degree that some chafe at the idea that someone, even God, could impose values on them.[8]

So the Enlightenment provided a framework that emphasized freedom. The Romantics went further and suggested that true freedom was a freedom detached from the obligations of society. Nietzsche warned that these ideas were problematic, but his response was to offer the idea of a "freedom of the strong," if you will, in which those with power could decide what was right and wrong. These ideas continued to develop and shape the contemporary notion of freedom into the 20th century.

---

[7] This was one of the key ideas of Nietzsche's that was re-interpreted by Adolf Hitler, who was an admirer of Nietzsche's work. However, it is clear that Hitler often misunderstood Nietzsche.

[8] The effects of nihilism, and the birth of the idea of the Enlightenment, are frequent subjects of Thomas S. Hibbs. One could look at his *Shows About Nothing: Nihilism in Popular Culture from The Exorcist to Seinfeld* (Dallas: Spence Publishing Company, 1999), especially pp. 11-53.

The Death of Common Sense: The 20th Century

The 20th century saw the birth of several new schools of thought in philosophy, as well as the development of divergent forms of modern psychology. Many of these ideas have had a profound influence on our present society.[9] However, three of these ideas that have had a particularly strong effect on contemporary moral confusion will be considered here. The culprits in this case are existentialism, emotivism, and post-modernism.

Existentialism was born of the author Sören Kierkegaard in the 19th century, but reached its fullest expression in the 20th century French philosopher Jean-Paul Sartre. A central tenet of existentialist thought is that "existence precedes essence." What this means is that who we *are becoming* is determined by what we *do*, and not the other way around. A Christian account of the human person says that what we do should express who we are. The existentialist instead holds on to the value of absolute freedom and the notion that one is constantly being created. The world itself is not rational, and therefore one cannot hope to make much sense out of existence. This remarkably dreary account of the world may seem to be too unappealing to achieve mainstream acceptance. In its purest form, that is perhaps true. However, the ideas that the world is not rational, that objectivity (the very idea that things are definitely one way and not another, especially in morality) does not exist, and that we are constantly becoming a new person are all alive and well today. Many people question whether life has any meaning, despite the fullness of life that God offers to us. Many people believe that everyone can have a different opinion about how the world works, despite that being the very definition of insanity. Many people consider

---

[9] For additional accounts of the effects of these ideas on modern society, see Grabowski, *Sex and Virtue*, 1-22 and Peter Gardella, *Innocent Ecstasy: How Christianity Gave America an Ethic of Sexual Pleasure* (New York: Oxford University Press, 1985). Both of these look at the development of the 20th century from an American perspective, specifically in regard to sexuality (especially Gardella's text), but they are applicable in a more general sense as well.

themselves to be a constant "work in progress," never content with themselves because they feel they need to experience more of *something* before they can feel "complete." This in itself is appropriate. We *are* works in progress, engaged in the constant, ongoing conversion that God calls us to. But by contrast, many people are ignorant of *why* we are works in progress. They have no idea what they are working to become. This specific breed of ignorance is what existentialism has provided.[10]

Emotivism is a moral theory from the early 20th century, articulated by Rudolf Carnap and Alfred Jules Ayer, among others. Emotivism states that there is no such thing as objective right or wrong, but merely our own preferences. When someone says that something is wrong morally, the emotivist says that what he or she really means is that they don't like it. This is an attitude that we may be able to relate to in our own lives. We are familiar with a variety of phrases that suggest this idea: "He has issues." "I have concerns." "That works for me." "I can live with that." But the emotivist denies *any* objective truth to morality. This means, for example, that murder is simply *not wrong*. If you have a problem with murder, that means that it affects you emotionally in a negative way. The reverse is also true: for the emotivist, helping someone out (for example) is not morally good. To think it is morally good is merely to express the sentiment that you like that course of action.

Emotivism has had a huge effect on the moral sense of the 21st century. While we may not specifically use terms such as "like" or "dislike" as expressions of preference in morality, many people do speak about morality as a matter of "opinion" and that when a conflict about morality comes up between two people, they just "agree to disagree." When questioned why a person holds a particular moral opinion, the effects of emotiv-

---

[10] While Sartre's existentialism is distinctly atheistic, this school of thought does not have to be. Kierkegaard himself was Christian; he found God to be the only relief to the anxiety brought about by this radical freedom.

ism really come to the fore: oftentimes, the reasoning is no more complex than, "I don't know why I hold this view — it's just the way that I feel."[11]

The last of the three ideas to consider in this section is a little different than the other two. It is certainly the newest of the ideas contained here, though its roots can be seen in the mid-20th century. Furthermore, this third idea is less a specific school of thought and more of a way to look at philosophy (including moral philosophy) as a whole. Post-modernism is a reaction against the perceived failure of the modern age, with its excessive emphasis on reason. In particular, the post-modernists do not think that reason can provide an accurate account of our life experiences that applies equally to all people. Many post-modernists are also reacting against what they see as a too limited account of the world, concentrated on the thought systems of only one dominant group in society, without due concern for the experiences and insights of other groups. For example, there are many post-modernist feminists, because they believe that the experience of women is not adequately addressed by the traditional approaches of Western philosophy.

So just what *is* post-modernism? While it defies easy explanation, one simple definition is the defense of equally valid but differing interpretations of language and reality. Philosophy recognizes a distinction between what something "is" (its objective existence, usually called its *ontology*; for example, a chair or a kiss), what that something "means" (its deeper unseen reality, referred to as *metaphysics*), and finally, how that something appears or acts in our external perception, our way of seeing, understanding, or interpreting it (formally termed its *phenomenology*). All philosophy up to the advent of post-modern thought recognizes that there is an objective reality to the world.

[11] For a detailed critique of emotivism, see Alasdair MacIntyre's landmark text, *After Virtue: A Study in Moral Theology* (Notre Dame: University of Notre Dame Press, 1984), pp. 16-35.

Things actually *are* a certain way, even if we disagree about how to explain that. We may disagree about the meaning of a chair or a kiss, but we would agree that the chair or the kiss exists. Post-modernism does not take that objectivity of existence or any deeper meaning into account. In other words, the chair does not necessarily exist; only our differing *experiences* of the concept we call 'chair' exist. The post-modern thinker questions an interpretation of an event, or an experience, or a word, because *your* experience of that event may not be *my* experience of that event. As another example, if two people both consider the color of the shirt a person is wearing, they may both agree that the shirt is red. However, they have no way of possibly knowing that what one calls 'red,' that what he or she experiences as 'red,' is in any way the same as the experience of the other. If that is even a possibility, how can one possibly ascribe a single meaning to that word or event? The post-modern thinker would say that we can't. There are as many meanings to the event or word as there are people to experience it.

How would this apply to morality? It would mean that there simply cannot be a *right* or *wrong* answer to a moral question, because one needs to take into account each individual's engagement with that experience. If we were considering a moral action, we could not judge whether the act of say, lying, was wrong in this instance because we cannot understand the experience of the person lying. This results in the purest form of relativism: everyone's morality is exactly their own, because we cannot possibly *truly, fully* understand each person's engagement with any given moral choice.[12]

A bit of good news is that post-modern thought barely exists outside the halls of academia. The problem with that, though, is that these are the same academics who are responsible for

[12] Critical responses to contemporary moral relativism are already a defining mark of Pope Benedict XVI's pontificate. There is no shortage of writings by him on this subject, both as Pope and previously as Cardinal.

forming the ideas of the next generation's influential thinkers. The long-term effects of post-modern thought on society still remain to be seen. Some philosophers already even consider post-modernism a failed idea. While it does seem to be a problematic idea, it is safe to assume that post-modernism's full legacy still remains to be seen.

For many of you, you may have had a gut reaction to existentialism, emotivism, and post-modernism. Despite recognizing how they have each contributed to the points of view of people we know, perhaps even ourselves, when presented in a concise form abstracted from a specific experience, these ideas do not seem to coincide with common sense. And that's exactly the point: these three thought systems create an understanding of our lives, our experiences, our morality that many people do not agree with when presented in the abstract, as has been done here, because these ideas fail to take into account what it means to be human. Any person can recognize this. The same academics who would champion these ideas might criticize the equally ambiguous concept of "common sense," but at least we all recognize that we call it that because it is "common"! But it's not so common anymore; in the past century, we have witnessed the death of common sense. And how can we define common sense? The life of God within us, calling us, inviting us to love one another, challenging us to *be* love for one another. It is this common sense that tells us that life *does* have meaning. It is this common sense that tells us that right and wrong *are* more than just opinions and feelings. It is this common sense that informs us that we *can* relate our experiences to one another because we are all human. Now we need to consider the relationship between two points of view: the ideas presented in this chapter and Christianity. Only then can one possibly make sense of Christian morality in the world today.

Moral Blindness, Moral Insanity: The Present Day

In looking at the whole gamut of ideas considered in this chapter, one can see the roots of present day moral confusion. The concept of freedom has disintegrated from a freedom to *be* who God has made us to be, a freedom to love, a freedom to make excellent choices that contribute to the well being of oneself and others to a freedom to simply do whatever one wants.[13] We recognize certain restrictions on our freedom: the civil law at least, and for some, an ambiguous concept to respect the rights or feelings of others. But provided that one does not violate these restrictions, everyone is free to do as they wish and furthermore, no one is allowed to suggest that someone's choice may be the wrong one.

These ideas have even infected the Church. As Catholics, people might find themselves challenged by Church teaching because they wonder what business the Church has telling them how to live their lives, or that the Church is behind the times, or that the Church has unrealistically high expectations for its members. More than any other aspect of Catholic thought, moral theology is vilified as being unreasonable or just wrong. The fact that these criticisms exist among otherwise well-intentioned Catholics demonstrates the pervasive power of ideas. We encounter the legacy of the Enlightenment everyday on television, in our conversations with co-workers, in the selective presentation of the news by the media. Sadly, even some theologians in the Church have been affected by these ideas and have advanced moral theology that fails to do justice to the Truth that the Spirit has revealed to us. This theology distorts our relationship with God and steers us in the direction of a disordered identity, away from who God created us to be. This criticism of the modern world is much more than just a case of complaining about how

[13] See Gal 5:13-15.

things are, or an appeal that things were better "back then." This is nothing less than a war over the Truth.

As Catholics, we have access to the Truth. We have to be careful to avoid falling into prejudiced ways of thinking that allege that "the Church is only a human institution that creates 'rules' based on the backward ideas of celibate old men." The Church is a community of believers, the People of God,[14] called into relationship by a God who wishes nothing more than to love us. As we recognize God as Creator (we affirm this every time we say the Creed), we also recognize that God has established the way that we must live. God is the author of freedom, and the sacrifice of Christ reveals that the fullness of freedom is experienced when we give ourselves away for the sake of another. This is the grounding for a just society, the goal of the modern project. The Enlightenment thinkers had the answer already, but in their pride and their selfish ignorance, they chose to ignore it. As Catholics, we must make this answer known to the world, for we have been called to be evangelizers, announcers of the Gospel of Christ, in both word and witness of our very lives.[15]

With this presentation of the modern world in mind, and armed with the call to make the Truth known to everyone, we are now at a place to examine the content of that Truth more closely. It's one thing to know the problem, and quite another to be able to be part of the solution. In the next chapter, the counterpoint to the moral blindness and insanity of the modern era will be revealed. The answer to moral minimalism, radical selfish freedom, and life without meaning is simply to accept God's invitation to love and to respond with that love in all of our relationships.

---

[14] See *Lumen Gentium* 1-8.

[15] Ibid., 1.

Chapter Two

A Brief Introduction to Moral Theology: The Importance of Relationships

In the previous chapter, the historical circumstances that led to the present crisis in moral theology were examined. But what exactly is moral theology? Clearly, giving a thorough answer to that question would require a much longer text. However, if we are going to consider how to respond to the modern crises and confusions in morality, we need to have some basis for understanding those responses, some solid ground on which we stand. Thus, this chapter presents the basics of Catholic moral theology.

The Christian faith is remarkably simple. However, in the past 2,000 years, Christians have often managed to make things more complicated. Sometimes this is good, born out of a desire to understand more fully what Christ would have us do. Other times, the complications are the result of silly humans getting in the way of God's plan for us. Moral theology has not been spared these complications. In order to make sense of this, we will need to look at a brief history of the subject, beginning with the critical understanding of why morality matters at all, and then moving into a presentation of some specific components of moral theology that developed over the centuries. This presentation will look at the subject through broad brush strokes, in order to understand the connections and distinctions between the two related ideas of *action* and *character.* Both of these concepts will be placed in the context of our *conscience.*

The problem in our time is that all three of these concepts, action, character, and conscience, have been taken to misleading extremes. In each case, the result is a crippled version of moral theology. In order to deal with this, this chapter will conclude with a reconsideration of a fourth concept: *relationship.* This concept is actually where morality begins, as will be explained in the next section, and so will also prove to be the easiest and most comprehensive way to understand morality in the chapters to come. So, let's begin with a story about why morality matters before moving into a consideration of action, character, and conscience situated in the context of Christianity's history.

A Love Story

God created us out of love. This statement is so simple in its presentation, yet so awesome in its meaning. And God created us out of love and *to* love, because He Himself *is* love.[1] A fundamental meaning of being created in God's image is that we are made to love. However, we would not know that or how to do that if God had not demonstrated this for us. The entirety of our existence is God's invitation to us and our response. This is the heart of morality.

After God created the human race, He entered into a relationship with us. This is the meaning of the biblical term *covenant.* He first established this covenant with Adam and Eve in the Garden (this covenant will be examined in more detail in Chapters Four and Five). He then established a covenant with Noah, and with Abraham, and with Moses. While the specific language may have differed slightly in each case, the essentials

[1] See 1 Jn 4:16.

were the same. God offered to us, "I will be your God and you will be my people." Based on that fundamental statement, God gave us instructions on how to live our lives, so that we might know Him and love Him. These instructions are not rules necessary for God to love us; His love is unconditional. But these instructions are meant to tell us how to love Him and love one another because, left on our own, we choose to love only ourselves. Understood in this way, the instructions are hardly "instructions" at all — they are simply the way we should live if we love God.

But the simplicity of that last point was lost on us. Consumed by our selfish desires, we turned away from the covenant. Even worse, sometimes we didn't turn away from the covenant, but instead just paid lip service to it. We followed all of the "rules," did everything we were "supposed to do." But there was no love. As a result of minimizing and ignoring the covenant, bad things happened, to individuals and to the whole People of God. When we realized what we had done (or failed to do) and turned back to God, our relationship was restored and things were right once again. This pattern continues throughout the Old Testament, and continues throughout our own lives now.

In the fullness of time, God gave us a more direct message. Rather than just give us instruction, He gave us a perfect example: God became flesh and dwelt among us.[2] Jesus Christ gave us the perfect example of love and taught us vividly what love meant when He suffered and died for us. Throughout the covenant relationship between God and His people, the covenant was also sealed with the shedding of blood. The sacrifice of Christ was the New Covenant, a covenant not established symbolically by the blood of animals, but by the blood of Christ Himself, the Lamb of God.[3] God loves us so much, wants so much for us to be free from our own sinful inclinations that

---

[2] See Jn 1:14.

[3] See Heb 9:12.

ultimately only do us harm, wants so much for us to just try to love one another as He loves us, that He died for us.[4] And along with this action, His words after His Resurrection, echoed by the Spirit throughout generations, remain: Do likewise. To be human, to be what God has invited us to be, is what it means to be holy.[5] We are called to die to our own selfishness and to live for one another, after the example of Christ who emptied Himself and offered Himself for us.[6] And for those who accept this, God has promised that He will come to us and make His home in us, and that we will remain together forever. This is the life of the Holy Spirit that began in us in Baptism, reached fruition in Confirmation, and is strengthened whenever we participate in the other sacraments. Most of all, it reaches its intimate climax in the Eucharist, when we take God within ourselves and become one with Him and with one another.

Now we can understand the very reason for morality. God has extended an invitation to us: to share in His divine life through His grace. That word "grace" can be understood as the very life of God living in us, the life of the Spirit. Sharing in His divine life is sharing in the very love that is God. We all experience this grace, regardless of our beliefs, when we recognize that we feel moved to act in one way and to avoid acting in another. By saying yes to this invitation, to these "moments of grace," we too are to be transformed into love. All of our "actions," all of our "choices," relate back to this central point: our response to God's constant invitation to love.

But love is more than just a feeling, of course. Love is a decision, and love is made manifest in action. This love story is the beginning of morality, but it is our response that continues the story. Now we can look at the ways in which we can understand the response.

---

[4] See Jn 3:16.

[5] See *Lumen Gentium* 39-42.

[6] See Ph 2:6-11.

The Response: Action, Character, and Conscience

When trying to determine what is the right thing to do, the loving thing to do in response to God's invitation to love, one can consider either the action itself or one can appeal to a consideration of character. These two concepts are not in conflict with one another. On the contrary, a full understanding of morality has to take both of these ideas into account. However, they are two different ways of *principally* looking at a moral situation. In other words, one can look at his or her actions primarily without much concern for character, or one could examine character without much concern for particular actions. Neither of these two perspectives is ideal. But for now, let's try to define the differences in approach.

If actions are considered in themselves, they are going to be evaluated according to some abstract principle, presumably with some consideration for the idea that there is an objectively "right" or "wrong" way of looking at the situation. This is "presumably" so because such objectivity cannot be taken for granted in our modern morally relativist world. If one considers actions primarily, one's evaluation of them will not consider any *personal* involvement in them. In other words, a person will not evaluate him- or herself as a person performing actions, but will instead be concerned solely with the actions themselves.

Perhaps an example here would clarify this last point. If you purchase a newspaper from a newspaper box, you have the opportunity to take the single paper that you have purchased, or more than one paper. Regardless of what you decide, you have only paid for one newspaper, and taking another paper would constitute theft, by strict definition. If you decide to take two newspapers, you or someone else could subsequently evaluate this moral choice by the objective standard that stealing is wrong (or at the very least illegal) and conclude that you had made a morally incorrect choice of action.[7] Note, however, that in all of

[7] It should be pointed out here that stealing is wrong in Christian morality. The

this, the kind of person that you are was never considered at all. We could replace you in this example with anyone else. The details of who that *person* is would not change our perspective on the situation.

Now instead let's consider morality principally from the point of view of *character* instead of action. In this case, instead of evaluating the action in the abstract, one evaluates one's choices according to the kind of person one is and/or wants to become. Put more simply, in considering your own morals, you could ask yourself, "What kind of person am I? What kind of person chooses to act in this way?" From a Christian point of view, this same question must be considered in a very specific way: "Does a Christian act this way? Is this behavior appropriate for someone who has died to him- or herself and risen again in Christ in baptism?"[8] This transcendental concern for ourselves as people redeemed by Christ raises our moral consideration above merely evaluating actions alone, and perhaps even avoids such an evaluation altogether.

Let's return to the "newspaper temptation" again. A person with concern primarily for his or her character would look at the situation and have to discern what kind of person he or she is. Is he or she the kind of person who would take two newspapers when they have only paid for one? A person with good character, one might argue, would not. The question of the legality of the situation or the morality of the action in the abstract is secondary to the person concerned primarily with character — there is an appeal instead to a consideration beyond the "rules" to the kind of person we are or wish to become.

These two approaches, action and character, give us differing information about our own moral choices and different

---

only reason I suggest that it might be "merely" illegal is to keep this evaluation of moral action as "religiously neutral" as possible. At this point, I am trying to explain the concept of action in a way that both the Christian and the critic of Christianity can understand.

[8] See *Catechism of the Catholic Church* 1227.

ways to consider human actions. However, as was said earlier, they should not be considered as two conflicting approaches to morality. Instead, they work together. To call oneself "Christian" is to define a fundamental aspect of one's very being. Therefore, the Christian must be concerned with what kind of person he or she is, whether or not he or she is conforming him- or herself to the person that Christ has empowered him or her to be. Because of this, the Christian must also be concerned with what *actions* he or she chooses to do or not do. These actions in turn should manifest the kind of person he or she *is*. To put it simply, actions reflect character. These two ideas can now be placed in the context of Christian history.

In the early Church, there was no distinction between action and character. From the earliest Church Fathers' connection to the historical experience of Christ through the development of the Church's ever-expanding role in the world, Christians understood that their actions reflected their character. They had not yet lost sight of the fact that Christ invited us into a love relationship with Him. Many theologians wrote about specific actions, but it was always understood in the context of the redemption offered in Christ. This is not an attempt to portray a rosy view of the Church's first few centuries as an idyllic wonderland of saints, free from sin. One must also remember that some members among the early Christian community provided us with Christianity's most pernicious and long-lasting heresies as well. But the Church's theology was still developing as they tried to understand more fully the lived experience of Jesus Christ and, for the best part, our minds had not yet run ahead of our hearts. Let's advance this history a few more centuries in order to clarify just what is meant in that statement.

St. Thomas Aquinas (among others), in the 13th century, provided the Church with a philosophical framework to understand the relationship between action and character. Always keeping in mind the notion of the person redeemed in Christ as primary,[9] Aquinas explained that a human action can be understood according to its *object*, the person's *intention* in performing it, and the *circumstances* surrounding the action.[10] In order for an action to be morally good, it must be good in all three of these aspects. If any one of these components is not good, then the action is not morally good. Let's look at each of these three components.

The *object* is simply what the action is. Why we do something and what circumstances surround our actions make a difference, but an action can also be considered by itself. Traditionally, the Church has always taught that certain actions are *intrinsically evil* in their object. In other words, there is no intention or circumstance that would ever make such an action right. Some examples of this would be abortion, fornication, or adultery. The reason for this is not because the Church is setting absolute "rules," but rather the Church is guiding us in the understanding that there are certain actions that a human person, made in the image and likeness of God, simply cannot do.[11] But obviously not every action is intrinsically evil in its object. For these other actions, one must examine other factors.

The *intention* is the reason why one does something. Is the intention to demonstrate one's faith in Christ to others? Is it to help someone else out of self-sacrificing love for another? Is it to ease someone else's burden? Does it contribute to one's own fulfillment as a human being? These are some good intentions for actions. However, if people do something to make them merely feel good about themselves, or to create a false impression in

---

[9] In fact, Thomas organized his *Summa Theologiae* according to the love story that began this chapter. He divided his text into three parts. The first part described God as Creator and why He created us. The second part described our response to the Creator, particularly through morality. The third part described our way back to God, particularly through the sacraments. The very structure of Thomas' work demonstrates the outline of the whole of salvation history, and serves as an excellent reminder of who God is, who we are, and where we are going.

[10] For more on this in much more detail, see St. Thomas' *Summa Theologiae*, I-II, q. 18.

[11] See John Paul II, *Veritatis Splendor* 80.

someone else, or simply to selfishly get their own way, these are not good intentions. The intention of an action ultimately relates to our final end: *Why* would I do this particular action? As Christians, our final end is to *realize* (that is, make real) the fulfillment of who we are called to be in the presence of God. Therefore, our intentions should ultimately (if not always directly) lead us towards this end.

Modifying the evaluation of both the object and the intention are the *circumstances*. In many ways, this is a "catch-all" for all of the other factors that might pertain to the evaluation of a particular action. If the object is the "what," and the intention is the "why," then circumstances are the "who, how, where, and when" of the action.

Another example will serve here to clarify these three concepts. Suppose you wanted to make a charitable contribution to a group that works with the homeless. You believe in the cause, it contributes to the building up of the Kingdom of God, and you make your donation with no exceptional fanfare. Aside from placing more details into this hypothetical situation, this is a morally good action. The object, contributing money to help the homeless, is clearly good. Your intention is based on a sincere desire to help the homeless. Furthermore, there are no circumstances that seem to affect this evaluation.

Now let's change the example. Suppose you are the CFO of a major corporation and you decide to donate a sizeable contribution to the same fund described above. You arrange for the donation to be announced in a press release for the company and, as CFO, your main reason for doing this is for the tax write-off that it will provide. This is not a morally good action. The object remains good, but the intention and the circumstances are not.

But, one may argue, surely the donation is a good thing, even if done for the wrong reasons, right? After all, the CFO could instead make a donation to a hate group. This is true. However, in our call to be like Christ, why we do things and the circumstances in which we do them are just as important as what we do. Christ tells us to be perfect as our heavenly Father is perfect.[12] Our intentions reveal what's in our hearts, and therefore they speak to the character of the person performing the action. As Christians, our primary intention must always be to love as Christ loves. The circumstances surrounding an action help to determine how reasonable the object and intention are, also thereby revealing what kind of character we possess.

We can now return momentarily to our historical perspective. St. Thomas placed the evaluation of these actions in the context of the kind of person one is, as noted above. Thomas was thus ultimately concerned about character. So how does one do this? How does one evaluate actions in terms of character? This is where the third concept from the chapter's beginning comes into play. Let's talk about *conscience*.[13]

The conscience is not some little voice of our parents or priests or police officers or teachers in our head. Conscience is God's life active within us, guiding us towards good choices and persuading us away from evil ones, encouraging who God has made us to be and dissuading us from becoming victims of our own selfishness. But the conscience is only as active and as strong as one allows it to be. A person has an obligation to develop his or her conscience and then utilize it, as it demonstrates our likeness to God. Our conscience allows us to act as human beings, rather than as just highly developed animals. Quite simply, the best way to develop a strong conscience is to follow the teaching of the Church, as it is guided by the Holy Spirit. By following Church teaching, one can be sure that he or she will be free from error.[14] This is an incredibly valuable gift! Catholic

---

[12] See Mt 5:48.

[13] The presentation on conscience in this chapter is extremely simplified! This is an unfortunate necessity given the needs of this chapter. However, the teaching on conscience is essential for a *thorough* understanding of Catholic moral theology. I cannot recommend further reading on this subject strongly enough. For a more detailed presentation, see David Bohr, *Catholic Moral Tradition* (Huntington: Our Sunday Visitor Publishing Division, 1999), 169-198, *CCC* 1776-1802, and *VS* 54-64.

[14] See *LG* 25.

teaching has always held up the primacy of the conscience in morality — we have a moral obligation to follow our conscience, for following it is actually following the will of God for our lives as we are able to discern it, leading us to surrender to the truth about ourselves.[15] This also emphasizes why it is so important to develop a strong conscience.

The problem in modern moral thinking is that some have misunderstood the role of conscience in terms of action and character. Our conscience does inform us of how we should act. The problem is how some people react to that information. Nowadays, a person is prone to hear the voice of his or her conscience; but at the same time, he or she has a different idea of what he or she "really" wants to do. In other words, they see what they want in contrast to what their conscience tells them, as if they were two different and competing voices. The conscience, the voice of one's innermost heart where God dwells, has become an outsider. How did this happen?

Our Minds Ran Ahead of Our Hearts: Nominalism

And now we have found our way back to our history story in earnest. While there were some bumps on the road along the way,[16] the thought of St. Thomas eventually became the dominant perspective in Catholic theology, and it remains in large part the foundation of much of the Church's theology today. But within a hundred years or so of his death, Europe became a much different place. The plagues that devastated so much of the population of the continent also ended up devastating a lot of the faith and

[15] See *VS* 58-59 in particular.

[16] St. Thomas based his teaching on the philosophy of Aristotle, which was unheard of at the time and more than a little suspect. Because of this, Thomas' teaching was initially derided by some, including the Bishop of Paris, where Thomas taught. However, God and history vindicated Thomas and did so quickly. He was canonized a mere 50 years after his death, and his teaching became the basis for Catholic philosophical thought.

hope of the people. It wasn't so much that people began to doubt God's existence — that is a much more modern phenomenon — but they did seem to wonder about the apparent arbitrariness of God who would allow such suffering to occur.

In the midst of the struggle with this age-old question of human suffering, a modification of Thomas' consistent moral vision occurred. The change came to be known as *nominalism*. Essentially, the perspective of morality changed from Thomas' concern for particular good actions that contributed to the formation of a good moral character to an emphasis on moral rules. Instead of understanding morality as a loving response to God's call for our lives, morality was about following the rules that God established. And while God established "rules" like the Ten Commandments, He could just as arbitrarily change them if He saw fit to do so. Needless to say, this is not the warmest image of God! But one must keep in mind the historical circumstances. With people dying all around you, a warm God may seem distant indeed.[17]

Unfortunately, this nominalist perspective influenced Catholic theology for centuries. The result of its influence on morality was to focus on rules and obligation rather than on good actions performed by people of good character. Theologians emphasized *what* one must *do*, rather than on *who* must one *be* in Christ.[18] Our minds had run ahead of our hearts. We had lost touch with the love story. But the effect on conscience was even more noticeable than on action or character. People understood morality as a limitation on their choices, rather than as a gift to guide them to excellent choices. Morality ceased to be a lived experience and instead became a burden that often seemed to make life more difficult.

---

[17] For a much more detailed presentation of nominalism, see Servais Pinckaers, *The Sources of Christian Ethics* (Washington: The Catholic University of America Press, 1995), 241-253.

[18] See Bohr, 88.

Take a moment now and consider your own thoughts about morality. Do you see morality as a gift from God to help you achieve your life's goal, which is living forever in His presence? Do you see it as a loving response to the One who first loved you? Or is morality instead something that keeps you out of trouble at the same time that it's also really making life a lot less fun? People may appreciate morality for ultimately "making the world a better place" or "making us good people." But this is not ultimately the point of Catholic morality. Morality is the fitting response of human beings as God's people to surrender to the mystery of Christ's saving act. It allows us to understand who we *really* are, and by living a moral life, we invite others to participate in the same invitation to grace that God offers to all. But for many, in their innermost thoughts, they'd much rather take the easy way out. Some people act well enough, but sometimes they don't want to. That constant conflict is the legacy of nominalism.

This unfortunate development in Church history goes hand in hand with everything described in the last chapter. An inadequate account of moral theology, combined with an overly idealistic account of human nature and human possibility apart from God and new legal and philosophical language to complement this account, results in 21st century moral confusion and moral minimalism. It's not inappropriate to say that only within the past 50 years or so has morality started to move back in the direction of the early Church's concern for actions in the context of character. With this renewal of focus, the Church can also more adequately respond to the moral challenges of today.

But as all who make up the Body of Christ do this, we are still faced with confusions within moral theology. While action, character, and conscience are all necessary components of moral theology, each of them taken to an extreme does damage to Catholic moral thought as a whole. We have already seen what happens when conscience is inappropriately over-valued in the nominalist conflict between obligation and what one really wants to do. Now we must look at what happens when we overemphasize the categories of action or character to the point of neglecting the other.

Furthermore, the relationship between objective truth, Christianity, and other religions must be considered. At first, this may seem to have little to do with morality. However, many contemporary discussions of moral issues devolve around the line of argumentation that Christian teaching doesn't apply if one isn't a Christian. In fact, one's religious self-identification does not matter as much as some would think.

Excess and Illusion: Problems in Moral Theology

Catholic moral theology is based on the interrelationship of action, character, and conscience. If one misunderstands one of these concepts, or overemphasizes or ignores one of them, a crippled version of moral theology results. Consequently, this generates the illusion that a person is faithfully responding to God's call of love. He or she unknowingly chooses to live a lie because it is easier. It has already been shown that if a person misunderstands the role of conscience in his or her life that morality ends up being seen simply as a matter of obligation. If a person overemphasizes action over character, he or she may end up subscribing to a flawed moral methodology such as *proportionalism* or *consequentialism*. If a person overemphasizes character over action, he or she may end up subscribing to a different flawed moral method sometimes referred to as *fundamental option theory*.

Proportionalism and *consequentialism* emphasize intention and circumstances over object.[19] In this moral method, a person may do an action that is objectively wrong (that is, wrong in its object, such as stealing or fornication), but that does not mean that the action is *morally* wrong for that person in those circum-

[19] This chapter cannot do justice to a full presentation of these moral methods or a thorough critique against them. If you wish to read more about Pope John Paul II's critique of these methods, see *VS* 71-83.

stances. Instead, a calculus is performed in which the good to be gained by the action is weighed against the evil to be endured. In this case, it is acceptable to tolerate evil for the greater good.

This seems like a reasonable approach to the often extraordinarily difficult situations of the modern world. If we were being honest, we would likely admit that we ourselves have used just such a moral calculation at some time in our lives.[20] But it fails to take into account several essential truths. The first is that, as people made in the Image of God, we can never willingly choose to go against God's will for us. Remember, this is not a matter of obligation, but rather because it is not who we were created to be (in other words, it ignores our character). Furthermore, one would need to be God Himself in order to understand all the possibilities that every circumstance and consequence could produce. Using these methods entails a risk that what we *think* is the best thing to do might turn out to be very harmful to ourselves or others. Finally, this "lowest common denominator" approach to hard moral choices fails to take seriously the idea that we are guided by the Holy Spirit, and that we will never be tested beyond our limits.[21]

The other extreme moral method is to emphasize character to the neglect of action. The *fundamental option theory* doesn't exactly understand the notion of character in the same way that it has been presented here, but this theory can still be used as a means to examine the importance of actions.[22] In brief, this

---

[20] Catholic moral theology does allow for the toleration of evil in some cases when it is unavoidable and unintended in order to achieve the good. This is called the *principle of double effect*. Proportionalism was a result of taking part of this legitimate principle to an inappropriate extreme. For an explanation of the principle of double effect, see, for example, Bohr, 226-227.

[21] See 1 Cor 10:13.

[22] Again, this is a very simplified presentation of fundamental option theory. Furthermore, not every theory that refers to a "fundamental option" is equally problematic from a theological point of view. There is a positive version of the fundamental option concept, which is an acceptance of the Christian Covenant and its Gospel vision without reserve among the various apparent "good" or indifferent options available. This would be a commitment not to second-guess the Lord's will, a *fundamental* grounding in the Covenant no matter what. However, for John Paul II's critique of the account as I present it here, see *VS* 65-70.

theory asserts that the decision to follow Christ is a radical, saving decision. Because it is such a monumental event in a person's life, it would take an equally monumental event to break that connection between the believer and Christ.[23] One would need to have a sort of "anti-conversion" experience. Therefore, according to this theory, for the one who has faith in Christ, who we might say has a Christ-like character, individual actions do not matter. The only exception would be an action that was deliberately aimed at severing one's relationship with God.[24] Hypothetically, this could mean that a saint who was faithful to God's will for his life for 50 years could then commit a single act of murder without it being problematic for his relationship with God! After all, all those years of service can't really be wiped away in a single choice, can they?

Actually, they can. Actions matter, because actions manifest character. Such a view is not only the perspective of Catholic thought; it also agrees with common sense (as Catholic thought generally does, contrary to popular opinion). Many people often think that the "little sins" they commit don't say anything about them. But that can only be true if one is willing to say that the big sins don't matter either, and that simply is not the case.

Before moving on to the final section of this chapter, let's consider the relationship between Catholic moral theology and other philosophical and/or religious perspectives. After all, doesn't Catholic moral theology really only apply to Catholics? In a sense, yes. But Catholic moral theology also appeals to the objectivity of truth, and herein lies the reason why it applies to all people.[25]

---

[23] To a very limited degree, this theory simply takes St. Paul's notion of justification by faith very seriously. See Rm 10:9-10. However, the counterpoint to this point of view can be seen in Jm 2:14-26. James understands that actions manifest character.

[24] Of course, this has traditionally been the definition of those actions we call mortal sin. See *CCC* 1472.

[25] On the objectivity of truth, see John Paul II, *VS* 1-27.

In the physical world, we all take certain things for granted as truth. If I walk off a building's roof, I will fall, no matter how badly I want to fly or believe that I deserve to fly. If I eat a steady diet of potato chips and nothing else, I will get sick, regardless of how much I love potato chips or how much I dislike more nutritional food. If I'm doing math, two plus two will always equal four, even if that means my calculations are wrong. We accept all this because we know that the world is structured on certain truths.

The same applies to the world of spirit. As spiritual creatures made by God, there is objective truth in the moral universe as well, whether one agrees with it or not. This is a simple explanation of what is called the *natural law*.[26] These truths can be demonstrated by an appeal to common sense: no group of people throughout history has ever said that murdering the innocent was a good thing. No society has ever sanctioned adultery as a good action. In our own lives, we know facts such as these in most cases without ever needing someone to tell us. Just a cursory evaluation of our own experience reveals these truths.

If two people completely disagree on a moral issue then, it stands to reason that one of them simply *must be wrong*. Two competing views of morality cannot both be right. There cannot be a point of view that expresses "my morality," even while it disagrees fundamentally with "your morality." This erroneous point of view is called *moral relativism*.[27] Therefore, how do we determine the truth?

Without the benefit of religious guidance, human persons still have the power of reason. With this, one can evaluate his or her own experiences and the experiences of others. Do certain actions seem to contribute better to human flourishing? Do cer-

---

[26] Much has been written on natural law. For some basics, consider John Paul II, *VS* 46-50 and the *CCC* 1954-1960.

[27] For a straightforward critique of moral relativism, see Peter Kreeft, *Making Choices* (Ann Arbor: Servant Books, 1990), 27-38.

tain actions seem to stunt a person's fulfillment or hinder the fulfillment of all people in society? Are the immediate effects clearly detrimental to one's self or others? Does a more balanced, rational exploration of an action's long-term effects on self or others reveal potential problems that were not considered? All of these questions, and other similar ones besides, can help to determine what the right thing to do is, apart from a specific appeal to religion.

So then, if that is the case, what is the point of religious moral teaching? Religious thought gives us a rationale for why the world is the way that it is and guidelines to help us understand the world. Regarding the first point, religious thought helps us to see that our lives do not exist in a sort of vacuum without meaning. Religious thought places human beings in the context of creatures created by a God with a specific purpose in mind. This should inform one's rational consideration of life experiences. As God is the author of morality, if we are trying to be good moral people, it makes sense to appeal to the designer's plan.

Perhaps more importantly, though, religious teaching gives us guidelines. While it may not be particularly difficult to determine that torture and murder are morally wrong apart from religious ideas, the same cannot be said for all moral issues. In fact, the issues that are probably a lot closer to our hearts, particularly sexual issues and medical issues, are the ones that are often a lot harder to wrestle through with reason alone. The reason for that can be considered in two ways (though these two elements are intimately related). From a purely secular, psychological point of view, feelings can sometimes confuse rational thoughts. From a specifically Christian point of view (shared by many other religious traditions), the experience of sin, a deep-seated desire to choose ourselves over others, makes us prone to choose our way of doing things rather than the way that we are supposed to act as God's creatures. So religious teaching gives us the guidance we need to be able to use our rationality wisely.[28] It is a gift from God that allows us to live more easily, if we just accept it.

This gives us some perspective for why religion is important for morality overall. But Catholics in the modern world seem to some to be particularly backward and behind the times. Why should someone accept Catholic moral thought?

The simple answer is that it is true. However, the full explanation of that statement would go far beyond the limits of this book. Instead, let us reconsider what was said above. Does an honest appraisal of lived experience suggest that Catholic teaching is wrong? Is Catholic teaching bad simply because it is perceived as difficult? If truth is objective, does morality really have to "keep up with the times"? Are humans somehow a fundamentally different creature now than they were 500, 1000, or 2000 years ago? Catholicism never asks us to leave our brains at the door of the Church. In fact, it demands that we use them to enter into a better relationship with God. Now, this is the point to reconsider the category of *relationship*. Recalling the starting point of morality will synthesize the concepts of action, character, and conscience, while navigating the unfortunate excesses previously discussed.

Saying "Yes" to the One Who Calls Us: Our Love Affair with God

In order to avoid the pitfall of thinking about morality in terms of rules, let us instead concentrate on relationships. On some level, most people disdain rules — they correctly surmise that they are restrictive in some fashion. Even if that restriction is for their own good, they feel an imposition on their freedom. However, if one instead considers morality in terms of relationship, then the person can more readily perceive that his or her

[28] For more on the necessary role of religion in morality, see ibid., 39-50.

choices are made in complete freedom; not a freedom to do whatever we want, but rather a freedom to be the best lover (that is, the best human being on God's terms) that we can be.

This concept of relationship in morality does not supersede the categories of action and character; rather, it subsumes them into a more holistic unity. This thus brings moral theology back in line with the thinking of the early Church and away from the mistaken excesses of later centuries. In terms of our conscience, one is guided by a different set of principles. More than just asking whether or not the action under consideration is good or what this particular choice says about one's character, the person can instead look at what effect this choice will have on his or her relationships.

But which relationships are meant here? First and foremost, our relationship with God. God first established a relationship with the human race, and then told us to be in relationship with one another. This makes perfect sense because God as Trinity is in a relationship with Himself: the Father, Son, and Holy Spirit are three distinct persons who all love one another.[29] We, in turn, are created in His Image. God also established a relationship with us. In biblical terms, this relationship is the *covenant* that God established with us. It means that God did not create us and then let us play in the world while He looked on in detached amusement. He wants to be involved in our lives. Furthermore, this involvement is not something big and impersonal. God is not just in a relationship with all of humankind in the abstract. No, God is involved in an intimate relationship with each and every one of us as individuals. This fact can have a strong effect on our understanding of morality. There is less danger of appealing to abstract rules; there is less danger of self-involved "navel gazing" while one reflects on character. Instead, each person can

[29] The dogma of the Trinity is an awesome thing! For a very readable explanation of this critical truth about God, see Frank Sheed, *Theology for Beginners* (Ann Arbor: Servant Books, 1981), 25-48.

concentrate on the intimate love-relationship that God desires to have with each one of us, if only he or she is willing to say yes to His invitation. In turn, as we recognize God in one another, we enter into love-relationships with others as well.

With all of these references to the love story between us and God, one might be wondering just how intimate this relationship is. The answer to this question was alluded to earlier. As it turns out, there is an easy example to explain the answer. There is one human relationship that is also a covenantal relationship: marriage. Marriage is an image of God's love within Himself and it is also an image of the love between God and His people, between Christ and the Church (the meaning of marriage will be further explored in Chapter Five). But as marriage is a symbol of God's love for us, that symbol can also be used to more easily understand what it means to have a relationship with God and how that affects one's morality. But even for persons who are not married, the analogy should still make sense.

Anyone who is in or has ever been in a serious relationship with another person understands that there are certain guidelines that establish proper conduct between two people. If a person doesn't like being called stupid, then we know we shouldn't call our loved one stupid. If we do, we understand why he or she is angry with us. Likewise, we would not punch our special someone in the face, nor would we talk about them disparagingly behind their back, nor would we try to sabotage the things that make them happy, nor would we deliberately try to thwart the things they do to make us happy. People who supposedly love and care about one another simply do not do such things; we care about who they are, and wish to honor them, respect them, and build them up. Chances are, nobody had to tell you that these were guidelines for a relationship. No one handed you a book that listed things not to do.[30] You just

[30] It's a sad sign of the times that perhaps we *do* need such a book!

understood that you were supposed to behave in a certain way, not because it was the "rules of relationship," but simply because you care for the other person.

Let's take the analogy a step further in another direction. Everyone knows that communication is part of a good relationship. This advice is so commonly known as to be cliché. Every reasonable person understands that if he or she purported to have a relationship with someone, then the quality of that relationship might be called into question if the person said they spoke to his or her loved one just once a week. By contrast, if a person is crazy in love with someone, that person wishes to spend all of his or her time with that someone!

If the relationship between Christ and the Church is a marriage,[31] then that means that we are married to Christ. Not just as a people, as a Church, but as individuals. We are in an intimate relationship with Christ. Therefore, all the guidelines that we understand as pertaining to relationships with other human beings apply here too. By using *this* perspective to guide morality, based on the foundations of action, character, and conscience, one can avoid all of the errors and extremes mentioned in this chapter.

Perhaps an example or two will help to illustrate this point. If we are in an intimate relationship with Christ, then we will not talk ill of Him or of His Bride, the Church. And yes, as we are all His Bride, then we should not speak ill of ourselves either! If Christ is our Spouse, then we trust Him to take care of us. Furthermore, we should try to do things that will make Him welcomed in our lives, by living according to His will for our life, while avoiding the things that will make Him unwelcome, which is when we sin and choose our own way instead of His way. When you love someone, you are so joyous about this that you wish to share that love with others. People who love one another truthfully also know that their love overflows from their

---

[31] And it is: see Eph 5:29-32.

own relationship so that it can be shared with all with whom they come in contact. This expresses our own call to evangelize, not just with words, but most importantly by the witness of our lives lived according to who God has created us to be.

Furthermore, we need to have good communication with our Spouse. We cannot hold this relationship together by having a mediocre conversation with Him in Mass on Sunday, mixed in with a few random short exchanges throughout the week. If that's all your communication is, your relationship will inevitably start to break down, and maybe fall apart entirely. If we don't want that to happen, we need to communicate with God through prayer, and we must do it often.

In the practical realm, discussions with others regarding morality can benefit from this emphasis on relationship. When considering why the Church teaches what it does, the Christian can understand the rationale not as some arbitrary ruling from on high, but instead as something that will ultimately make us happy and our relationship with God better. In addition, as we the Church make up one Body in Christ,[32] then any time we improve our relationship with God, we can improve our relationships with one another, and vice versa. Conscience can be our guide in this, as we choose those loving actions that ultimately form our character into the loving, Spirit-filled, Christ-like people that God has called us to be.

The background in moral theology presented in this chapter, combined with an understanding of the modern situation presented last chapter, can now permit an examination of specific moral issues. In each case, some of the principal arguments against Catholic teaching will be considered, along with responses to them. Throughout these presentations, there will be an emphasis on moving beyond the perspective that simply sees the Church's teaching as a series of rules. Instead, they will use a well-formed conscience as the expression of the divine proof

---

[32] See 1 Cor 12.

about ourselves to choose loving actions in conformity with God's goal for our life (union with Him), to develop a strong character that images God, because we are carefully mindful about the integrity of our relationship with Him.

The first issue will be examined more briefly than some other topics. This is not because it is less important. On the contrary, in many ways it is the most critical issue of our day. The reason for this brief treatment will be explained in the next chapter. Armed with this basic foundation in Catholic moral thought, let us begin our examination of the issue of abortion.

Chapter Three

The Usual Suspect: Abortion

Nothing strikes more to the heart of the question of personhood than the question regarding the morality of one person killing another. And nothing potentially causes more debate about the very notion of human personhood than the status of the unborn child. The philosophical, political, biological, theological argument over abortion has been particularly noisy over the past 30 years, but this can be misleading. From the beginning of Christian history, those who have accepted the saving grace of Christ's sacrifice and become his covenant people have also rejected the possibility that it is ever acceptable to deliberately take another person's life.[1]

Of course, even the word "person" is a bone of contention for some. Many people would agree that killing another person deliberately is always morally wrong,[2] but might also insist that the fetus in the womb does not constitute a person. A lot of ink has been spilled in trying to define just what a person "is." We will consider some of the morally inadequate definitions that

---

[1] This can be seen as early as the *Didache*, or *Teaching of the Twelve Apostles*, an early Church document that some scholars date back as early as apostolic times (around 70 AD).

[2] This, of course, immediately suggests the question of soldiers killing one another in times of war. We will examine that question in Chapter Seven.

have been proposed.[3] We will then consider what definition God has provided for us through His Church, and examine the issue through that lens.

This chapter will follow a slightly different order from the other chapters in this book. We will begin with a bit of a caveat explaining why abortion is being handled separately from other issues. Then, we will consider some of the common arguments against the Church's teaching on personhood, followed by a presentation of the Church's response. Finally, the chapter will conclude with some special consideration of common counter-arguments and related issues.

There Can Be No Lifelong Love Story Without a Life

Of the many moral issues that we will look at in light of the love relationship we have with God, this first one is going to be examined a little bit differently. In particular, this topic will receive somewhat shorter treatment than some of the other broad topics in this book. The reason for this is rather simple: there are dozens and dozens of books, articles, and web sites that address both sides of the issue, often in far greater detail than a single chapter could provide. Despite all of these details, however, everything about this issue comes back to the fundamental principles here considered and which often get lost among all the arguments. As proof of that danger, some Catholics even roll their eyes when the topic of abortion comes up, for they feel that the issue has been "talked to death," and that everyone is more or less committed to their views and are just not going to change their minds.

---

[3] As stated at the outset, the number of sources available on abortion is huge. For some fairly straightforward accounts about the philosophical question of personhood in regard to abortion, consider the Congregation for the Doctrine of the Faith's 1974 *Declaration on Procured Abortion*, especially paragraphs 8-18, and Peter Kreeft's *Making Choices: Practical Wisdom for Everyday Moral Decisions* (Ann Arbor: Servant Books, 1990), 116-118.

So if that is even partially the case, then why spend any time at all on abortion? The reason is twofold, and both reasons are contained in this chapter's title. Abortion is first of all "the usual suspect" for the reason mentioned above and because it is the most common issue that people are going to identify when they hear the phrase "Catholic teaching on moral issues." In this sense, it may seem like the treatment of abortion first is to "get it out of the way," so that we can move on to more provocative issues.

Indeed, such a point of view would demonstrate how insulated or desensitized we sometimes get about the most important things. We sometimes experience similar feelings about prayer, or the Mass, or the Bible. As Catholics, we sometimes make presumptions that we know all that we need to know about something, and anything more in depth should be left for "the experts." As long as we go to Mass, we sometimes reason, it doesn't really matter if we understand why we do the things that we do there. Or, as long as we pay attention to the Scripture readings at Mass, we don't really need to study our Bibles. Would we trust in our bank accounts simply by the fact that we still had blank checks left in our checkbook? This attitude promotes a thoroughly minimalist account of our faith experience that has contributed directly to the present crisis in catechesis in our Church. The issue of abortion fits into this same category.

This is unfortunate. Abortion can also be considered "the usual suspect" because, in its own way, it can be connected to every other chapter in this book. Our society has lost sight of what it means to be a man or a woman. In the pursuit of legitimate goals of equality, we make the mistake of assuming that *equal* means *identical*. Abortion ends up depriving women of the very characteristic that makes them literal miracle-workers and men are deprived of the opportunity to participate in the awesome gift of co-creation, to be the fathers that God has called them to be.

In a related way, the vast majority of people in the modern world fail to understand the full purpose of sexual intercourse.

Intercourse is a means of both expressing a unique kind of human love as well as the way in which human beings are given the privilege to raise human life. In the perverse selfishness by which this profound act is debased, it becomes a recreation, a vehicle for emotions and physical sensations. When this cross-purposed activity actually results in the new life that is its natural end, abortion becomes a way to deal with an unwanted "consequence." The result: an evil act born from an evil act, crime on top of crime.

Sexuality is one aspect of our identity as persons. While it is a profoundly important aspect, it remains a subordinate aspect. We recognize our personhood most especially in our freedom. Extending this to our bodily understanding, some people conceptualize that we must have ultimate control over every function of our bodies. Pregnancy then is viewed as an imposition on our freedom. Therefore, abortion becomes "necessary" to preserve this misguided notion of freedom.

Finally, our very society is based on foundations both pragmatic and sublime. On the pragmatic level, society needs new members to perpetuate its existence. Abortion prevents this or, perhaps even worse, puts control of who becomes a new member of society in the hands of selfish individuals or even selfish governmental agendas. But we also hold lofty ideals of respect and dignity for all human individuals. Abortion forces us either to ignore these ideals in the case of a targeted group of people (the unborn) or else to create a pseudo-philosophical language to de-value that same group of people out of their humanity. Furthermore, if we stigmatize one group of people as undesirable in society, it is an easy logical step to apply the same stigma to another group of people. If we can kill the unborn, then why not the elderly, or the handicapped, or a particular race? Even if we ourselves do not directly engage in this activity, our silence threatens to de-humanize us just the same.

So we see that abortion is an issue the importance of which cannot be exaggerated. The way that we consider the issue of abortion speaks to the way that we look at many other critical areas of life. If we understand Christian moral life to be living out the love story between God and His people, all of His people, throughout all of their lives, then we need to allow God's people to live. Moral living is impossible without this foundation. There can be no lifelong love story without a life in the first place. For this reason, let's consider the specific moral teaching of the Church on the issue of abortion.

If You Have Any Questions, Consult the Manufacturer

There are many reasons given in an attempt to justify why a woman should be "permitted" to have an abortion. Some people even go so far as to suggest that, while abortion is admittedly a bad thing, it is a "necessary evil" in some instances.[4] Such cases often include rape, incest, situations in which the mother is still a teenager or in which the health of the mother is at stake, and the like. The similarity between all of these cases is that they constitute extraordinary situations. But that's an important point to consider: these are *extraordinary* situations, and therefore shouldn't be cited as the best cases to endorse the morality of abortion. We will return to these considerations a little later on. In any event, evaluation cannot be decided by "cases," no matter how difficult the circumstances involved. Moral evaluation must be rooted in sound moral principle.

Furthermore, despite the lip service given to these unusual situations, the vast majority of abortions are done for convenience.[5] This is not to ignore the severe emotional stress that women may go through as a result of having to deal with this decision, but rather to point out that in almost every case, a

---

[4] This "necessary evil" approach often follows the pattern of consequentialism or proportionalism discussed in Chapter Two.

[5] According to the Alan Guttmacher Institute, up to 96% of abortions in the United States are for reasons that have nothing to do with the health of the mother or extraordinary circumstances such as rape and incest. See "An Overview of Abortion in the U.S."

woman could choose to have a child, and yet does not so choose. How can this be rationalized? Interestingly, by something as simple as word play.

When people disagree about something, their argument often breaks down on the level of semantics. Simply put, the parties involved disagree about the very meaning of a term, and therefore, may not even be speaking about the same thing.[6] This miscommunication can often be completely innocent. But semantics can also be used quite deliberately. If we voluntarily change the meaning of a word, we can change how we evaluate it. This can enable someone to make a concept attractive to someone who might otherwise be opposed to it. For example, we can change the term "used" to "pre-owned," or a company can deprive whole groups of people of their livelihood for a greater profit margin and call it "downsizing." This technique is used frequently in advertising, marketing, and politics.[7] It has also been used to effectively promote abortion.

In America, the argument over the legality of abortion refuses to consider fully the notion of personhood. In fact, "Roe v. Wade" tried to concentrate instead on the question of when human life begins and failed to answer even that properly, despite tremendous scientific evidence available to the contrary.[8] However, in the 30 years since that decision, many people have come to accept the fact that human life begins at conception. This is not a religious opinion. It is a scientific fact.

---

[6] This also relates to our consideration of post-modernism in Chapter One. If we can't agree on the very meaning of a term, then we cannot achieve a moral consensus. Hence many of our contemporary difficulties.

[7] This was even formalized as "doublespeak" in the society described in George Orwell's dystopian novel, *1984*.

[8] Roe v. Wade states in its argument: "When those trained in the respective disciplines of medicine, philosophy, and theology are unable to arrive at any consensus, the judiciary, at this point in the development of man's knowledge, is not in a position to speculate as to the answer." A commentary on this erroneous position was offered by several biologists in 1981 before a Senate Judiciary Subcommittee. For still more on the biological origin of human life, see Dianne N. Irving, "When Do Human Beings Begin: 'Scientific' Myths and Scientific Facts," *International Journal of Sociology and Social Policy*, 19 3/4 (1999): 22-36.

But that still does not address the question of personhood. Yes, a fetus may be human life, but does that make it a person? Here is where the semantic argument in favor of abortion comes into play. Instead of defining all human life as human persons, we can more specifically define exactly *who* is a person. Thus, one may conclude that the unborn fetus is human, but not necessarily a person. Despite the qualitative difference, a fetus is sometimes likened to being no more human than the human material used to create it, the sperm and the egg.

So what is a person then? Many competing definitions have been posed. Some would say that when a baby is born it becomes a person. Others say that when a child is capable of life apart from its mother it is a person. Some would say that when a fetus looks like a baby it becomes a person. And finally, some would even go so far as to say that when a human being is desired by another person, that's what makes them a person.

This question of personhood is critically important in determining the moral evaluation of abortion. If the unborn fetus is in fact defined as a person, then the unambiguous conclusion is that it is legally permissible to kill some innocent people solely on account of our desire to do so.[9] Most people who support abortion do not think it permissible to kill innocent persons. But they also do not believe that the fetus is a person. Hence, the centralityof personhood to any moral discussion.

So, in looking for a way to understand abortion that also takes into account the overarching truth that we are created by God in love and for love, we will first consider some brief responses to the definitions of personhood presented above.

The first definition considered above was that a baby becomes a person when it is born. This is a particularly strong example of the bending of definitions, for it is purely an arbi-

[9] Sadly, while uncommon, there are some pro-abortion thinkers who are this intellectually honest about the issue. This speaks to the larger problems in contemporary morality discussed in Chapter One. If we misunderstand freedom to be freedom to do whatever we wish, then why should abortion be prohibited?

trary distinction. How is this human "thing" explicitly different in the moment it comes out of the womb from a mere moment earlier? There is here no clear defining concept for personhood, except perhaps "not in a womb." This definition is too flimsy to hold weight.

Another alleged definition of personhood seemingly more thorough is that which affords the child the status of "personhood" when it is capable of life apart from its mother. This can seem to make a certain amount of sense. This view offers as evidence of its validity that the unborn fetus is completely dependent on its location within its mother's "geography," if you will. But this argument, too, does not hold up. Birth does not constitute any independence not enjoyed by the pre-born. A newborn child is not capable of independent life apart from his or her mother's nurturing. Nor is a two-year old. If the continued nurturing of basic psychosomatic needs remains critical until one gains "independence," then one could even argue that there are 18 year-old kids going off to college that are still incapable of living apart from their mother! While this definition tries to make a distinction between persons apart from one another physically, it still arbitrarily defines personhood without adequately demonstrating why the unborn child is *not* a person.

The third and fourth arguments are a little different from the first two insofar as they allow the possibility of granting personhood to the child while it is still in the womb. The third argument is based on the external appearance of the human life. This idea contends that a six-week old fetus doesn't *look* like a human being; therefore it *isn't* one. By contrast, a seventh-month fetus looks like a baby, and is therefore a human person. This reduces personhood to a matter of appearances. What about an adult human being who is charred severely in a fire? This human no longer resembles what a "normal" human being looks like according to an arbitrarily defined criterion; do we therefore deprive them of their personhood?

This leads to the final "definition" presented above. Even going further than appearances, some would grant personhood on the basis of one being desired by another person. When a baby is wanted, it is a person. How many thousands of human beings would be deprived of human personhood by this definition! The orphan, the widow, the elderly, the homeless — and all those human beings constantly threatened with marginalization by society — are thereby bereft of their personhood! If this definition were promulgated, it should be legally and morally permissible to eliminate whole unwanted sectors of society. Tragically, the 20th century actually witnessed this idea become policy and attempts at its implementation were horribly effective against millions.[10]

However, even if personhood *were* defined solely by the desire of another person, all human beings would be persons from the moment of conception to their deaths and beyond, for God the Father is a Person, and He calls us out from the beginning of time to be His. This also leads us to our alternative definition. Moving away from semantic wrangling, it seems impossible to escape the logic that a concept like personhood has an objective meaning. The reason for this is that there *is* such a thing as objective truth.[11] Therefore, if we would know the truth about when personhood begins, we should be able to learn the answer.

When we have questions about a product that we own, how it operates, what it does, what it can't do, we have two choices. We can either experiment on our own, which may lead us to a correct or incorrect understanding of the item, or we can get a more confident answer by consulting the manufacturer. We might consult the instruction manual that came with the product or we might contact the manufacturer directly.

---

[10] Furthermore, Margaret Sanger, the founder of the organization Planned Parenthood, advocated the study and practice of eugenics. While she may be distinguished from the practices of the Nazi regime, what she did advocate is still utterly dehumanizing. To claim that she was merely a product of her time (a debatable statement to begin with) does not legitimize these beliefs, especially held in the (comparatively) recent past. One can read more about this in Planned Parenthood's own printed biography of Sanger.

[11] Review Chapter Two for more on this.

The same methods apply to the concept of personhood. Some people have tried to define personhood based on their observations of the world. As we have seen, most of these definitions are necessarily deficient in some way, for they fail to see the person beyond his or her physical form or our relationship to a physical form. But if we wanted to know for certain who is considered a person, we can consult the manufacturer: God the Creator.[12] And, in order to do so, we have both the option to consult the Instruction Manual (Scripture and Tradition) or to thereby contact the manufacturer directly (through prayer and rational evaluation of our experience on God's terms). So what do we find there?

Let's look at the Instruction Manual first. The Scriptures, particularly the Old Testament, provide us with a number of statements that seem to suggest personhood defined even beyond human ways of perceiving and leave no doubt concerning its living presence from the moment of conception. In Jeremiah, we read that "before I formed you in the womb I knew you, before you were born I dedicated you."[13] Similarly, we read in Isaiah that God "formed me as His servant from the womb."[14] The wisdom text of Job includes even the biological observation that "with skin and flesh you [God] clothed me, with bones and sinews knit me together."[15] This idea is echoed in Psalm 139: "You knit me in my mother's womb."[16] The first two passages reveal personhood, for God gives purpose to the person before they are even born. God creates all things for a purpose, but He does not *call* "things" into being by name. He calls *persons.* These latter

---

[12] I realize that human beings are neither "products" nor exactly "manufactured" by God in our contemporary meaning of the term. But "manufacture" does mean "made by the hand" in Latin. And are we not, in fact, made by God's hand? See Ps 95.

[13] Jr 1:5.

[14] Is 49:5.

[15] Jb 10:11.

[16] Ps 139:13.

two passages, on the other hand, one might argue, speak only of God creating the human being, not directly of creating a person. God intervenes directly in the creation of persons, in a way in which He does not in creating animals or plants. Even giving the power to reason for humans to create chairs or alarm clocks or anything else differs from God's creative act. God intervenes because something unique is being created: a person, made in His own image and likeness, formed by His hand.

We could continue investigating the Instruction Manual by looking at the whole living Tradition of the Church, an experience as vibrant as the Covenant relationship it sustains. Aside from specific injunctions against abortion itself, we could find numerous sources throughout the Church's vast experience of God's revelation that indicate that God creates human *persons* and calls them to Himself. God made every*thing* else in creation from no*thing*; He made *us* from Him*self*. God has revealed that human personhood begins when human life begins.

This is fine for someone who is willing to accept the authority of Scripture and Tradition. But what if one doesn't? Aren't these just religious arguments based on individual beliefs? While this is not in fact the case,[17] an appeal can still be made to the very intention of the "manufacturer" by examining the idea of personhood through the gift of human reason.

Each of the definitions of personhood examined previously has a certain arbitrary character to them. Personhood, in which we include the recognition that a human being is born into a community and is called to be a responsible member of that community, must begin when the possibility of that person's involvement in the community also begins. This statement would seem reasonable to one who held to any of the definitions considered previously. However, the unborn child, from the moment of conception, not only possesses potential to influence the human community in adulthood, but from the very moment of

---

[17] Review Chapter Two again! The concept of objective truth is extremely important!

his or her existence, that child has an effect. Even in the decision to have an abortion, that decision is predicated on the undeniable effect that the unborn person has on his or her mother.

If this is the case for the unwanted child, then it is all the more demonstrable in the case of the wanted child. The evidence for an unborn child's personhood is most clearly seen in the love and enthusiasm of the child's parents when that child is wanted. This is a universal, primeval, instinctual response. For those parents, the child's conception changes everything in a way that no other major event in their life can do. Even if they have welcomed a previous child, this cannot diminish the unique joy of the new child's future birth. This experience demonstrates that, from the moment of conception, we instinctually intuit that the human life is a human person. Why else discuss names, dreams for the child's future, prepare a nursery, or get anxious over the responsibility for this new life?

Previously, we said that abortion was wrong primarily because it is the killing of another human person. The role of community mentioned above also provides another, slightly different, argument against abortion based on human personhood that complements and supports the previous one. As persons in society, we recognize that we have rights and corresponding responsibilities.[18] These rights are based on our recognition of being part of a community of other persons, governed by laws meant to protect those rights. The most fundamental right of a person is the right to life itself. Therefore, it is debasing for human persons to deprive other human persons of life, regardless of differences between them.[19] In the case of the unborn, while one might still try to argue that the unborn child's status as a person cannot be proven without an appeal to faith, the reverse

[18] The exact nature of these rights and responsibilities is one of the great arguments of the modern world. However, few will disagree that people do have rights and, with them, certain responsibilities.

[19] This argument is further explained in the Congregation for the Doctrine of the Faith's *Declaration on Procured Abortion*, 8-12.

is also true: the child's status as a person cannot be *dis*proved. Therefore, with at least the rational *possibility* that the unborn child may be a person, it would be dangerously foolish for a human being to kill that human life, and it would be equally foolish for a society that claims to respect all people to permit the killing of that human life.

But all of these appeals to Scripture and rational arguments must be understood in the context of the basis for morality that we introduced last chapter. What effect does abortion have on our relationships? Undeniably, in the case of the parents and the child, abortion literally terminates the relationship, closing off the possibility that love be given or received. But the damage to relationships doesn't end there.

Studies constantly reveal a host of negative effects that accompany abortion. Women who have abortions not only put their own health and future fertility at risk, but there is strong evidence that severe psychological damage occurs as a direct result. Many women report incidents of depression, suicidal impulses, and an overwhelming guilt over what they have done.[20] This damages the relationship the mother has with herself, encouraging self-destructive patterns of thought and behavior, as well as damage to the relationships around her. She is unable to effectively love others, for she is damaged by a single profound decision not to love.

And finally there is the alienating effect it has on the relationship between the woman and God. God has called us to be loved by Him, to welcome His will for our lives into our own wills, to love as Christ modeled love for us. Abortion, the decision to deliberately end the life of one of God's people, necessarily

---

[20] See, for example, "Adverse Psychological Reactions – A Fact Sheet," located at www.hopeafterabortion.com. Numerous sources exist detailing the effects of post-abortion syndrome, despite some within the psychological community denying its existence. On the methodological flaws, see Emil J. Posavac and Todd J. Miller, "Some Problems Caused by Not Having a Conceptual Foundation for Health Research: An Illustration From the Studies of the Psychological Effects of Abortion," *Psychology & Health* 5 (1990), 13-23.

rejects that offer from God. It is a specific decision to choose one's own will over God's will, to reject His meaning both for the woman herself who chooses to abort and for the child that is killed. And this, above all, is the reason why abortion must be considered unequivocally immoral: not just because it takes another life, but rather because taking another life is a rejection of God's will for us and for others, a rejection of our relationship with God. It corrupts our very identity as human beings.

All of the above is necessary knowledge if we are to properly understand what is at stake in the issue of abortion. However, there are still a few related issues that deserve consideration. While none of them changes the immorality of abortion (some of them, in fact, reinforce it), these issues do represent the unusual "cases" that often come up in contemporary discussions of abortion in general. As we are focusing in this text on our ability to evangelize through both our moral lives and our understanding of moral truth, we must address these common counterpoints before moving on.

Ideals, Reality, and What's Really Real

Everything that we have said so far considers abortion in its most basic form: a woman finds herself pregnant, chooses not to be, and has an abortion. As noted earlier in the chapter, however, controversies over abortion often result from a focus on the "hard cases" or "the bigger picture" rather than abortion simply understood. In this section, we will briefly consider these extraordinary cases, as well as how our own beliefs matter in regards to this issue, and the wider question of the world's population.

There are some who contend that abortion needs to remain available in society in order to deal with extraordinarily difficult situations. As mentioned earlier, these situations would include when a woman is raped, when pregnancy results from incestuous sexual assault, or when the prospect of carrying a baby to term poses significant health risks to the mother. No one can deny that these are far more difficult situations than many of us will ever have to deal with. But do they change the meaning of abortion?

Despite the circumstances surrounding the action, abortion remains what it is: the deliberate killing of another human person. This fundamental value cannot be weighed against other concerns such as social impropriety, risk of birth defects, quality of life, or even another person's life. God alone is the giver of life. To usurp that authority is to necessarily circumvent His sovereignty over all life and to reject His will for us.[21] This is not to say that God demands or approves of these tragedies. The vagaries of human existence are not the result of God's malice or His disinterested authority, but rather emanate as the fallout from one tragic source: the reality of sin. While not the only definition, it seems that sin can simply be described as the fact that human beings choose their own selfish will instead of God's will. This is not simply a judgment that the one who procures an abortion is a sinner. It's much bigger than that. The fact that we live in a world that has abortion in it and the circumstances that lead one to consider this "option" enables us to perceive how sin has marred the beauty of God's design. When we face tragedy, Christ empowers us to love as He loved — to accept suffering, rather than to add to it, to see through the darkness to the light hidden therein. And as God the Father raised Christ to new life through His acceptance of suffering, so too can we experience this Resurrection in our own lives when we accept the suffering that comes our way. But even so, we must always remember that suffering is only the doorway, not the destination! Christ did not come to remove or exalt suffering, but to reveal

---

[21] More can be said about the principles involved in these situations. See Chapter Six. For more information on "arguments for life," one could consult any number of sources. See, for example, the links offered at www.priestsforlife.org, or Dr. and Mrs. J.C. Willke, *Abortion Questions and Answers: Love Them Both*, 2nd ed. (Cincinnati: Hayes Publishing Company, 2003).

its meaning as the "admission booth" to life. To accept the reality or even "necessity" of abortion in the world is to implicitly deny this truth.

These same tragic situations often lead well-intentioned people, especially politicians, to conclude that they are "personally opposed" to abortion, but that they wouldn't want to deprive someone else of their right to choose. Such statements are couched in language that erroneously suggests that we have the freedom to do as we wish. We cannot do as we wish; we can only choose between God's will for our lives and our own will against His. Depriving another person of life, or even permitting someone else to do the same, fails to take seriously God's sovereignty and the love that He has shown to us.

Would we accept another person's decision to kill his or her own sibling or spouse? Would our understanding of freedom restrict us from stopping such a person? In saying that we cannot stand in the way of another person's choice regarding abortion, we are doing just that. This attitude utterly ignores the truth that we, as God's people, are responsible for one another — not just the unborn child, but also for the woman who would do such great harm to herself, and who deserves the care of the community.

In the political arena, lawmakers will support abortion legislature because they believe that it is their mandate to support the positions of their constituents. But that is not their job. Their responsibility is to support the human community and make sure that all members of that community (not just adult voters) are treated with dignity and respect. Authentic civic authority shares in God's authority inasmuch as it upholds this principle. But abortion is a profound disregard to one especially helpless and vulnerable section of the lawmaker's constituents: the unborn. Therefore, abortion laws are an abuse of the lawmaker's authority. No one would support a politician who advocated the legal murder of one class of people, or who thought child abuse was an acceptable practice, yet a politician who supports abortion does both of these things. Regardless of his or her position on any other issue, a society that elects lawmakers who tolerate the killing of its members cannot hope to be a just society.

This leads to one final issue. Some will support abortion on account of the growing population of the world. Some believe that the world cannot support so many people, or that new births hinder the development of peoples who are already struggling to survive. There are two points that need to be raised in regard to this issue. The first is that, while there may be some truth to the idea that new births compete with existing children for available resources in some developing Third World countries, the solution to the problems of adequate human development must be just, and it must keep the larger picture of the community in mind. Abortion as population control policy, aside from depriving a community's members of their autonomy, doing significant harm physically and psychologically to those who undergo it, and fundamentally devaluing *all* life, is based on the absurd notion that being killed is better than suffering. Rather than controlling the population through violence, efforts should be made to improve conditions in the community more broadly, to make more resources more equitably available for all.[22]

The second point relates to developed countries. In many developed countries, factors have combined to actually produce a *negative* birth rate.[23] In other words, more people are dying than are being born to replace them. While abortion is of course not the only factor relating to this, it is one of the factors. It also dem-

---

[22] The argument that abortion is ultimately necessary to stave off overpopulation is based on the spurious notion that overpopulation is in fact unmanageable in the world. See Herbert F. Smith, "The Proliferation of Population Problems," *Homiletic and Pastoral Review* 87, no. 5 (February, 1987): 11-23. Given the increase in the spread of AIDS and continued developmental challenges in the Third World, the age of this information does not invalidate it. See also Michael Schooyans, *The Demographic Crash: From Fatalism to Hope* (St. Louis: Catholic Central Union of America, 2001).

[23] Ibid. See also the February 27, 1998 declaration from the Pontifical Council for the Family, which speaks directly about the factors involved.

onstrates that abortion is not necessary for population control, because the population of developed countries is not growing. Furthermore, as the still developing countries of the Third World rely on the economies of the developed nations for assistance, and as the economies of these nations need people to run them, the negative birth rate in these countries has a negative effect on the world as a whole. Abortion fails to aid the world as its proponents suggest.

Some people bring up all of these issues related to abortion when discussing the legality and/or morality of abortion because they believe that they are making rational appeals. A "realistic" view of the world demonstrates that we need to have abortion available, even if only for hard cases. A "realistic" view of the world says that abortion will allow the people of the world to live better. Many will claim that a world without abortion would be a nice "ideal," but that it's just not practical. All of this ignores the "really real": the world as God has created it, redeemed it, provided for it, and sanctified it. All of our worldly wisdom can create comfortable illusions to mask the challenges of our lives, but it cannot change the truth, and the truth is that abortion is the murder of an innocent human being. In the most fundamental way possible, this distorts the divine purpose for human existence.

In summary, then, we have examined the issue of abortion from the point of view of personhood and from the point of view of relationship. The unborn child is a person, and therefore must be treated, like all other human persons, with objective and divinely endowed dignity. This precludes doing deliberate harm to him or her. Furthermore, abortion does damage to all of our relationships, in ways that are profound and sometimes unnoticed right away. In a special way, abortion is a rejection of God's invitation to relationship with Him. It is a distinctly unloving response to a call to love made manifest in the conception of a new person in God's family.

This approach to the issue of abortion must also color the

way we evangelize. Aside from choosing not to have an abortion ourselves (obviously), we must take every opportunity we have to explain exactly what is at stake. The issue far transcends politics and strikes at the very idea of what it means to be human. We must work hard with our lawmakers to eliminate abortion from society. We need to be cognizant of "family life" policies around the world that advocate abortion and fight against them. Perhaps most importantly, we have to be willing to stand up for what we believe and not only condemn the act of abortion itself, but also extend God's love to those people who find themselves in the position where they believe abortion seems like a viable option, or seems perhaps, their only option. In this way, we demonstrate the love that Christ modeled for us in His life, death, and resurrection. In this way, we build up the Kingdom.

Our character is made manifest in our attitude towards abortion. When we oppose abortion, we implicitly recognize and consciously affirm who we are as human persons created in the Image of God. To accept abortion, under any circumstances, is to lose sight of this same truth. This question of personhood will remain extremely important as we continue our examination of how we are to live out the love story, the life of love and truth that God has called us to for the salvation of the world. The next chapter will not examine a specific set of moral issues, but rather will reflect on an important concept for understanding personhood in light of all the other issues we will examine: what it means to be a man or a woman in God's design.

Chapter Four

Men are from Muck and Women are from Ribs: The Question of Gender

Despite the fact that it seems self-evident that men and women are different, the modern world still seems to spend an inordinate amount of energy proving that we are all "just the same." On the one hand, people often converse about certain fairly childish attitudes as being a "guy thing" or a certain overly sentimental movie being a "chick flick," or a certain way of seeing a situation as a man or woman "thing," that the other gender would fail to understand. But when it comes to important matters, matters of the law or of corporate policy, the modern world is quick to assert that men and women are the same. Are our differences really mostly incidental? This chapter will consider the question of gender and the effect it has on our lives and lifestyles.

The contemporary difficulty with this question can be demonstrated by considering some specific elements of modern science and social thought, especially as these ideas come into conflict with the Church's wisdom, which provides a more holistic account of gender, and in which we glimpse the design of the Creator. This design serves as a blueprint for relationships between men and women. This deserves attention, not because it is some kind of archaic biblical sociology, but because of another, more essential "design": the relationship between human beings and God. Only in this context can one ask: is the question of gender really that important?

For some people, the question of gender is thoroughly *un*important — a biological mask that we overemphasize in society already. For others, gender is the key to improved civil rights and social accessibility. Still others characterize gender as a means of control, defined in any number of ways. However, none of these approaches to the issue addresses the question of whether or not gender has any effect on our morality. Does being a man or a woman mean anything in regard to the way that we live our lives?[1]

The complexity of some contemporary moral issues seems to urge us to answer this question in the affirmative. The chapters to come will explore how our understanding of the meaning of masculinity and femininity affects our understanding of sexual behavior.[2] This in turn leads to understanding the meaning of fertility in the larger vision of the person and the huge effect this has on certain "hot topics" discussed in medical ethics today. Finally, the fact that we still appeal to gender as a factor in social discourse indicates that it has an effect on our social ethics as well. Clearly, this aspect of being a gendered human person "made in the image of God"[3] is worth our attention!

---

[1] For a much more academic discussion of this issue, especially in regard to the way women and men develop their morals specifically, one could consider Christopher P. Klofft, "Moral Development, Virtue, and Gender: A Comparison of the Differing Accounts of Lisa Sowle Cahill, Servais Pinckaers, and Paul Evdokimov" (S.T.D. diss., The Catholic University of America, 2000).

[2] In regard to discussions on gender, the careful use of language is extremely important for some thinkers. Distinctions can be made between "sex and gender," "male and female," and "masculinity and femininity." While I respect the distinctions made between these terms, for our purposes here, I will be more fluid in my use. Generally speaking, I will be referring to "gender" as that component of the person that manifests in both physiological and psychological differences between persons identifiable as "men" and "women." I will be using the terms "male" and "masculine" and "female" and "feminine" interchangeably, except where specifically noted otherwise. One could consult a large body of writing, both theological and otherwise, on the question of sex and/or gender for more on the use of this terminology.

[3] Gn 1:27.

There are two broad schools of thought on the issue of gender. At either end of the spectrum, scholars refer to these approaches as *essentialism* and *constructionism*. *Essentialism*, in its most extreme form, states that gender differences are inherent in our very biology. From outward appearances, to genetic makeup, to neurochemistry, humans are either male or female. In the logic of this narrow approach, it is appropriate to say that men and women are very similar, but essentially different, creatures.[4] By contrast, an equally extreme *constructionist* account of gender difference states that our visible biological differences are nothing more than a necessary evolutionary mechanism to facilitate fertility among the human race.[5] Aside from our genitalia and the necessary hormonal components that make them work, our identity as male or female is entirely a social construct. Whether one is actually male or female is not a matter of birth, but an almost entirely arbitrary distinction and even a matter of "free choice."

Needless to say, one can identify accurate aspects of gender identity in both theories. Most people subscribe to the very common sense notion that men and women are indeed different in some ways that go beyond the blatantly physical differences noticeable when men and women are naked. But at the same time, we also recognize that much of what it means "to be a man" or "to be a woman" seems to be a social construct or at least socially reinforced. Therefore, in considering issues of gender, all the possibilities should be kept in mind. While Christian thought does not endorse either of these extremes, it certainly discerns truth further along one end of the spectrum than the other and, with good reason, insists on the exploration

---

4 The language of "essence" here is deliberate in its philosophical meaning. One can make a distinction between what something *is* and the properties that something *has* (e.g., color, shape, feel, etc.). The former is its *essence* or *substance*, while the latter are its *accidents*. In the case of extreme essentialism, men and women differ in their substance, not merely in their accidents.

5 In this case, it would be appropriate to say that all of our biological differences are merely accidents of an ultimately genderless concept called "human being."

of this question in a much broader context mentioned above, i.e., the Image of God. Only by a thorough understanding of that context can we understand the challenges sometimes offered to the Church on this question.

Gender Equality and Gender Relativism: Mostly Equal, Most of the Time

Contemporary Western society strongly emphasizes the notion of gender equality. Men and women, many believe, should have equal and unfettered access to all the same rights, responsibilities, and especially vocational choices. In a world in which children are seen as a burden as much as a cause for joy, where self-identity is more readily identified with material gain, and where questions of relational responsibility are left ironically up to the will of the individual, complete gender equality is the only option that could make sense in society.

This causes some friction when confronted with other values, including values important to a Catholic understanding of the world. Some of this friction within the Church specifically is likely born from misunderstanding of the Church's teaching, but some of it is also based on the insistence of the social approach of *gender relativism*. This phrase not only refers to the idea described above that men and women are complete equals in all things, but also to the contradictory notion that *sometimes* being male or female entitles one to special consideration. A couple of examples here: many men are happy with women being able to support themselves, and perhaps even their husbands. But some men still insist that men should remain the primary decision-makers for the household. Women, in turn, espouse this same degree of social equality, but are sometimes offended if men do not treat them according to old standards of chivalry.

An even more common example would be the demand of some women for equal pay and equal professional opportunities and responsibilities, while at the same time also demanding time off without restriction to be mothers at home.[6] Where is the equality for men in this case? Some would propose equal time off for fathers as well, which would be appropriate. Some, however, note that since men cannot have babies, the comparison doesn't make sense and therefore men do not factor into the equation. But if this is indeed the case, why is it that no one has pushed for research that would allow men equal access to motherhood? This would create real gender equality. Of course, this seems a little absurd. But the point remains: sometimes social attitudes towards gender stress absolute equality, while maintaining exceptions when they are convenient. It should also be noted that all of the examples provided here have been based on access to money, which speaks more broadly to the problematic materialistic obsession of society.[7]

Despite the problems of gender relativism, the insistence on otherwise absolute gender equality is based on either a scientific notion that gender cannot be neatly stratified into male and female or that society can only be just if absolute equality is in place. We must examine each of these in turn.

It is true that scientific research has continued to reveal a more complicated picture of gender than what was once originally thought. In fact, some scientists distinguish between as many as six different components that determine a person's "gender," and it is unusual that a person will have a unanimous agreement among all six.[8] Even if one questions this specific scientific model, more established data does recognize that a

---

6 Before continuing, I must note that women's choosing to take time off to be mothers at home is a proven benefit to the children and should be avidly supported by society. I am using this case merely to illustrate a point.

7 This is a decidedly Western problem, as many of the moral controversies in this book are. Not all societies across the world have such divisive discussions about gender, nor do they see any problem with specific gender roles as a means to organize society.

8 For more on this, see Robert L. Crooks and Karla Baur, *Our Sexuality*, 9th ed. (Wadsworth Publishing, 2004), 47-53. The six categories are chromosomal sex, gonadal sex, hormonal sex, sex of the internal reproductive structures, sex of the exterior genitals, and sex of the brain.

combination of physical and neuro-chemical traits comprise the full picture of a person's gender.

This scientific ambiguity has led some to consider gender equally a matter of psychological identification as well as physical identification. This can be seen, for instance, in the extreme case of transsexualism.[9] Transsexualism is a condition in which a person is biologically one gender, yet firmly believes that he or she is, in fact, the opposite gender. At a point in the not so distant past, such a condition was universally considered a psychological anomaly, a disorder. Only in extraordinarily rare cases in the past would any counselor actually suggest that the person's psychological identification was actually correct, that their physical appearance was somehow an accident of nature.

In the early 21st century, however, attitudes towards trans-sexualism have changed. While most still find such a condition odd at best and a serious disorder at worst, others are more willing to permit the possibility that nature does seem to make mistakes. Scientific work in line with this idea has advanced tremendously the technological possibilities of "gender re-assignment surgery."[10] The attitude behind such a notion is important if subtle: male or female does not matter. What really matters is that one is comfortable with him- or herself *as he or she defines him- or herself.* There are fewer more radical examples of "freedom" than the decision to supposedly reverse one's very gender! Science and technology are supporting the social need for absolute gender equality by providing the means to modify it as we see fit.[11]

---

[9] This condition is now often referred to instead as "transgender," further demarcating the specific use of language such as "sex" and "gender."

[10] This title is something of a misnomer, as it ultimately does little except to change the outward appearance to match the individual's self-perception.

[11] There is a paradox in the science of gender re-assignment. If the work of some contemporary scientists mentioned earlier is accurate, gender is far more complicated than any hormonal or surgical adjustment alone could change. This is evidence for the elimination of social ideas based on "male" and "female." Yet, the philosophy behind such researchers would have to equally allow the freedom to "change" one's gender, even though there is an inherent recognition that such technologies probably, at best, modify gender, but do not change it.

But this is not the only way in which contemporary science has affected our understanding of gender and indirectly emphasized absolute gender equality. A brief mention must be made here about homosexuality.[12] As homosexual persons fight for and receive increasingly equal "access" to all areas of society (e.g., marriage, having and raising children), there has been a corresponding increase in the popularity of the idea that homosexuality is a matter principally or solely of genetics, or at least of prenatal conditioning. If homosexuality is ever proved to be, for example, completely genetic, it seems unjust to deny the homosexual person any right available to a heterosexual person, especially in the specific examples presented above.

There are problems with this notion. The first problem is that there is no definitive evidence that homosexuality is solely a matter of genetics or prenatal conditions. The available evidence for a genetic component to homosexuality is still inconclusive or has been proven unreliable.[13] However, this hypothesis is often presented as if it were established scientific fact. While equally inconclusive, if an attempt is made to demonstrate that homosexuality may instead be purely psychological (and therefore, arguably, "not normal"), such a theory is discounted as being hateful or discriminatory.[14]

The second problem resulting from the idea of homosexuality being completely genetic relates more specifically to gender. If sexual orientation bears no intrinsic relationship to reproduction, what does it mean to be a man or a woman? Does

---

[12] The morality of homosexual activity will be considered in Chapter Five, and the question of homosexual marriage will be considered in Chapter Seven.

[13] Perhaps the most provocative evidence came about in the early 1990's from the work of Simon LeVey, such as *The Sexual Brain* (The MIT Press, 1994). However, as all of his research was conducted on homosexual men who had also died of AIDS, it was impossible to determine with certitude whether AIDS or homosexuality accounted for the physical differences he discovered.

[14] It is crucial to note at this point that any actual attitude or actions motivated by hate or discrimination against another human person due to his or her sexual orientation (or on any other basis for that matter) is directly contrary to Christian teaching.

homosexuality end up proving a strict constructionist account of gender? Some would happily say that it does, but this truth would result in a massive re-working in the understanding of human society as a whole. Some would readily assert that this also is both true and a good thing. Conversely, however, it seems one would be hard-pressed indeed to imagine that 4,000 years of more or less successful and functional human society (across all times and places) is fundamentally flawed in its understanding of the human person as both an individual and as a member of a community of persons.

Aside from these scientific approaches, there are even louder voices asserting the need for absolute gender equality purely from a social point of view. Social views on gender in the past 50 years have loudly protested against "patriarchal" approaches to social organization, politics, and history. This term is used disparagingly to refer to a male-centered or male-dominated approach to and interpretation of society, without due consideration for the specific concerns or needs of women. In fairness, there is undeniable truth that women have most often not been treated as equals with men throughout most of human history. That said, this sweeping condemnation still fails to take two other points into account. The first is that thousands of years of patriarchy in no way necessarily demonstrates a specifically intended malice on the part of men across history. As a result, one could offer the counter-proposition that perhaps it should be sufficient for society to note and correct the errors of history and then move on. The second is the much more controversial discussion over what degree of patriarchy still remains within society today. Is society still male-dominated? Has there been an honest attempt to increase the social accessibility of women in all critical areas of our society? We will not participate in this debate here. However, it does serve to introduce one specific complaint voiced by many people today that is more germane to the evangelical intent of this book.

The Catholic Church has been accused loudly and often of its purported patriarchal structure. An organization with its origins in another male-dominated religion, based on the teaching of a man, founded by a group of men, with a restricted hierarchy of men (unmarried, no less, at least later on in the Church's history) that remain "in control" to this day: with this description, it would seem that the accusation is not without merit.[15] It also seems that the structure of the Church stubbornly militates against the trend towards absolute gender equality. When faced with this image, there are two approaches one may take: to assume that everything is exactly as it appears to be, and thus discount the Church's place in modern society, or to find out why things are the way they are, resisting the pull towards one's personal agenda and issues. It is worthwhile to note that whichever approach one takes inevitably says something about that person's character.

There is one specific area of the Church that seems to cause more problems than any other in terms of the discussion about gender: the issue of women in the ministerial priesthood.[16] From the point of view of someone standing outside the Church, there simply is no good reason to restrict women from becoming priests. It just seems "unfair." Even within the Church, some theologians and Scripture scholars present evidence in favor of changing this tenet of the Church, either wholly or at least in part (such as the ordination of women as deacons). While this text cannot adequately consider all the elements that make up the reasoning behind this stance on the part of the Church, so controversial to some, we must at least consider what God has revealed to His people regarding gender that has led the Church

---

[15] This description, of course, ignores several critical truths about the Church, such as its divine founder or its essence as a divine, not human institution. But this is the view many people have of the Church: as a merely human institution. The lack of the feminine in this description has been fuel for conspiracy theories for centuries, most recently brought to life in the wildly successful novel *The DaVinci Code* by Dan Brown.

[16] Of course, women are not in fact restricted from priesthood: all people, male and female, are baptized as priests in the sacrament of baptism. This priesthood calls us to offer ourselves, our lives, as a sacrifice to God. See *LG* 10.

to understand that the ministerial priesthood is restricted to men.

Having examined the modern insistence on absolute gender equality (with the exceptions provided by lingering gender relativism), and also examining some of the critiques launched against Catholic teaching, we must have a framework in which to examine the truth revealed by God through His Church. It seems only logical to begin with the Catholic version of gender equality and then examine the specific role of men and women in more detail.

In Christ, There is Neither Male nor Female...

So what is the Catholic response to all that has been said? Is absolute gender equality congruent with the Christian experience of God or not? If it is, why is it so hard to bring it about in society? If not, how does one discern the truth about men and women? To answer these questions requires an approach considerably different from what has been presented so far.

The short answer of Christian tradition to the question of gender equality is: yes. God did make men and women equal. In the story of creation, we read: "God created man in His image... male and female He created them."[17] Both men and women are made equally in the Image of God. Furthermore, in the salvation brought about by Christ, a new life of intimacy with God is possible for both men and women. St. Paul writes: "There does not exist among you Jew or Greek, slave or free, male or female. All are one in Christ Jesus."[18] The invitation to fullness of life in Christ is thus revealed as equally available to both men and women.

The equality intended by God and the equality sought in society differ in key ways. Referring back to the two approaches

[17] Gn 1:27.

[18] Gal 3:28.

to gender equality considered above, equality based on scientific evidence and equality based on social demand, a brief outline of the differences is in order before moving on to a more comprehensive theology of gender difference and gender meaning.

To begin with, the Scriptures clearly indicate that God intended two genders, that despite scientific evidence positing new variables in the question of gender, human beings are fundamentally constituted as either male or female. These variables may prove useful in helping to understand ourselves, they may help explain certain social behaviors, such as why some men act "feminine" and some women act "masculine." They may even ultimately contribute to medical advances that address specifically male or female health issues. But the revealed intention of the Creator is for human beings to be men and women.

Is this conclusion too facile? Is this a simplistic appeal to the Bible while remaining utterly ignorant of scientific advances? If this were a mindless fundamentalist approach, perhaps, but that is not what is asserted here. This answer can be further explained on the basis of faith, on the basis of science, and on the basis of common sense.

On the basis of faith, Christians believe that the Scriptures are the inspired Word of God, alive and active and as true now as they were when they were written. The Bible hasn't lost its relevancy simply because the world is more complicated (contrary to prevailing opinions among many groups in the modern world). As the People of God, it makes sense that we take God's Word as truth. For believers, nothing about human existence makes any sense without reference to the Creator.

On the basis of science, we must note that there is nothing in the view of equality as presented in the Scriptures that is contrary to modern science. Modern science may claim to have a more thorough or more detailed picture. But at the same time modern science hasn't been able to alter the fundamental truth that human beings, as well as almost all mammals and most other animals besides, have two genders; not one, and not more than two. Even if this were solely a way to facilitate reproduction (and it is, in fact, much more than that), this scientific fact corroborates what God has revealed.

Finally, there is the truth that comes to light on the basis of common sense. It simply doesn't take much reflection on the world or on daily experience to realize that there are both men and women in the world, and that they are not exactly the same creature. Reflecting on this for two millennia, Christian tradition discerns the basis for this common sense. It is the natural wisdom perceived by human beings by the light of God's revelation and by means of the created universe. Theologians and philosophers refer to this insight (in part) as *the natural law,* and this title is no idle claim. For example, if one were to encounter a person who insisted that there was only one sex, or that there were more than two sexes, we would *naturally* find this person to be deranged or at least seriously out of sync with what readily appears as common knowledge. Some modern thinkers despise an appeal to common sense but there is a reason that we call it this: because it makes sense to most people.

So if men and women are in fact deemed equal in the eyes of God, how does one explain the apparent disparity between the roles of women and men in His Church? While the answer to this question is composed of several elements, at this point at least it is evident that God's revealed will concerning gender equality in no way prevents women from taking an active role in the community. The stumbling block of absolute gender equality, however, is its specific insistence on equality in *roles.* By contrast, the equality revealed by God is equal access to God's grace, an equal invitation to intimate relationship, an equal calling to redemption by the power of Christ, an equal opportunity to grow in charity, and an equal challenge to holiness. In other words, God has already provided us equality in everything that really matters.

Yet some would claim that this too is too simple an argument, especially when spoken by a man! Women do not appear to have equal access to authority, to the ability to make decisions and changes in the Church. One could debate whether or not this is indeed the case. For instance, with dwindling numbers of priests, especially in sparsely populated areas of the United States for example, women do have positions of authority as pastoral administrators, running all aspects of community life as pastors, with the exception of sacramental ministry. Besides these increasingly common cases, women elsewhere in the Church are able to hold prominent positions in all areas of community life, again with the exception of the administration of all of the Sacraments.[19]

The question of hierarchical "authority," though, deserves more probing consideration. There is a valid perception that the clergy possess authority over the laity, and that without being a member of the hierarchy, one cannot possess real authority in the Church. How one defines authority is crucial here, and repeatedly needs to be measured — by clergy and laity alike — against the criteria Christ gave us for leadership among His followers. If one equates authority with the ability to make policy changes for the whole Church, to arbitrarily interpret Scripture as one sees fit, or to change the basic way the Church is organized, one encounters two related problems. The first and more important is a misunderstanding regarding the purpose of power and authority. Having "authority" within the Church is not the power to control others. It is a responsibility to be a steward for the spiritual well-being of others.[20] It is a sad fact that some people within the Church who do exercise "authority" act as though they "possess" it as a personal prerogative. On the other side, there are many people who seek that type of "authority," and fail to understand just what that means. The second

---

[19] This odd choice of phrase is due to the fact that all baptized believers can baptize if necessary, and the sacrament of matrimony is conferred by the couple on each other. Thus, women have always been able to be ministers of some sacraments as a function of the lay priesthood of all the baptized.

[20] St. Augustine warned about the danger of seeking "authority" in the Church. "When I am frightened by what I am to you, then I am consoled by what I am with you. To you I am the bishop, with you I am a Christian. The first is an office, the second a grace; the first a danger, the second salvation." See *Sermon* 340, 1: PL 38, 1438. See also *LG* 32, in which this is quoted.

problem with the model of the hierarchy posited above is based on a false notion of the scope of the Church's governance. No one possesses the authority within the Church to change what Christ has revealed about His Church, not even the Pope or the bishops acting as a college.

The role of women in Christian history, from the ministry of Jesus Himself to the present, is a valid concern. For all its misfortunes in different epochs and periods, the Church can nonetheless claim the affirmation of this premise: Women should by right be afforded opportunities to assume their positions of responsibility and stewardship within the Church.[21] These opportunities presently exist, though often they are not pursued as avidly as they might be. In part, this is due to a lack of education that such positions are available and that people are needed to fill them. However, there is no escaping the sad truth that too many members of the hierarchy fail to understand their role as shepherd, and instead become more concerned with maintaining administrative control.[22] This emphasis unfortunately creates the impression that women, or even lay people in general, have no authority in the Church. But in any case, one must keep in mind that these approaches to authority are matters of changeable policy, not doctrine or in any way constitutive of the Church.

All of this has been an attempt to respond to the question about God and gender equality. The evidence from the input of faith, science, and common sense all point to a clear conclusion: that God has created men and women as equals. Yet we are *distinctly* men and women, two equal but *different* genders making up one human race. Why? What is the identity, the constitutive difference, even the "destiny," if you will, of being a woman or being a man? We can begin to probe the question by a return to

---

[21] Examples from history would include the prominent leadership role of women in the churches of the apostolic period, the role of Abbesses as spiritual leaders in the Patristic Church, the prophetic witness of women such as Catherine of Siena, and the mystical insights offered by women Doctors of the Church.

[22] See *LG* 27.

human genesis, way back "in the beginning," in a story about God and a very special creature made of the muck of the earth. So let's meet the muck creature.

The Tale of the Muck Creature

We traditionally know the muck creature by its more common title: "man." The muck creature has, from the start, been fascinated by himself: observing himself, judging himself and his fellows, eventually establishing standards about himself. "Man" is *anthropos* in Greek, and this fascination with self eventually evolved into a systematic study (usually indicated with an "-ology"). Hence, the muck creature's disinterested assessment of self and others came to be known as the discipline of *anthropology*.

The final section of this chapter will be concerned specifically with *Christian anthropology*. This term does not refer to a specific study of Christian culture or society, as we might normally envision when we hear the word "anthropology." More broadly speaking, anthropology can be understood as the study of what it means to be a human being. Thus, if one is studying *Christian* anthropology, one must then consider what Christianity has revealed about what it means to be a human being.

As the basis for this explanation, there is no better foundation than the extensive teaching of Pope John Paul II on this subject. In a series of lectures delivered between 1979 and 1984, the Holy Father explained an extremely influential set of teachings now referred to as *the theology of the body*.[23] As this relatively

[23] While we will be considering many of the critical foundational ideas of the theology of the body, this is not a thorough treatment of the theology as a whole. Fortunately, what is provided in this chapter can be easily supplemented by a reading of the compiled teaching itself. It is available as *The Theology of the Body: Human Love in the Divine Plan* (Boston: Pauline Books and Media, 1997). That text may be too daunting for some; fortunately, there are a number of excellent works that present the theology of the body in very readable form, such as the works by Christopher West.

straightforward term suggests, the pope articulated a detailed theological reflection on what it means to be an embodied spiritual creature, what it means to be a body in a world of bodies, what it means to be men and women, why men and women are able to relate to one another in a very special way, and why it seems so difficult sometimes for women and men to actually relate to one another at all.

John Paul II begins his reflection on the meaning of the body by a careful reading of the Book of Genesis, especially Chapter Two. In this second, older story of creation,[24] we read that God fashioned "man" out of the muck of the earth. The word, *adam*, is usually translated as "man," in the sense of "human," but not necessarily "male." Nor is it a proper name. Adam instead refers to the substance of which the muck creature is made, for *adamah* means "earth." "Adam" is thus the earth or muck creature.[25] The Holy Father points out that the creature cannot be understood as a "man" (male) when there is no complement, i.e., woman (female). So the status of the muck creature "Adam" is representative of humanity in general, called into being, given bodily and spiritual existence by God.

The muck creature understands itself as a "self." This is a very specific way in which it is like God, for it understands itself as a person, as a being set apart from the rest of creation. At this point in the story, no other part of creation is like this being. For this reason, the creature is thankful to God who made him. Despite the thankfulness of the creature for its existence, however, it also experiences profound loneliness, for there is nothing else like it to share its personhood with. John Paul II notes that this is the first of three *original experiences* before the experience of Original Sin in Genesis 3. This first experience he calls *original solitude*.

---

[24] Gn 2:4b-3 is actually the older creation story, composed in the 10th c. BC. Gn 1-2:4a was composed during the 6th c. BC.

[25] See Gn 2:6. The word play here is quite deliberate.

In response to this solitude, God gives the creature companionship, in the form of the animals. The creature names each of the animals, signifying dominion over them. But despite the increased population of the garden, there is still no fitting response to the creature's solitude, for none of the animals is made in the Image of God; none of the animals is a person like the creature. The creature is not alone; it has all the other animals with it. But it is *lonely*, for something (someone) is missing. God then puts the muck creature into a deep sleep and fashions another creature out of its rib. When he awakes, he realizes that the new creation is one different in wonderful ways, yet still like himself, another person, also made in the Image of God. This is the origin of woman, and by extension, the "origin" of man, for he can now understand himself as a unique sort of person apart from woman, and vice versa.[26]

Their differences are a cause for celebration, however, not division. The man and the woman recognize that each of them complements the other, each is the missing part of the other, and that the two of them are capable of forming a union. The writer of Genesis gives us an important comment at this point: "That is why a man leaves his father and mother and clings to his wife, and the two of them become one body."[27] The two become one body or one flesh. Aside from this being a blatant sexual reference, confirming the goodness of sexual activity in marriage, this language speaks of the special relationship that exists between the two of them. The Holy Father calls this second of the original experiences *original unity.* In the next chapter, we will consider this experience more fully when we look at the meaning of marriage.

Finally, before the original sin in Chapter Three of Genesis, John Paul II points out the third of the three original experiences.

---

[26] Even the language referring to them changes, for now in Hebrew the man is referred to specifically as *ish*, not *adam*, while the woman is referred to as *ishah*.

[27] Gn 2:24.

At the end of Chapter Two, we read: "The man and his wife were both naked, yet they felt no shame."[28] This is the experience of *original nakedness.* Note the two parts of this simple phrase: (1) they were naked and (2) they felt no shame. We are more concerned with the first part here. The nakedness here does not refer only to a lack of clothing, or even an understanding of them being comfortable in one another's presence without clothing. To understand this more completely, one must understand a deeper meaning to the idea of nakedness. Nakedness implies vulnerability, a recognition that one can be hurt, not just physically, but emotionally as well. Among the many reasons why people are not just regularly naked in front of one another is the fear that one will be used, objectified, manipulated, or judged. In a similar way, we guard ourselves from being *emotionally* naked in front of one another, unless we know and trust the other to not hurt us or take advantage of us. But the Genesis writer invites us to reflect on the fact that the man and his wife did not have that fear, that shame. It expresses the truth that their relationship was free from those forms of abuse.

All of this reflection on the man and the woman and the three original experiences is also part of a bigger revelation about humanity. While we are made in the Image of God in that we are capable of knowing and loving,[29] we are also unlike God in that we are embodied. Unlike angels, we live in a physical world and we relate to one another through the medium of our bodies. If we wish to communicate, we speak with our mouths, make gestures with our limbs, write letters with our hands. Our abil-

---

[28] Gn 2:25. The Hebrew that is rendered as "wife" here is the word for "woman." This is a continuation of the Hebrew wordplay of verse 24. While every biblical translation is at the same time an interpretation, the consistent and ancient understanding of the word as "wife" here suggests the appropriateness of understanding these chapters as an explication of marriage (among the other things here being discussed).

[29] We are made in the Image of God according to the first creation story. See Gn 1:27.

ity to perceive the world through our five senses requires our brains to process information. We *are* bodies, and this is the way that God made us. This cannot be considered an incidental fact, though we readily take it for granted in our day-to-day lives. If we wanted to go into the realm of the highly speculative, we could *imagine* the possibility that God *might* have chosen to create us without bodies. But He didn't. And this must be considered an important part of understanding who we are. It gives us a way to appreciate and celebrate all of God's creation, as well as giving us a way to appreciate one another, serve one another, love one another. We recognize that our deepest relationships are matters of the heart, or the "soul," if you will, but even then, we *manifest* that love through the things that we *do*, the words that we *say*, the *physical* actions that we carry out, with and for one another. According to God's revealed design, our bodies *do* matter. The ultimate proof of this fact is the Incarnation: The Son of God became flesh and dwelt among us, and through His bodily death and resurrection, we embodied creatures are restored to the capacity for wholeness, divine intimacy, of being brought to new and eternal life.

If our bodies matter, then it also follows that being a "man body" or a "woman body" also matters. From this insight follows the need to ponder the meaning of being a man or a woman, as well as the meaning of the unity between them. Begin with the man. It is interesting to note that, in the entire theological tradition of the Church, much *less* is said about man's role in creation than about woman's! One particular aspect of manhood stressed by Pope John Paul II's reflections in the theology of the body is fatherhood. While this specifically relates to having and raising children, this is not the only way that fatherhood is made manifest. The role of the father is to be a protector, provider, and a guide for the children. Of course, this is the role of the mother as well. But the man's outlook on the world tends to go outside himself and his family. Men tend to think in terms of directed approaches towards specific goals, to a concern for "the rules" of human interaction and justice.[30] This colors the way that men interact with the world, and is distinctive and complementary to the way that women interact with the world.

Women have the unique capacity to give, restore, and fulfill life. A 2004 document by the Congregation for the Doctrine of the Faith states, "Women preserve the deep intuition of the goodness in their lives of those actions which elicit life, and contribute to the growth and protection of the other. This intuition is linked to women's physical capacity to give life."[31] Based on this, we can see that woman already exercises a form of priesthood that the man is incapable of in her capacity to be a mother. What the man is by grace as a member of "Holy Mother Church" (i.e., as the bride of Christ), the woman *is* by her very nature *as woman*. As the fullness of the meaning of man is contained in fatherhood, the fullness of the meaning of woman is motherhood, in the many ways "motherhood" is understood. Sadly, this understanding of woman has been minimized or worse, vilified, in the modern world as a limitation or an imposition.

The specific parental strengths of the woman differ from the man's. As the man deals abstractly with situations and arrives at concrete solutions to difficulties, the woman nurtures the interpersonal relationships of the family and so insures the stability of the community. The CDF wisely notes that whenever society loses sight of the distinctly feminine, violence inevitably

---

30 There has been no shortage of material written in psychology in the past 50 years dealing with the supposed differences between the way men and women think. One of the most thorough conversations is the one between followers of the writings of Lawrence Kohlberg, who basically insisted that men are more concerned with justice and moral abstraction, and the writings of his student Carol Gilligan, who posited that women are more concerned with interpersonal relationships and caring for one another. On the other hand, some psychologists find significant weaknesses with both approaches, instead positing that men and women are more or less alike. This brings us full circle to the beginning of the chapter once again. I invite the reader to seek out some of these debates for him- or herself; however, I believe the psychological evidence for behavior differences along gender lines is compelling.

31 CDF, "Letter to the Bishops of the Catholic Church on the Collaboration of Men and Women in the Church and in the World," 13.

increases.[32] It is the intuitive and intrinsic feminine strengths of woman that allow society to exist and to grow in holiness.

These categories of fatherhood and motherhood also extend beyond the bounds of immediate family. The celibate priest is called to be father, as the chaste woman religious is called to be mother, and as married couples who are physically incapable of having children are called to be parents. Broadly speaking, the role of parents is to be stewards for those in their care. We are charged with loving, nurturing, educating, and protecting those that God has entrusted us with. In the family, this specifically includes one's children. For the priest and the Religious, it includes the members of their parish or the community which they serve. For others, the unmarried and those without children of their own, parenthood is an invitation to serve the community in taking care of the hungry, the homeless, or those without hope or direction.

Because of this emphasis on parenthood, the meaning of the unity between man and woman is more important than the isolated meaning of man or woman alone. After all, parenthood cannot exist without both man and woman! God's design, as revealed to us in the Garden of Eden story in Genesis, teaches that men and women were intended to live together in a relationship of equality, reciprocity, complementarity, and love. The very meaning of human existence only makes sense as a result of this relationship. This reaches its fullness, of course, in the sacrament of marriage. But even aside from that very special union, men and women must still relate to one another with respect for both their God-given equality as well as their God-given differences. The community that lacks either the strength of its men or its women will not be an authentic human community.

This all seems rather idealistic. Even within marriage, it seems that men and women can hardly get along today. Why is this? How did we fall so far from the pattern established by the Creator? The key word here is "fall."

---

[32] Ibid.

Genesis 3 records the account of the first sin, the first time that human beings used God's gift of freedom against Him: to make a choice contrary to God's will. Blame should not be placed solely on the woman or on the man. Each of them made this fatal decision. When this sin is revealed for what it is, the effects of it are immediate and universally far-reaching for the human condition. This is the theological category of Original Sin, into which we are all born.

And the litany of these effects is dismal. The relationship between creature and Creator broke down. Humanity chose to turn away from God's love, the very love that sustains everything in being. Therefore, as we try to make it on our own (consciously or unconsciously) without God, we are inevitably faced with failure. This is particularly so in the fundamental relationship between man and woman. No longer was their relationship characterized by equality and innocence. They now knew that they were naked, and they hid in shame from one another. The culmination of this breakdown occurs at the end of Chapter Three in Genesis, when the man names his wife Eve, just as he named the animals before her.[33] So begins the history of disordered male domination. Note well that this is *not* God's design! The effects of the ever-expanding misuse of the precious gift of freedom are everywhere evident and still rampant in so many parts of life.

To talk of sin brings new focus to the point of our present project. Morality seeks to re-orient our freedom away from sin and toward the will of God. Morality is the name we give to our voluntary response to God's plan for us as men and women. Moral reflection, especially for issues that are rather specifically gender-related, such as sexual ethics, is essential to understanding that freedom. The revelation that God intended us to be equal but different is the foundation for us to respect the unique gifts that men and women offer to society. Modern insistence on absolute gender equality destroys the possibility of appreciating one

[33] Gn 3:20.

another for our differences, which is ironic in a Western culture that seems to put such a high premium on "diversity."

In Chapter Two, the methodological categories of action and character, the role of conscience, and the priority of relationships as our guide for morality were considered. Each of these categories has far-reaching implications in terms of gender. Beginning with action, we can see that certain choices available to us are based wholly or largely on gender. For example, a man can use his ability to procreate more prolifically than a woman, to abuse his gift of sexuality and have children with many different women. The man who does this may do so out of a misguided desire for a legacy to carry on his genetic identity, or it may simply be promiscuity. Similarly, a woman who is pregnant is faced with the distinct choice to have the child or end its life with abortion. No man is faced with this personal bodily decision. A man may abuse his gender to exploit prevailing currents of male dominance in society. Gender indeed can have an effect on our actions.

All these examples relate to the issue of character as well. How one uses one's manhood or womanhood speaks of character in general, but also more specifically to one's character as a gendered person. The choices that one makes, and even the *thoughts* about those choices, are always going to be made as a man or as a woman. In interpersonal relationships, certain character traits are understood to be indicative of "good" male or female character and "bad" male or female character. Of course, some of these ideas are culturally determined and so of lesser value in moral evaluation. But all that was said above about the meaning of being man or woman, especially in terms of parenthood, strongly suggests that we can validly speak about the virtues of a man or woman of exceptional character.

Because gender relates to both actions and character, it is a fitting category to engage the conscience. Obviously, one does not need to use his or her conscience to ask, "Should I act as a man or a woman?" As we saw above, this is inherent in the very fact that we *are* men and women. Gender is, however, another category of moral knowledge that can be used by the conscience to determine the best way to act. In this way, we realize our character as people whom God has loved.

The most important category of all is relationships. Based on all that has been said thus far, it is obvious that gender impacts all our relationships. Relationships generate responsibilities. We have a responsibility to take seriously the way that God has made us. We have a responsibility to understand what it means to be a man or a woman created in the Image of God. We have a responsibility to demonstrate that understanding in a way of living that makes use of the unique strengths, talents, and gifts that only woman possesses and only man possesses. If we fail to honor these responsibilities, *all* of our relationships will suffer. We will be acting as men and women who have failed, deliberately or by our negligence, to be who God has called us to be. Understanding our anthropology, the meaning of why God made us the way that He did, is not just an option useful for our spiritual growth; it is, in fact, a moral necessity. These relational responsibilities are fundamental to the examination of specific moral issues.

God created human beings as two different ways of being a person: male-persons and female-persons. Speculation whether or not God could have created us differently is fruitless. One could wish that gender differences were not so problematic in society. However, women and men are different. These differences matter, even when we don't want them to, and they cannot be rationalized away. Rather than fighting the truth (which, by the way, is a perfectly workable definition of sin), the believer must instead embrace the responsibilities that truth entails: that we are persons made in the Image of God. This is the script of the love story. Life is simpler when it is true to its nature. Relationships are happiest when they are connected to their source. We are only capable of living the love life that we have been called to if we are faithful to the script. Living in this way makes this truth more accessible to others, and encourages them likewise to the truth, a sharing of "character," if you will. As is the case in moral life as a whole, love generates love.

How does all of this relate to the Church's insistence in upholding the constant tradition that only men can be ordained to the ministerial priesthood? Part of the reasoning behind a male priesthood is the teaching of Christ Himself, from which the Church discerned a practical theology from the start. This cannot totally be blamed on a historically conditioned mindset or simple bias. Jesus was certainly remarkably open in His attitude towards women, contrary to prevailing views of the day.[34] More than once in the Gospels, Jesus' own disciples are shocked by His affirming behavior toward women.[35] In choosing those who He commissioned to spread the Gospel and shepherd the community, He chose both men and women. The central figures at the dawn of the Christ Event are the Virgin Mary and Elizabeth, the mother of John the Baptist. But those twelve men He chose as His constant companions for three years, to whom He revealed the mysteries of salvation, in whom He laid the foundations of the Kingdom in terms of leadership, were given a specific role the night before He died. They were empowered for that role by a charism shared only among themselves: to shepherd the community through the priesthood of the New Covenant. If Jesus wanted to, He could have chosen women to be among them. In fact, however, He did not. Later theology would assert that "grace builds upon nature." And that is the heart of the issue here.

Human nature is created by God as distinctly a male version of this nature or as a female version of this nature. Whatever other rationale is set forth to support the traditional practice of ordination in all the valid apostolic succession Churches of East and West, this fundamental mystery that conjoins maleness and priesthood is basic. It is the complement of the divine mystery that conjoins femaleness and motherhood, both physical and spiritual. It is only in this light, in a wisdom that defies firm

[34] In the centuries that followed, Christianity was also at the forefront of recognizing the rights of women in society in general.

[35] See, for example, Jn 4:27.

articulation (as all mystery defies being chained to human comprehension) that we can actually see the fallacy of the commonly held notion that it would have made perfect sense for Christ to choose His own mother to be one of His first priests. After all, no one is more fitting as a model disciple than the Mother of God. As Catholics, we hold Mary to be the best human creature that has or will ever live, most perfect of the redeemed, united to the Holy Trinity in a unique personal intimacy and holiness. Yet Jesus chose *those* twelve men to be the first bishops of His Church.[36] And there were other men He did not choose (e.g., Joseph of Arimathea, Nicodemus, John the Baptist).

Thus, the theological congruence between the role of the priest and maleness further sheds light on why only men — and specifically chosen men — can serve in the ordained priesthood: the ordained priest acts *in persona Christi*, in the person of Christ.[37] This is irreducibly important: the priest acts as Christ for the community, not only *in* His name, but *as* His living presence among His people to feed, to heal, to strengthen, to teach, and to love "as He has loved us." Contrary to some contemporary thinking, the biological fact that Jesus Christ is a man is not the reason why the priest must also be a man. Such narrow symbolism would in fact ignore that all Christians are baptized as "a chosen race, a royal priesthood, a holy nation, a people of his own."[38] Rather, the key to grasping the Church's deeply rooted reasons that the *ordained* priest must be a man has to do with the essential meaning of the Covenant relationship between Christ and His Church. Like spousal Eve, taken from Adam's side, the spousal Church is born in sacraments of Baptism and Eucharist from the pierced side of Jesus on the Cross.[39] There He is forever Priest, Altar, and Victim. And *there* He sums up all these roles as Spouse. In the marital imagery of the Church articulated in the

---

[36] See *Inter Insigniores* 4.

[37] See CCC 1548-1551.

[38] See 1 P 2:9.

[39] See Jn 19:33-35.

Letter to the Ephesians, Christ is the Bridegroom and His Church is the Bride.[40] Therefore, acting *in persona Christi*, the priest acts as the Spouse, as Christ the Bridegroom, who loves His Church and gave Himself up for her. All of us together make up the Church, the Bride of Christ, but the priest, specifically *as priest*, acts as Christ the Bridegroom.[41] This actually leads us back to our consideration of the meaning of gender. The priest, acting as Christ, as spiritual father, is ordained to do what Jesus did, with His authority and with the efficacy with which the Spirit flourished Christ's ministry: to announce the Gospel from the Father, to foster a community of faith, and to celebrate and make available the Sacred Mysteries with His own hands. The priest does not do this on his own, of course, but rather through the celebration of the sacraments as specific encounters with God's grace, which, through the Church, Christ's Bride and our Mother, give life, restore life, and fulfill life.

This idea of priest as Bridegroom explains how the priest acts *in persona Christi* in a re-presentation of the Sacred Mysteries of the ever-present reality of salvation. More critically and at the core of this great charism, the priest acts *in persona Christi* because of the *ontological constitution of the priesthood*. What this means is that a man who has become a priest has been radically, literally changed. He has been "marked" by God as priest. It is this that distinguishes the priesthood most distinctively from being a simple career choice or even the choice made by a community about the persons who are going to shepherd them. Priests do not simply choose to become priests, or become priests by popular acclaim, but rather are *called* by God and *anointed* by God and affirmed as such by the community.

The basis for this claim can be found throughout the history

---

[40] See Eph 5:21-32. Also see Jn 2:35-36 and Rv 21.

[41] Again, it is also important to note that *all* Christians are baptized as priests. The role of the priest (in general terms) is to offer sacrifice to God. While we make a special distinction for the ordained priesthood of some men, we are called to offer our very lives as sacrifices to God. See *LG* 10.

of God's people. Abraham is called into Covenant and begs the royal priest Melchizedek to offer sacrifice. During the time the Old Covenant was made known to the newly liberated Israelites by Moses, his brother Aaron was named by God to be priest. "Naming" for the ancient Hebrews was "to call into being" or "to make a new being" of the one so named.[42] The inference here is that Aaron did not choose to become priest, any more than he chose to be created. Nor did Moses or the people choose him to be priest. God named him priest. Furthermore, the sons of Aaron were also named priest. From this point forward, Aaron and his descendants held a unique place among God's people — they were priests, called apart specifically for this role. Aaron in particular was named High Priest by God Himself.

In the fullness of time, God sent us a High Priest, Jesus Christ, who would do more than offer sacrifice on behalf of God's people. He Himself would be both Priest and Sacrifice, such that no other sacrifice would ever again be needed. The one Sacrifice of Himself was complete and eternal, all sufficient, and so, fully operative now and forever in the priesthood of the Church. As the Word made flesh, Jesus is sent to be the Reconciler; hence He is forever Priest and Sacrifice according to the will of His Father. "No one takes this honor on himself."[43] Thus, a priest, called to act *in persona Christi* must be called according to the pattern set forth by God in Christ: chosen, sent, and empowered to unite humankind with God.

Fatherhood indeed remains the male complement to the vocation of motherhood. There is also a complementary relationship between priesthood and motherhood revealed in Scripture. In every case in which a woman was called by God to be mother

---

[42] There are plenty of examples of name changes in the Old Testament. In every case, the name change itself signifies that the person has changed, that they no longer are who they once were.

[43] Heb 5:4.

in order to further the mystery of salvation revealed through history, the woman in question is married to a man chosen as a mediator to realize a covenant with God. In the early Old Testament, a wider concept of priesthood empowered the patriarchs and prophets. They offered sacrifice as a sign and seal of their spiritual fatherhood, shepherding their people as "God's flock." All of these men foreshadow the Levitical priesthood of Aaron and prepared human understanding for the fulfillment of these "types": the messianic priesthood of Christ. In a literary convention almost unknown in the literature and folklore of the time, women are mentioned in pivotal roles — a paradigm for the Church to come. Abraham's wife, Sarah, Isaac's Rebekah, Jacob's Rachel and Leah, among other strong women of the Old Testament, are essential to the story. The role of these extraordinary women — mothers, prophetesses, and even warriors (Hannah, Ruth, Esther, Judith, Susanna) — is the underpinning of the male priestly role. We have already pointed out the New Testament figures of the Virgin Mary and Elizabeth, the mother of John the Baptist. The work of God is made manifest through mothers and fathers, but priesthood is another specifically male way in which one's vocation may be lived out. As much as it may grate against the modern insistence on absolute gender equality, this is not an arbitrary decision on the part of the Church. Rather the Church is doing nothing more than what God has revealed to us, only what God has given us permission to do.

This charism-oriented understanding of being male or female naturally affects the greater picture of the Church's understanding of itself. So, necessarily, gender has a self-evident effect on many moral issues. This is nowhere more true than in the realm of sexual ethics. Catholic sexual teaching will likely remain one of the most controversial topics in any modern discussion of morality, somewhat ironic when one considers how infrequently Jesus Himself spoke about it. This has less to do with the value that He placed on it, and more to do with His greater concern for other ways we abuse our relationship with

God and with one another. That observation into human nature by the Christ is still wholly relevant, but our culture has created a situation in which sexuality increasingly figures in those relationships in an unavoidable way (no matter how hard one tries even!). So let's talk about sex.

Chapter Five

Let's Talk About Sex: The Linchpin for Many Other Issues

We live in a world that has become fixated on sex. This is not merely a matter of opinion. It is readily evident from even a casual perusal of our culture, especially in the realm of popular entertainment. Discussion about sex, products designed to help people have sex, more products and clothing designed to make one more sexually appealing, presentations of sex on TV, movies, and the Internet: it seems the only way one can escape this barrage is to avoid popular culture altogether; admittedly that is not an easy task. Given the challenges offered by the present context, we must continually ponder what God has revealed to us about sexual activity and what place it is supposed to have in our relationships with ourselves, with others, and even with God.

At Fatima, the Virgin Mary reportedly appeared to a group of Portuguese shepherd children and said that more people end up in hell for sins of lust than any other sin.[1] This may or may not be shocking to us, or we might think that such a succinct statement is "proof" that Catholicism itself is hopelessly fixated

[1] As private revelation, it is true that the Church does not require belief in this event as necessary for salvation, and it is not strictly theological. But the fact remains that the Church approved the content of this vision because it was congruent with the Gospel and Tradition.

on sex. But the assumption that sex is inherently damning or the idea that Christianity is utterly against sex both miss the more important truth of Mary's message. Sex is not only a series of isolated actions,[2] but also a way of looking at the world, as we discussed last chapter. One of the difficulties in the modern world is a confusion between our gendered ways, or if you will, our sexual ways, of looking at the world, and actions that specifically involve our biology.[3] As a result of this confusion, we become fixated on sexual activity or on actions and attitudes that facilitate sexual activity. This is a problem for both believers and those with a purely secular world view. The problem is that sometimes those with a secular mindset, who have a selfish interest in justifying their own sexual behavior, invariably criticize Catholic teaching primarily on this topic. As a result, they misunderstand Catholic sexual ethics and so end up discarding the rest of Catholicism: the life-giving truth that frees us to be who God called us to be in order that we might truly be happy. The modern world is full of otherwise good-intentioned people who have settled for a lesser good, sexual pleasure, mistaking it for something that it is not. Let's unpack this idea a little bit further.

While this popular fixation on sex may be problematic, the basic drive towards sexual activity, the appreciation of it, in some cases even the curiosity about it, are not. God is the designer of sex and the earliest chapters of the Bible contain His unambiguous support for it.[4] It was clearly the Creator's intent for human beings to engage in and enjoy sex!

But as sinful human beings, we have historically lost sight of the Creator's design and pursue instead what we think is

---

[2] Remember first and foremost, sex isn't something that we *do*; sex is something that we *are*. To isolate actions apart from persons would be to fall into the heresy of dualism, distinguishing the person from his or her body.

[3] This is about more than just our genitals; sex is primarily a matter of our brains.

[4] The blessing of fertility in Gn 1:28 is also a command for human beings to reproduce.

best. We have a propensity to substitute lesser goods for greater goods, or even for the greatest good, God.[5] These lesser goods may not in themselves be evil, but they lead us to make bad choices when we give them more value than they should have. Because of the immense goodness of the gift of our sexuality, there is a strong temptation for us to misuse it, to ascribe to it a more important, and hence distorted, role than it should have in our lives, or perhaps worst of all, to let it become a god for us. This is the reason why so many people have difficulty with sexual sins. It is not because sex is bad, but rather because it's *so* good, that we make it the *only* good. This is not what God has revealed to us.

In this chapter, we will look at many of the ways that sex is abused and overused, as well as some of the principal arguments put forth to justify such behavior. In response to this, we will once again look at what it really means to be created by God, what it means to be incorporated into the Body of Christ, and what meaning human sexuality has because of these realities. This will provide us with some practical responses to the excessive emphasis on the use of sex as marketing tool, entertainment, means of establishing or improving self-esteem, and so many other things in our culture. These principles recall us to a way of relating to others that concentrates on the true sexual self created in the Image of God.

While the frequency and intensity of sexual sin in the modern world encourages this chapter to be slightly longer than the rest, the present work offers an introduction to the subject. Fortunately, there are a number of excellent texts available that focus solely on the questions of Catholic sexual ethics, and which are written for a general audience. With this caveat in mind, we can review the recent past for the roots of this modern problem.

[5] For a simple explanation of God as the greatest good, see Peter Kreeft's *Making Choices* (Ann Arbor: Servant Books, 1990), 73-91.

Sex Without Babies, Babies Without Sex

At the risk of oversimplification, the fundamental disconnect between Catholic sexual ethics and the actual behavior of so many people can be traced to a *contraceptive mentality.* Technological advances and cultural changes have divorced sex from its most fundamental meaning: an intimacy that leads to procreation. While human sexuality is clearly about more than just reproduction, it seems illogical to ignore the fact that this is the natural purpose of the act. And yet reproduction hardly seems acknowledged in the popular understanding of sexual activity. Nowadays, we can have sex without babies and babies without sex! How did this come about?

The root of this curious dichotomy goes back to our discussion of philosophical history in Chapter One. In the Enlightenment, people imagined that one did not need any external authority to guide him or her in how to live a good life.[6] These philosophers contended that, simply by the power of human reason, humankind would rise above the "restricting" authorities of Church and the nobility and form a just civilization. While these thinkers' intentions may have been good, and while they demonstrated a certain intuitive understanding of natural law, the actual lived results of the project were far less successful. Many of the Enlightenment thinkers discounted the influence of human sinfulness. This is why the utopia they sought never came about.

So, while the project may not have succeeded, certain ideas took root in modern culture, contributing strongly to our present misunderstandings of sexuality. Principal among these is the modern understanding of the term "freedom." Freedom

---

[6] Of course, this idea is flawed from the very beginning, for we as Christians also do not believe that any external authority guides, but rather the very living presence of God active within us. The notion that Christian morality comes from an outside authority is part of the legacy of nominalism, also discussed in Chapter One.

should be properly understood as a *freedom for excellence,* the gracious option to know the Truth and to live in Love. But instead, we understand "freedom" to mean that we are free to choose to do what we want, free to define ourselves as we wish to be rather than as God has made us to be. The result is a world of "free" people that feeds our illusions about ourselves and masks selfishness as a debased form of "love."

This version of "freedom" has allowed people to re-define the meaning both of sexuality and of relationships for themselves. Historically, the symptoms of this first appeared in a subtle form, with the increasing acceptance of pornography, experiments in alternative family structures, and studies that investigated the link between fertility and people's actual sexual experiences.[7] The influence of these symptoms began to become even more pervasive in the 20th century. Two events in particular occurred that ultimately have had a profound effect on our modern understanding of sexuality. The first is the work of Margaret Sanger, the founder of Planned Parenthood, and her insistence that reproductive control was critical for women's rights. The second was the 1930 Anglican Lambeth Conference, which was the first time in history in which a Christian community permitted married couples to use contraception.[8] This latter event would set the stage for the social explosion that occurred with Pope Paul VI's encyclical *Humanae Vitae* in July, 1968. But, by and large, there was still a strong social sentiment that sex was to be reserved for marriage, and marital sex was primarily for having children.

---

[7] Contrary to perhaps many people's understanding, some of these ideas began long before the past 50 years. For more on the history of the Enlightenment and its effect on sexuality, see E. Michael Jones, *Monsters From the Id: The Rise of Horror in Fiction and Film* (Dallas: Spence Publishing Company, 2000) and Peter Gardella, *Innocent Ecstasy: How Christianity Gave America an Ethic of Sexual Pleasure* (New York: Oxford University Press, 1985).

[8] These were not the *only* critical events of the 20th c. before 1960; they are just particularly germane to the contemporary disconnect between Catholic thought and Western secular thinking on sexuality.

This changed radically in America in the 1960's. The sexual revolution that had begun almost two centuries before in Europe in elitist circles had a breakthrough in American culture due to a number of social factors. Common to many of these factors was an increased public awareness of the notion of "freedom," combined with a distrust of authority (fundamentally the same kind of distrust that murdered priest and noble during the French Revolution), and combined further with advances in medical technology that made contraception more reliable. The result: a new openness to sexual experiences apart from procreation. No longer was sex something that "belonged" solely to married couples. Instead, sex could be used by unmarried couples for recreation, or for friendship, or as a celebration of a nascent New Ageism, or any number of other possible reasons.[9] And while America may have come later to the party, America's position of world prominence and its extraordinary media machine made these ideas even more widely accepted elsewhere in the West.

This set the stage for what occurred within the Catholic Church. The story of the encyclical *Humanae Vitae* is a very interesting one.[10] Basically, the shift in values mentioned above, combined with an increasing number of non-Catholic Christian denominations which now permitted the use of contraception, led many to believe that it was only a matter of time before Catholicism would also permit the use of contraception by married couples. In fact, Paul VI gathered a special commission to address that very topic. The final result of those deliberations was the encyclical itself, which concluded that contraception was *not* acceptable, *contrary* to the consensus of the very commission assigned to examine the issue. This sparked an immediate

[9] It was an unfortunate naïveté that the many developers of contraceptive methods thought that they would only be used by married couples!

[10] For those interested in exploring both the content of the document and its history of controversy, there is no better resource than Janet E. Smith's *Humanae Vitae: A Generation Later* (Washington, DC: The Catholic University of America Press, 1991).

rebellion in the Church,[11] leading from levels of dissent ranging from "respectful" disagreement with the teaching to complete exodus from the Church's ranks. The wisdom of the Holy Spirit in this regard, however, will be manifest as we continue onward in this chapter.

Clearly, *Humanae Vitae*'s teaching fell on deaf ears. The sexual revolution established an important (albeit erroneous) modern premise: sex and procreation did not have to be essentially linked. Procreation was reduced to being an optional extra for sex. In fact, technology would soon advance that would even go further and assert that sex was not even necessary for procreation: sex without babies and babies without sex.

What are the repercussions of this critical shift in our understanding of human sexuality? There are many, but they are all specifically related to our understanding of both fertility and relationships. At the risk of oversimplification, once sex and procreation are no longer understood together, almost everything becomes justifiable: contraception, premarital sex, artificial reproduction, pornography, homosexual marriage. If sex is not for having babies, and if both sex and having babies have nothing to do with the meaning of marriage, then how can we possibly hope that people would understand Christian teaching? How can we possibly be surprised by the rapid social changes of our world that wish to redefine such fundamental concepts as marriage and family? This is the unfortunate situation that we have created for ourselves in Western culture. We Christians find ourselves stunned or disheartened by things we see or read today. Do we also understand that these are the inevitable consequences of our decision to see fertility as a problem to be dealt with rather than as a gift to be respected and celebrated?

---

[11] In this case, this is a literal truth: official statements of dissent existed the very day after the encyclical's release. Of course, this misses the point of the encyclical, which is about marriage as a whole, not just the prohibition against contraception.

With this brief history in mind, we can turn to the modern view of sex and relationships in more detail. It seems worthwhile to consider all of the arguments presented in favor of the modern view before offering a detailed but concise refutation of these same arguments based on Christian anthropology and what it tells us about marriage, procreation, and chastity. Morality is about developing and maintaining loving relationships, so the thinking person must strive to be clear about how love is actually made manifest between people, separated from the illusions spawned by selfishness, brokenness, and self-loathing.

The Most Important Thing and the Least Important Thing in the World

One of the psychological advantages of moral relativism and emotivism as moral methodologies is that they free a person from the confines of logical and rational thought. Flippancy aside, there is a truth here. In conversation with someone who wishes to justify his or her own sexual morality (or lack thereof), it is not uncommon to hear that, on the one hand, sex (or whatever specific aspect of sexual experience is being discussed) is so great that any attempt to limit its expression with some "code" or "rule" fails to consider how wonderful it is. One should have sexual freedom because everyone should be able to experience "how great sex is." Limitations seem prudish, or maybe even unloving in some way.

On the other hand, a Catholic should agree that sex *is* great, it is important, and it is an amazing gift of God. For all of these reasons, the gift of sexuality deserves deep respect. The Catholic might explain how the marital act is an opportunity for integral human persons to experience something analogous to the inner life of the Triune God, or that it expresses the love of Christ for His Church. At this point, the conversational partner is likely to screw up their face in confusion and even go so far as to respond: "Why are you making such a big deal about this? It's just sex." And therein lies the essentially logical inconsistency of the modern approach to sexuality: people treat sex as though it is both the most important and the least important thing in the world. But we can't logically have it both ways. Either it is important enough to deserve special respect or it is not important and should not be such a "big deal" in our culture. Christian anthropology asserts that in fact it *is* important and *does* deserve special respect.

But that is clearly not the dominant view of modern secular culture. Certainly, many of the ideas supporting this view are as ancient as pagan antiquity, but some are "modern" in the sense that even traditions of appropriate sexual behavior spanning centuries have been ignored. To grasp the latest bout in the struggle between the sacred and the secular, one must consider the various points of view put forth by people to justify a skewed perspective on human sexuality. The fundamental place to begin this consideration is by investigating "relationships" in broad terms.

Due to changing social conditions, the process of "courtship" has also changed drastically.[12] While one should strive to avoid an excessively romantic view of the past, it seems reasonable to state that, at a time not so long ago, a man and a woman would date, perhaps beginning in high school, and would eventually make the decision to marry and start a life together. While there was no guarantee that this picture-perfect model was without difficulty, couples generally stayed together, raised children, and lived their lives. Sexual activity was highly restricted or (ideally) non-existent before marriage, and an emphasis on sexual activity within marriage was certainly not stressed or advocated in popular culture.

---

[12] For the purposes of this explanation, I will be concentrating on the experience principally of the developed West, especially the United States. This description would certainly not be accurate for the whole world in all aspects.

Hardly a single element of this simplified account of dating and marriage exists in the First World of the 21st century. Instead, a young person is likely to date several different people, not only in his or her teenage years, but also into his or her 20's. While this is not necessarily a problem in itself, an important difference is that now young people will more often than not experience some form of sexual expression in many of these different relationships. "Sexual expression" refers to anything along the spectrum of activities ranging from various forms of "petting" all the way to sexual intercourse. Eventually, after a person has had the opportunity to explore different relationships and different world experiences, and often after establishing a career, he or she might finally consider marriage. Two young adults marry, bringing into the marriage not only their careers and life experiences, but also the history of all of their previous relationships. One can only hope that the couple is able to navigate through this history while making the decision of whether or not to have children. Oftentimes, interest in career, freedom to travel, or just desire for material gain defers childbearing until later in life, or else it is avoided altogether.

The differences between the "then and now" accounts described above can be further investigated by considering specific aspects of modern sexual experience. To continue to move from the more general to the more specific in this section of the chapter, having describing relationships in general, the next step is to examine modern attitudes towards marriage in particular.

Because of the modern secular mindset regarding sexuality (often misnamed "freedom"), marriage is no longer deemed a necessary condition for sexual activity. In fact, the recreational view of sexual intercourse (and this includes attitudes ranging all the way from blatant promiscuity to serial monogamy and to intercourse as a sign of love and commitment) means that the decision to get married is instead relegated only to a desire for children. In other words, if a couple is sexually active, yet does not plan to have children, there is no need to make the relationship "socially permanent" through the institution of marriage.[13] In the interest of encompassing as many views along the spectrum of modern secular thought as we can, a couple might also decide to get married because they wish to make their relationship "socially permanent" in the eyes of their family and friends, with or without the possibility of children in the future.

At this point, yet another logical inconsistency is encountered in the modern secular mindset. While some couples will insist that marriage is for having children, this seems contradicted by the reality of contraception, so widely used by many married couples. In America, for instance, statistics seem to bear out the fact that most married couples regularly use some form of contraception.[14] So what *is* the reality? Is marriage for having children or not?

These related questions are the key to understanding the problem of the contemporary fixation with sexuality. The reality of easy, reliable forms of birth control has consequentially invited couples to define marriage for themselves. Some couples hold to traditional notions of the place of sexuality within marriage and its connection to children. Other couples will insist that sex is for any committed couple and that marriage is only necessary when a couple is ready to "have kids." Still other couples will instead define marriage as a public proclamation of a permanent love commitment that has little or nothing to do with children at all. Some couples see marriage as a necessary step in order to have access to specific social and economic benefits. Finally, some couples will find marriage to be an antiquated and unnecessary institution altogether. Marriage then apparently has

---

[13] In fact, even this point of view is not necessarily the case. Some would hold that marriage itself is nothing more than a choice made for social, legal, and/or economic purposes. Other than these purposes, it has no meaning for the relationship itself.

[14] According to UN statistics for 1996, 76.4% of married women, age 15-49, use contraception. About 6% of women use "non-modern" methods which, in this survey, would likely include methods of natural family planning (discussed later in this chapter).

no objective identity of its own; it is a notion that one has a right to define as one wishes.

In fact, "rights language" is prominent in modern social discourse on sexuality. After all, if one is "free" to do as one wishes, it makes sense that one has a "right" to do as one wishes, especially in a country as thoroughly connected to the notion of freedom as is the United States of America. Yet even the very use of rights language (and so "freedom") in philosophical and political discourse has changed. Instead of a concept of human rights based on some objective criteria of what it means to be human, we have simplified the definition to apply "rights" to whatever suits our fancy, provided it doesn't "obviously hurt" someone else. For example, most 21st century secular Americans would not say that he or she has the right to randomly shoot someone else, as that plainly hurts someone else, and thus one does not have a right to do that. However, the same person may assert that one has a right to have consensual sex with any adult they wish, as that does not plainly "hurt" anyone.[15]

This modern re-envisioning of rights language can be seen not only in discussions of marriage, but also more tellingly in discussions about birth control. In the early 20th century, Margaret Sanger asserted that birth control was necessary in order to secure the full "rights" of women. As long as women were tied to childbearing, Sanger believed that women would not be able to participate fully in society. This represents a change from understanding motherhood as something good for its contribution to society to understanding any number of other concepts (career, material gain, direct political participation) as more important than motherhood. This is not to deny the importance of these other concepts, or even to suggest the proper

[15] Whether it actually does hurt anyone remains to be seen. But also note how carefully I had to choose my example: "consensual sex with any adult." This rules out rape and/or pedophilia, for instance; yet to rule those examples out requires an appeal to some objective law that says such activities are wrong or inappropriate. Once again, we encounter the logical fallacy of moral relativism.

place of motherhood in a hierarchy with these other concepts. It does, however, demonstrate that a logically sound, experientially proven understanding of society has been rejected in favor of newer ideas, and for no better reason (despite language to the contrary) than that these newer ideas are more attractive to our own selfish desires.

Moving on from the specific category of marriage and children, an examination of the subject leads to even more specific aspects of human sexuality, constantly referring back to the modern revisionism which "frees" us to define with impunity the meaning of marriage and sex as one chooses. In this way, many of the principal arguments used in favor of these practices are manifest. The remainder of this section will consider extramarital sex, other forms of sexual expression outside of intercourse, masturbation, pornography, and homosexuality.

The category of extramarital sex includes both premarital sex and adultery. Adultery is easier to analyze, so it's helpful to begin with that. As a subtle testament to the common sense notion of natural law, most people, regardless of their moral development, still tend to see the violation of the marital relationship as unacceptable. There is a monumental irony here in the fact that we cannot agree on what the definition of marriage should be, but most agree that it cannot be violated! Despite this traditional repugnance towards extramarital sex in the form of adultery, some people would still advocate its practice. Some may protest that seeking "love" outside of a loveless or abusive relationship is understandable and therefore also morally acceptable. Others will claim that having sex outside the marital relationship is merely an extracurricular exercise or a practice to help strengthen the more serious and committed marital relationship. People who are not married may not be adverse to sex with a married person for, they reason, if the married person has no respect for the marriage bond, why should the extramarital "lover"? Hence there are some rationalizations offered for adulterous behavior, but these are generally considered "exceptional" cases.

Turning to premarital sex, however, one encounters a much wider array of rationale. Premarital sex is not an exception; rather, it is the norm for most developed Western societies.[16] Within the past 40 years, this has become so much the case that the idea of *not* engaging in premarital sex seems exceptional and noteworthy. When questioning why people would have sex before marriage, the answers are many, but all these lead back to the basic human desire to choose to do as one wishes. However, before writing off all instances of premarital sex merely as promiscuity, it should be pointed out that, while some people do have sex purely for recreational, selfish, and/or hedonistic reasons, others seem willing to admit that sex is generally to be reserved for the context of a "serious" relationship.

One of the subsequent issues then, of course, is defining what constitutes a serious relationship. In the hormonal storms of adolescence, teenagers are quick to embrace the notion of dating seriously and so make choices about sexual activity accordingly. As they get older, they start to have more reasonable understandings of commitment, but they often already have begun active sexual lives at that point. As a result, some young adults are quite willing to say that if a person is worth going on three actual "dates" with, then they are also worth having sex with. Others possess more self-control and may wait months, occasionally (though rarely) years, to have sex with a partner.

But the timetable is not the issue; the justification is. In all of these cases, there is a belief that genital activity is acceptable within a committed relationship, because sexual intercourse is nothing more than an especially intimate way of showing affection. After all, sex is usually fun for both people, and it often has the effect of strengthening the relationship. Further, with contraception (and possibly even abortion), one can even control

---

[16] According to Robert T. Michael et al, in *Sex in America: A Definitive Survey* (New York: Warner Books, 1994), only 7% of men and 21% of women are virgins on their wedding night.

the consequences. The contraceptive mentality is demonstrated again: there is no necessary connection between sex, marriage, and procreation.[17]

People not only engage in sex outside of the marital context but also in a host of other sexual activities as well. We can include in this category all forms of sexual contact that are sometimes covered under the broad term "petting," and all forms of non-vaginal intercourse, i.e., oral and anal intercourse. The attempt at justification for these behaviors varies, largely dependent on the age of the participants. Generally speaking, young adults and adults who engage in these behaviors rather than sexual intercourse may offer the explanation that these activities are "safer" and/or less intimate than vaginal intercourse. As such, the "commitment level" needed to engage in these activities is correspondingly lessened. They offer the pleasure of sexual activity, without any of the concomitant physical or emotional risks.

For younger people such as adolescents, these activities allow them to experience sexual pleasure without the complications of vaginal intercourse. There is a curious distinction made that oral intercourse and especially anal intercourse are somehow considered less intimate than vaginal intercourse. It would seem that there is a certain inherent understanding of the vaginal sexual act to be an act that expresses a special intimacy between people and there is the conscious or unconscious awareness that pregnancy can only result from vaginal intercourse.[18] Thus, despite what may be involved in the physical act of oral intercourse,

---

[17] Despite all that has been said on this issue about commitment, many young people who would tend to reserve sexual intercourse for "serious relationships" might also admit that sometimes, more casual sex "just happens" on occasion. This demonstrates that if one lacks the self-control to remain chaste outside of marriage in general, one's resolve is weakened in exceptional circumstances, opening up the possibility of even worse moral decision-making.

[18] This is not technically accurate, of course. Depending on the nature of "petting," and whether the couple is naked or not, the possibility of pregnancy still exists.

it is somehow reasoned that it is a much less significant activity than vaginal intercourse.[19]

Because of the difficulty of remaining chaste in our sex-saturated popular culture, some people will claim that masturbation is unavoidable, ultimately harmless, and after all, "better than the alternative" (i.e., having casual sexual relations with someone else). Statistics bear out not only the overwhelming frequency of masturbation among the general populace, but also the interesting increase in women masturbating.[20] Many psychologists assert the "normalcy" of masturbatory activity and attribute no moral weight to it at all.

When we look at the issue of masturbation more closely, though, we see a somewhat more complicated picture. Regardless of the moral evaluation of masturbation itself, one must also consider the social elements that contribute to both an increase in the desire to masturbate and also to its increased social acceptance (for, after all, "everyone does it"). In particular, it is hard to properly evaluate masturbation without also considering the role of unrealistic fantasy and pornography.

But aside from these important social modifiers to our understanding of masturbation, we cannot ignore the basic meaning of the action itself. For whatever reason a person masturbates, and with whatever mental aids he or she may use in doing so, a person deliberately pursues sexual pleasure apart from the context of any relationship whatsoever and objectifies any person involved in his or her fantasy. The fantasy image becomes a useful "thing" whose personhood is irrelevant. Here

---

[19] One might imagine that oral and especially anal intercourse could not be so common among adolescents. Unfortunately, it is a choice many young girls make in order to avoid the complication of regular sexual intercourse, ignoring or unaware of the unique difficulties of these alternative activities. A "morally neutral" presentation of this phenomenon can be found in "Oral Sex Among Adolescents: Is It Sex or Is It Abstinence?" *Family Planning Perspectives* 32:6 (November/December 2000).

[20] According to *Sex in America*, about 70% of men masturbate on a regular basis, as do about 35% of women.

there is not just the divorce of sexuality and marriage, but even of sexuality and relationship itself. It makes sense that a culture that loses sight of the connection between sexuality, marriage, and procreation would inevitably also seek sexual pleasure apart from any relationship whatsoever.[21]

The increased availability in pornographic material relates to this issue as well, both in the increasing amount of material available and, perhaps even more significantly, in the ease with which it is made available. In the 21st century, no one needs to surreptitiously slink into a bookstore or movie theater where someone might see him or her, thus creating a socially embarrassing situation. In fact, some people are so comfortable with their engagement with pornography that they would feel no embarrassment even if they did have to go to such places. Instead, pornography is available anonymously by mail, on cable, and especially on the Internet. Studies yield widely varying results about the specific number of pornographic sites on the Internet, but other studies have revealed an increase in pornography addiction through the Internet, and users' increased likelihood of finding pornographic material on the Internet, whether or not it is explicitly sought out.[22]

Is the increase in the prevalence of pornography a result of our skewed attitudes about sexuality or have our improper attitudes about sexuality allowed pornographic material to proliferate? It seems likely that the relationship goes both ways. As a result of societal changes in attitudes toward sex, pornography doesn't seem like such a big deal. And with more people being

---

[21] An additional psychological complication in masturbation is that there is a sort of relationship present between the masturbator and the mental subject of the activity. The danger here is that one creates unrealistic expectations about relationships when they remain selfish ideals in one's mind. See William Kraft, *Whole and Holy Sexuality* (Abbey Press, 1989), 102-108.

[22] A 2002 survey by the Online Computer Library Center revealed only 3% of all public sites were sexually explicit, but due to various marketing techniques used by such sites, there is a much greater chance of someone unintentionally encountering one than their numbers might suggest.

exposed to pornography (especially the young), these impoverished attitudes about sex are reinforced.

Even pornography itself has changed its face. Now one can legitimately speak of the "pornography industry," and adult film "stars" have a much higher degree of recognition than ever before and even a bizarre form of "critical acclaim." These changes have led some people to say that this is proof of pornography's harmlessness. After all, the people who act in these movies are celebrities (of a sort), and they are paid to do this, and they seem to like doing it. Who are we, one might say, to tell a person they can't have sex on film for money, as long as it's consensual and no one gets hurt?[23] As in all of the cases we have considered thus far, the same mindset applies: there is no connection between sex, marriage, and procreation. Pornography reduces sex to a mechanical process used as a commodity. The psychological and emotional ways that people "use" pornography suggests that something much more than just the mechanical is operative here.

The last topic to be considered in this section is homosexuality. In some ways, this is a more complicated issue than the others, as discussions today about this issue often have less to do with the morality of homosexual activity and more to do with the place of homosexual persons in society. This latter issue will be examined in the chapter on social ethics. Yet even this change in emphasis reveals something about the modern perspective on the morality of homosexual activity: few people seem to consider the activity itself (understanding, of course, that "activity" actually covers a number of activities) to be morally problematic for persons who are homosexual.[24]

The reason claimed for this is because many find homosexuality to be "natural," that is, different than, but equal in all other ways to heterosexuality. This has certainly become largely

[23] See n. 12 above.

[24] One might even make the case that people find little difficulty with heterosexual persons, especially women, acting in a homosexual manner.

the case in the public consciousness, whether or not there is any scientific evidence to actually support such a point of view. Many people find this approach attractive because of the intuitive recognition that sexuality, while not entirely defining a person, does contribute much to one's self-understanding. For many, to criticize homosexual activity is not a judgment on the activity, but rather on the homosexual persons themselves, as if the distinction cannot be made between the two. How does this relate to all of the issues considered above? The answer is this: no one would consider homosexual activity equivalent to heterosexual activity except for the disconnect that exists between marriage, sexuality, and procreation.

This is the necessary conclusion to this section. Having considered an array of rationales offered in defense of various forms of sexual activity apart from the context of a married heterosexual couple open to new life, all of these rationales reveal one fundamental component in common: none of them is valid if sexual activity is properly reserved for the marital relationship, and is understood as intrinsically related to the possibility of procreation. Hence to explain to someone why sexual morality is so important, what Christianity teaches us about sexual activity must be explored. While it is true that there is a lot of sex in the Bible, scriptural teaching on sexual morality is considerably more limited, at least on the face of the texts themselves. However, the tradition of the Church has articulated key foundational principles about what it means to be human which are found in the Scriptures. These principles reveal how human beings are to celebrate the awesome gift of sexuality and behave sexually. It is in both understanding these principles and in cultivating the virtue of chastity that one is able to integrate sexuality into relationships with others, establishing relationships that are both wholly accurate according to the truth of the human person and also holy in recognizing the sacredness inherent in every human being. Needless to say, this is a much different approach than the secular rationalizations offered above.

Active Participation in the Love Story

In order to understand how human beings are to celebrate God's gift of sexuality and thereby to contribute proactively to the building of loving relationships in the world, we must ponder the Christian definition of what it means to be human. This definition includes four fundamental components: human beings are created by God, human beings are created in God's Image, all human beings are called to be incorporated into the Body of Christ, and men and women in particular were created to be in relationship with one another in a unique way. From this anthropological framework, we can understand the meaning of marriage, and how that constitutes the morality of sexual activity.

Human beings are created by God. This simple fact also contains a simple truth: the definition of what it means to be human is not decided by human beings. It has been decided by their Creator.[25] Contrary to the currently pervasive point of view, we are not free to define ourselves however we wish. Rather, we have the free will either to accept God's definition of ourselves or to reject it in an attempt to make ourselves into gods.

And what is that definition? Scripture tells us that God made us in His Image and Likeness.[26] This means that we are like God. We have the capacity to know and we have the capacity to choose. More importantly, we have the capacity to love, like God. God extends His invitation of love to us, and we have been given the ability to respond to it. Every other decision to love another person is fundamentally connected to this ability to respond to God's love for us.

Furthermore, in Christ, we have been brought together as a community, as His Body. We are literally "incorporated," i.e., "brought into the body," through Baptism.[27] All human beings

[25] See Is 45:9.

[26] See Gn 1:26-27.

[27] See 1 Cor 12.

are called to this unity, human and divine. Christ reveals that we have an obligation to one another, to contribute to the building up of one another in every way. His Gospel also reveals the truth that to hurt someone else is ultimately to do damage to ourselves. To be anything less than what God has made us is to be alien to our human dignity, blind to our own meaning, opaque to the One Who made our hearts for His dwelling. A fundamental tenet of our baptismal covenant is living up to our corporate responsibilities to one another.

The truth of our identity in the Image of God is revealed to us in the first creation story, in the beginning of the Book of Genesis. But we are also able to glean many more important details about God's design by examining the second creation story. As we mentioned in Chapter Four, Pope John Paul II highlighted several important insights into the meaning of being man and woman in chapter two of Genesis as part of his comprehensive theology of the body. These insights illuminate the meaning of the relationship between man and woman. The experience of the first man's original solitude reveals that human persons are not meant to live alone, but rather in communion with one another. The experience of that original unity reveals that man and woman exist in a specially constituted relationship in marriage, and that it was God's design for them to come together in one-flesh unity in this permanent relationship. Finally, the experience of the original nakedness reveals that the intimacy of this relationship requires a total commitment, a total gift of self to one another, free from the fears of manipulation or abuse on the part of either person. All of these insights combined speak to a profound understanding of God's true design for marriage.

So what is the meaning of the marital relationship? Grounded in everything that has been said above about the human person, marriage provides a unique opportunity for a man and a woman to share in a life that mirrors and radically participates in the intra-Trinitarian life of God, a unitive life which also participates in God's creative power.

To explain this more fully, we need to look at the Scriptures as the description of the love story between God and humanity. We see constant references to the Covenant. We discussed the meaning of this term in Chapter Two as it applies to understanding morality in general. Here the focus is the idea of the Covenant and its strong resonance for God's people in terms of the meaning of marriage. Israel discerned this through the inspired words of the prophets, who were led to understand the Covenant relationship between Yahweh and the Israelites as a marital relationship. When the people of Israel were unfaithful to Yahweh (as they so often were!), it was as if Yahweh's bride, Israel, was being unfaithful to Him as His spouse. As they continued to reflect on this image, the Hebrews came to understand the critical truth that this symbol was also to be understood the other way around: the people's relationship to God was a marriage as well, because a marriage, in fact, *is* a covenantal relationship. In covenant, the two partners freely give their whole selves to one another in a permanent union that cannot be broken.[28]

Even this still does not fully explain the meaning of marriage. Marriage is also a mystical participation in the intra-Trinitarian life of God. Nice, big theological words, but what do they mean? While a detailed explanation of the dogma of the Trinity is a bit out of place here,[29] we can at least understand enough to validly compare it to human marriage. The Son, or second Person of the Trinity, is the perfect Word (*Logos*) or image of the Father. As a perfect image, the Father and the Son love one another. This perfect love that exists between Father and Son is itself another Person, the Holy Spirit. The Holy Spirit is the Personal emanation of the love between the Father and the Son.

---

[28] Thus the meaning of Jesus' words in Matthew's Gospel (19:6): "Let no man separate what God has joined." See also John S. Grabowski, *Sex and Virtue: An Introduction to Sexual Ethics* (Washington, DC: The Catholic University of America Press, 2003), 23-49.

[29] Inasmuch as we poor humans can talk about a "detailed explanation" of the Trinity at all! Still, further research into this essential truth is a worthwhile endeavor, as it helps us to understand who God is more fully. If we profess to love God, we owe it to ourselves to learn as much as we can about who He is.

In a similar fashion, the relationship between husband and wife is grounded in joyful and reverent reciprocity. As husband and wife love one another fully, offering their whole selves, their whole lives to one another, that love actually becomes manifest in a third person, the couple's child. It is clear, both in Tradition and in experience, that the marital relationship is a gift from God to us so that we can love one another in an all-encompassing way, at the same time that we both understand God ever more deeply and share in His creative power. The ability to conceive a child is a participation in the very Being of God, a cooperation in God's activity in the world, and a unique form of stewardship. The birth of a child is irrefutable truth that "giving away" love doesn't deplete it, but rather increases it — children give us more opportunities to both demonstrate and share our love for one another. All of this is possible because of God's love for us. In turn, this shared love invites us to love God more effectively in response. The love story continues.

The central concept of Covenant allows us to understand the meaning of marriage. It also leads us to a fuller understanding of the meaning of sexual activity within marriage. Why is it that people do not, in fact, have the "right" to have consensual sex with any other adult they wish? Why is it that sexual activity only belongs within the province of marriage? It is because of the irrevocable gift of self that sexual activity inherently entails and this can only happen in a covenantal relationship. To put it very simply, once we have given ourselves to another person, we are no longer available to give ourselves to anyone else![30] This total self-giving can only make sense in the context of a permanent relationship. This is not merely a religious argument; this is demonstrated in the makeup of our very bodies and readily understood by anyone truly honest or prudent enough to reflect upon human experience. Sexual intimacy automatically gener-

[30] This is also a good explanation for the deeper meaning behind Paul's discussion of "marital rights" in 1 Cor 7:3-5.

ates a certain degree of relational intimacy on the emotional and spiritual levels. To abuse that intimacy generates a unique kind of hurt — not (only) because God's will for our lives has been ignored, but also because of the very meaning of human identity.

Within marriage, sexual activity means many things. At its most basic level, sexual intercourse in particular inherently expresses an openness to the possibility of new life.[31] But we also realize that sexual activity (including more than just intercourse) means much more than this. It also articulates the longing of spouses to express their love for one another in a unique way. It enhances the happiness of the couple as they experience an equally unique form of pleasure. And, underpinning these aspects, it also creates the opportunity for the couple to reflect on God's love for them. While elements of these meanings may somehow exist in the intentions of an unmarried couple that engages in sexual activity, it is impossible for these elements to be fully present. The reason for this can be explained by appealing to another one of John Paul II's concepts, the idea of the *language of the body.*

We are all familiar with the concept of body language. We understand that certain postures, facial expressions, ways of standing, all communicate certain feelings without words. The body itself expresses all of these. We are usually only half conscious (and sometimes completely unaware) of this body language. This suggests that our body-selves convey truths beyond our conscious intentions. For example, if a person falls asleep while listening to someone speak at a conference or in church, the message is pretty clear that the speaker failed to excite the listener. If the listener instead slapped the speaker afterwards,

[31] Regardless of the intentions of the couple! While morally good sexual expression requires at least tacit human assent to the openness to new life, that openness is also present in the very nature of the act itself. See also Christopher P. Klofft, "The Licitness of Pleasure as an End of the Marital Act: The Theological Approaches of Janet E. Smith, Lisa Sowle Cahill, and Christine E. Gudorf" (S.T.L. thesis, The Catholic University of America, 1997).

the speaker understands without words spoken that he or she has evidently caused offense! In a more positive way, the smiles of the audience might generally indicate enjoyment or approval, again without words ever being spoken. The body-actions of the persons in the audience communicate on their own.

Such is the case also in sexual activity. Beyond the person's intention to engage in such activity, the very nature of the activity *itself* conveys *meaning,* the meaning of self-giving to the other. To give an example of this, a couple engaged in sexual intercourse is, by the very *nature* of sexual intercourse, expressing an openness to new life. This can be demonstrated by the simple biological fact that pregnancy is possible when two people have sex (unless they do something specifically to prevent this from happening). This *meaning* to the act is present regardless of the couple's *intentions* when they decide to have sex.

Thus, to engage in sexual activity without that fullness of self-giving that is contained in and unequivocally intended by the acts themselves, is to engage in a lie. We may not mean to lie, but what we intend and what our body-self is conveying contradict one another.[32] Because of this, sexual activity outside of marriage can never be morally good.

At this point, especially among the young, the discussion then seems to beg the question: what *is* "sexual activity"? Many people are especially curious about the answer to this question! Is kissing always appropriate? Is anything "beyond" kissing ever appropriate for the unmarried?[33] People often think it would be terribly convenient if God or His Church simply drew a "chastity line" in the metaphorical sand with a sign saying, "Do not cross." But every attempt historically to draw such a line not only has

---

[32] Note that I avoided using the language that we "make the body tell a lie." To use such a construction implies a dualism, that somehow our body is separate from ourselves. Remember we *are* our bodies; they are not just possessions of ours.

[33] In fact, actual conversations with high school and college age students rarely yield such chaste speculations!

run into potential difficulties over particulars; more importantly, it entirely misses the point.

The meaning of marriage and sexual activity within marriage point to more fundamental issues for human persons than isolated reflection on specific acts alone. As such, a discussion of sexual ethics should move away from a focus on *acts*, and instead concentrate on the more important moral category of *relationship.* That is, rather than trying to discern the morality of specific sexual acts, instead one should focus on what those actions indicate about ourselves and our relationships. In this way, we reflect on our sexual *character*: what kind of person acts this way? What kind of relationship will be established if it is defined by these particular choices of action rather than other sorts of action? Do my actions accurately reflect the truth of my own being or of my relationship with another?

This is not necessarily a normal way of thinking, especially among the young, who often have such difficulty discerning the truth about relationships (for all sorts of reasons). But it does urge us to develop the virtue of prudence and a more intuitive engagement with the natural law. Put more concisely, if one understands "sex-in-context" honestly, one can readily admit that almost all sexual behaviors outside of marriage are simply inappropriate; they do not accurately reflect a valid human relationship one has with the other.[34] People engage in these activities because they are fun; because they are, in the right context, a powerful good; *and* because they are, in that same context, an awesome opportunity for joy given to us by God. Any truthful and objective reflection on the intrinsic meaning of sexual activity, however, will lead the reasonable person to conclude that its place is solely within marriage.

Does this leave us completely without specific principles for guidance? Yes and no. As explained above, in order to main-

[34] By "valid human relationship," I mean one that is honest, motivated by a sincere desire to donate oneself, and with a willingness to serve the other in love.

tain the proper focus for morality, it is more productive to avoid generating a list of "Thou shalt nots" for sexual ethics (as with ethics in general), beyond the fundamental principle that sexual activity belongs properly within the context of marriage. At the same time, a guideline seems necessary. For example, what constitutes a kiss at the end of an evening that will lead a person further into sexual sin in mind or body later may differ from person to person. One who has not developed a strong sense of the virtue of chastity may have to decide that such a kiss is too much and should be avoided. Another couple may realize that this particular expression of affection represents a truthful portrayal of the intimacy and maturity of their relationship, with no fear that any internal or external moral failing will result. This sort of judgment occurs based on one's self-knowledge and a prudent evaluation of one's own maturity and the maturity of the relationship in the light of objective truth.

Some may be unsatisfied with this conclusion, as if the question of concrete principles altogether has been sidestepped.[35] While a more detailed version of this fundamental principle is articulated in the last section of the chapter as it applies to specific issues within sexual ethics, this in no way detracts from the assertion here that this is all the principle that is needed. This is an accurate presentation of the Church's consistent teaching, as affirmed in God's revelation to us: sex and marriage go together because sex and procreation go together and procreation and marriage go together. Any activities that we label "sexual activity" that are *not* "sexual intercourse" point ultimately towards sexual intercourse, and are thus subject to the same moral evaluation.

In our behavior, the focus is to concentrate on improving the quality of our relationships by being honest with ourselves and with others. This in turn will affect the choices that we make, thus improving our "sexual character," if you will. As this

---

[35] Or worse, accuse me of being lax in my presentation of moral truth!

character improves, we will be participating in the development of virtue.

Virtue is that quality that allows us to act well and to avoid acting badly.[36] One theological term for this quality is *habitus*.[37] While this is the root for our word "habit," the original meaning has an important difference from our contemporary usage. When we think of habits, we think of largely unconscious actions that we perform. These are often actions that we might wish we didn't perform and usually find quite difficult to avoid. Habits like chewing one's nails or smoking come readily to mind as examples. But *habitus* is different in that it is a *willed* action; it is something we choose to do in each and every instance. In choosing to do these actions, we eventually find it easier to do them (thus the similarity with our modern understanding of habits).

So virtues can be included as habits in this specific philosophical definition of the word. This means that we willingly choose to do good things, even though that choice to do the good might sometimes be very difficult. However, we also recognize that, as we do good more consistently, it becomes easier to do good in general. This is how virtue develops. The converse is also true in the opposite of virtue, called *vice*. If we consistently make bad choices, it becomes easier to continue making bad choices. Because of the powerful draw of the goodness God intends in our sexuality, it is especially easy to make continually poor choices when it comes to sex. The way to avoid this pitfall and, even better, to make it easier to feel confident about the right choices, is to develop *virtue* in our moral lives.[38]

Again, the particular virtue that applies to our sexuality is the virtue of *chastity*. The chaste person recognizes that our sexuality, the fact that we are men and women, is a large part of our

---

[36] See Augustine, *Retractiones*, I, 9.

[37] For more on this, see Servais Pinckaers' treatment of Thomas in *The Sources of Christian Ethics*, trans. Sr. Mary Thomas Noble, O.P. (Washington: The Catholic University of America Press, 1995), 225.

[38] Pinckaers offers an awesome description of moral growth in *Sources*, 359-374.

self-understanding, but it does not have to dominate it. Chastity allows us to see other persons as *persons*, not as potential objects for our sexual pleasure. In the person who has developed the virtue of chastity, the temptations of our sexuality, specifically the temptation to use another person physically or mentally for our own selfish ends, is mitigated by our desire instead to foster good relationships.

In the secular world, we have come to believe chastity is, at best, a nice ideal and at worst a denial of what it "really" means to be human. Neither extreme is true. Chastity allows us to respond to the truth of what it means to be human in ourselves and in others. In terms of our sexuality, it is what allows us to live the love story. When they live chastely, married persons exercise their option for a unique participation in the love story, by loving as God loves and experiencing His presence. Ignoring this spiritual component of our sexual ethic undermines its very meaning. This is more than just reflection on the connection between sex, procreation, and marriage (though that is where we began). This is far more fundamental: it goes to the heart of what it means for human beings to be made in the Image of God. Now a return to the topics considered earlier in the chapter is possible, enlightened by this guiding perspective.

Truthfulness: The Mark of a Good Relationship

Each of the topics considered in the beginning of the chapter was examined from the perspective of the modern secular point of view, including the most common rationale for various behaviors, in each case noting how the connection between sex, procreation, and marriage has been lost. Now with that background, it is possible to re-examine each of those same issues, placing them in the context of Catholic sexual ethics outlined in the previous section. In doing so, the truth of the Church's teaching becomes more cogent. As morality in general, and sexual ethics in particular, is about forming good relationships, it is obvious then that relationships need to be based on truth, not on falsehood or illusion. Even secular "relationship experts" know that truth and honesty are the hallmarks of a good relationship!

The first topic considered was birth control, a critical issue for the present misunderstanding on so many other issues. As marriage and procreation are essentially linked, it is easy to conclude that deliberately thwarting the procreative possibility in the marital act violates the very meaning of the act. This is expressed in the Church's teaching through the insistence that, in each occasion of the marital act, there must be both an expression of the committed love and unity between the spouses, as well as an openness to the possibility of procreation.[39] These two ends are usually referred to as the *unitive end* and the *procreative end* of the marital act. This terminology demonstrates that this uniquely marital expression of love is necessarily connected to the possibility of procreation. Expanding this one step further, one can conclude that procreation is one of the purposes of marriage itself, a dominant theme in Christian theology since the beginning, even if at times this overshadowed other essential aspects of marriage.

This understanding of marriage is not subject to manipulation as one sees fit. Instead, one can see, by understanding the relationship between sexual ethics and personhood as a whole, that the definition of marriage is an objective reality apart from our cultural attempts to re-define it.[40] This truth has been lost in the widespread attempt to manufacture more convenient illusions about marriage, sex, and procreation, hidden behind a language of "rights," a smokescreen that has been created out of pure subjective desire.

---

[39] See *HV* 11-12.

[40] And keep in mind that this fact is not necessarily conditioned on religious belief at all. This definition of marriage makes rational sense even as a purely *natural* reality. However, the advantage our Catholic faith brings to the definition is a better understanding of and appreciation for the *gift* of marriage that God has given us.

But this objective truth offered to us by God is not easily practiced or integrated. In light of the complexity of the modern world (whether we imprudently choose that complexity for ourselves or it is thrust upon us by others), it seems difficult to maintain that essential openness to procreation in *every* occasion of the marital act.[41] While this openness is non-negotiable in order to maintain the integrity of what the marital act and marriage mean, this does not require a married couple to actively *try* to achieve pregnancy with *every* marital act (an oddly common misconception of Catholic teaching). The 1968 papal encyclical on Christian marriage, *Humanae Vitae,* talks about *responsible* parenthood, and one could question a couple's "responsible choice" to blithely continue having children without regard for the upbringing and education of those children. Upbringing and education requires time, and resources, and attention, and the basic health of the parents. Thus, there are often very good reasons why a couple should responsibly refrain from having a child, either for the time being or perhaps even indefinitely.[42]

This is why the Church permits a married couple to take advantage of either the naturally fertile or infertile times in a woman's cycle in order to encourage responsible parenthood.[43] Natural Family Planning (NFP) makes use of the best scientific knowledge to predict fertility or infertility with remarkable accuracy.[44] Rather than discuss the specifics of NFP itself, it

---

[41] In fact, such a position was even considered by the committee that conducted the research that ultimately led to the document *Humanae Vitae*. See *HV* 2-3.

[42] Pius XII, in his 1951 "Speech to the Catholic Union of Midwives," said that there may be circumstances that could "exempt [the spouses] for a long time, perhaps even the whole duration of the marriage, from the positive and obligatory carrying out of the [marital] act." Some examples of such circumstances could include a woman with a medical condition by which she would risk her own life simply by being pregnant or a spouse who has the AIDS virus.

[43] *HV* 16.

[44] The treatment here of NFP both scientifically and morally is covered in brief only. Fortunately, numerous other sources are readily available. One of the most comprehensive is *The Art of Natural Family Planning,* 4th ed. (Cincinnati: The Couple to Couple League International, Inc., 1996).

will be more useful here to address one of the most common and challenging critiques that arises in regard to this aspect of the Church's teaching. That criticism can be summed up this way: If NFP and contraception both prevent a child from being conceived, and this is the couple's intention, what is the moral difference? In both cases, aren't the parents closed to the possibility of procreation?

The answer to this question has two parts. The first part has to do with the couple's intentions. If the couple does in fact choose to avoid having children, not out of a sense of responsible parenthood, but rather because having a child is something they seek to avoid in order, for example, to maintain an affluent lifestyle to which they've become accustomed, or to further their careers for the sake of mere financial gain, or for a woman to maintain her physical shape "unmarred" by pregnancy, then the use of contraception *or* NFP is equally illicit, i.e., they are *both* wrong because of this *intent*. The method of NFP is not automatically morally permissible. There must be sufficient moral reason why the couple chooses to avoid the possibility of a child in the marital act.

The second part of the answer has to do with the critical difference between contraceptive practices and NFP. When a couple uses contraception, they choose to engage in the marital act on *their* terms, that is, they act in such a way as to deliberately thwart the possibility of procreation. By contrast, the couple practicing NFP cooperates with a natural design that is already contained in the woman's cycle of fertility. God has made it so that women are not fertile 100% of the time. In fact, most of the time a woman is *not* fertile. Thus, the couple can prudently decide *not* to engage in the marital act when the woman is known to be fertile. This is not an action against the possibility of procreation (in fact, logically, abstaining from an action is not an action at all). The difference between contraception and NFP can then be summarized as the difference between choosing to engage in the marital act on one's own terms or engaging in the marital act according to God's design and the prudent decision to use God's gift of sexuality as a means to contribute to both the couple's relationship and responsible parenthood.

The difference doesn't end there, however. When a couple chooses to use contraception, they choose to imagine themselves as masters of their own fates, if you will. They decide to have sex whenever they want to do so, and they decide what consequences will or will not be allowed to occur. How does this demonstrate a healthy relationship with God, when one acts so specifically to thwart His design? How does this demonstrate a healthy relationship with one whom we call "spouse" when we make liars out of our bodies' language? How healthy is it to enjoy another, even ostensibly with sincere loving intent, while damaging the fundamental meaning of the action? Where is the truthfulness in this relationship?

By contrast, the couple practicing NFP engages in a unique school of virtue.[45] By learning to develop self-control about whether to engage in or avoid the marital act, by treating one's spouse fairly and justly as a genuine partner in the marital relationship, by prudently deciding when to engage in the marital act and when to responsibly bring children into the world, and by having the courage to trust in God's design rather than making human agenda into gods, NFP enables husband and wife to grow in holiness. The couple honestly practicing NFP lives and loves as God has called them to do in marriage. That is how marriage is meant to contribute to the building up of His Kingdom.

The Church's teaching regarding the meaning of the marital act is truly foundational. All the other issues considered at the beginning of the chapter in particular categories fall readily into place upon this essential cornerstone of sexual ethics. It gives us a solid basis to comment on specific concerns germane to each of those categories of behavior.

To begin, it makes an evaluation of the related activities of adultery and premarital sex rather simple. Adultery is always

---

[45] For an excellent treatment of this, see Grabowski, 142-154.

wrong because it ignores the fundamental meaning of sexuality and the exclusivity of the marriage bond: the giving of one's whole self to another. Regardless of the circumstances involved, if one is licitly married to another, then there is no way in which a violation of that covenantal relationship could ever make sense morally.[46]

As we noted in the beginning of the chapter, the ethic is not as clear to many when it comes to premarital sex. First, a quick summary of the response to cases of outright promiscuity is in order, in which sexual activity is used by one or both partners for selfish enjoyment or even financial gain. As has been explained, the marital act carries with it a significance inherent in the act itself, and this significance can be readily understood by a rational person. This meaning goes far beyond mere pleasure, even when both parties consent to it. While the pleasure of a good act is in fact good, pleasure's *moral* goodness only applies *when the good act itself is also good*. But promiscuous sex is *not* good; it is a lie.

Promiscuity is not the principal motivation of many people in the modern world. Instead, motivated by sincere if insufficient notions of love and affection, most people today cannot see why sexual activity must be reserved solely for marriage. After all, the couple asserts: (1) that their love for one another is genuine, and (2) that the sexual act is a demonstration of that love. Therefore, it could seem that the unitive end of the "marital act" has been kept intact. For most couples, however, there is a deliberate thwarting of the procreative end of individual acts, often combined with an overall intent that is not at all open to the possibility of procreation. The intrinsic meaning of the sexual act is egregiously violated. It is no longer an honest act of two spouses, but rather a

---

[46] It would take us too far off course here to discuss the related issues of divorce and annulment. For the purpose of our discussion here, it is sufficient to remember that a decree of nullity means that the sacrament of marriage did not exist in the first place. Therefore, while *adultery* is never morally permissible, it *is* possible that a person who was once married according to civil law may be able to "give himself or herself fully" to another.

display: an act intended to convey deep meaning, when in reality it remains an ultimately self-serving act. This is not the kind of action performed by people called to love. The call to love is one of total self-giving, and pre-marital sex is not that.

One may counter with the, perhaps, more exceptional case: the sexually active unmarried couple who not only assert their love for one another, but who also insist that they are in fact open to the possibility of procreation. With the denigration of marriage today, some couples see no value to marriage, even as a symbol or for its purely civil status. Why is *marriage* specifically required for sexual intercourse if the couple honestly "means" what the "marital act" itself signifies?

The problem in this case comes from a limited perception of marriage. Marriage appears to be reduced to the status of a religious and/or social category, a label to be placed on those who want it and which legislates certain civil circumstances for the couple. While marriage encompasses these things, it is also something more, even if it is understood solely as a natural (as opposed to a supernatural, or "religious") reality. The marital act makes manifest the couple's commitment to one another. It demonstrates that two people have given their whole lives, their whole selves, to one another. Once validly given to another, one cannot "take oneself back." The reality of marriage then protects both of the partners. It establishes formally the commitment expressed in the marital act. Therefore, marriage serves as an assurance to both spouses that their gift of self will not be thrown away as soon as it is inconvenient.

Finally, marriage protects the children that come from the union of the two parents. While many people in the world today are forced to grow up in circumstances ranging from unconventional to dangerously dysfunctional, no one can reasonably deny the benefits to growing up under the care of two loving parents, especially when they both teach that child the meaning of love by their example to one another. Without marriage, there is no stability to the family, aside from the changeable "promises" made by the parents. For even with the best intentions, those promises are subject to the vagaries of circumstance and exigencies of human selfishness. Therefore, either parent could leave at any time, leaving the child without a stable environment in which to mature and develop as a person. The effect on the child consequently has an effect on the larger community as well. In every way in which that child's development is hindered, his or her contribution to the community in the future is also hindered. Failure to take seriously the responsibility to be parents has contributed significantly to the reasons why we have ceased to be a society of "good" people and have become a society of "good enough" people. The commitment of marriage is the guardian of the long-term promise that the partners have made to one another and to their children in both word and action.

Premarital sexual intercourse is not the only issue that needs to be considered here. There is also the issue of appropriate displays of affection short of intercourse in which the unmarried often participate, while still protecting their dignity as persons as well as demonstrating honesty in their actions toward one another. This is not an easy issue to address, especially to the young, but we must attempt to articulate some principles that take seriously the meaning of human sexuality in God's healthy plan for us at every stage of our lives. The following specifics would seem to apply to all reasonable people outside the context of marriage. Engagement with the genitals that leads to orgasm or the possibility of orgasm is not morally valid for the unmarried. Orgasm is a physical sign representative of the spiritual reality of sexual intercourse. Even independent of sexual intercourse itself, orgasm signifies the same total self-giving. Furthermore, physical contact that arouses the senses beyond what is reasonable for a particular person to deal with, based on his or her moral development, is at best imprudent and more likely dangerous. As a reminder, in all of these cases, the choice of how to act or not to act is based on a recognition of both the self and the other as *persons,* not as objects for sexual satisfaction, and also that sexual activity signifies a total self-giving to the other. As a total self-giving requires a permanent commitment, such activities must be restricted morally to marriage. These two guidelines promote growth in chastity, which ultimately lead to happier, healthier, and holier sexual activity in the context of marriage.

It should be obvious that, if sexuality's meaning only makes sense within the context of the marital covenant, solitary sexual experience in masturbation fails to be an honest or truthful experience suited to the building up of our relationships. In fact, masturbation provides a unique impediment to the building up of relationships on account of its inherent selfishness and the fantasy component that often accompanies it. Masturbation's statistical normalcy does not in any way create a "moral normalcy"; rather, its statistical normalcy is a testament to many other things simultaneously: one's need for self-affirmation (ironically through self-degradation), our cultural context which makes the development of chastity so difficult, and our own selfishness as sinful beings. Regardless of intention, all of these facts are present at once when a person masturbates.

These reasons all demonstrate a profound yet prevalent misunderstanding of the gift of our sexuality. As such, it is easy to see why masturbation is wrong from the perspective of the evaluative category of relationship. Masturbation demonstrates a weakness in our character, evidence that we have not fully responded to God's invitation to love, and are still in need of healing. While one's personal culpability in the act of masturbation can be very little (on account of age, maturity, habit, isolation, or trauma, for instance), there is no way that masturbation can be said to be a good, or even a neutral, activity.

The structure of the masturbatory act itself fails to do justice to the meaning of the marital act. As it is a solitary activity, there is clearly no unitive dimension to it. One cannot claim that masturbating to the image of one's spouse somehow contains a unitive dimension, for one is still using the image of the spouse for a non-spousal, one-sided activity. Motivated perhaps by an insufficient or immature or even a false love, one unintentionally objectifies the beloved for one's own selfishness. Likewise, lacking a spouse, the masturbatory act (in a special way for men[47]) deliberately thwarts the procreative dimension of the marital act.[48] Finally and in sum, there is no self-giving involved in the act. No relationship is genuinely fostered and one puts oneself in the position instead to foster habitual behavior in a direction away from the virtue of chastity and away from the fulfilling intent of healthy sexuality.

Much of what has been said about masturbation also applies to the issue of pornography. These two activities are inextricably linked in our society. Needless to say, participating in the production of pornographic material is immoral. Even if one wished to propose the odd hypothetical of spouses working together to produce pornography, the gift of our sexuality is something holy, sacred; it allows us to share in both a foretaste of the joy of God's presence as well as God's creative power.[49] As something sacred (reasonably evident even in a "natural" sense of the word "sacred"), it must be accorded a certain dignity. The sexual act is not to be shared in any sense with anyone outside of the covenantal relationship: the spouses and Christ. Furthermore, the sacredness of sex means that it cannot be used as a vehicle of commerce or exhibitionism.

But the number of people producing pornographic material pales in comparison to the number of people who make use of

---

[47] I mention men specifically here because there is a definitive correlation between male orgasm and procreative possibility. Science is still unsure whether or not female orgasm contributes to the possibility of procreation, though it is definitely not required for it. Thus, the affront to the procreative end of the marital act is more readily demonstrated in male masturbation.

[48] This rather mechanical explanation for the immorality of masturbation was offered by the Congregation for the Doctrine of the Faith in their 1975 document *Persona Humana*. See *PH* 9. While not particularly long, this document contains the longest "official" statement by the Church on the subject of masturbation.

[49] There is also the matter of exclusivity of the marital act, not only in the act itself, but also in its availability to others. Therefore, it would be equally wrong, for instance, for a married couple to have sex in public, as this too violates the dignity of this sacred act.

it, usually as some sort of direct or indirect masturbatory aid. Pornography increases the spiritual danger inherent in masturbation, for instance, by validating another person's supposedly willing degradation of him- or herself. Thus, the masturbatory act not only affects the relationships and the relational ability of the masturbator, but also perpetuates the illusion of the producer of the pornography (be it film maker, "actor," model, or what have you) that his or her activity is acceptable, harmless, even beneficial. All of this is indeed an illusion; there is no honesty or truthfulness in the engagement or production of pornographic material.

Concluding the survey of the topics discussed earlier in the chapter, we arrive at the issue of homosexuality. The reader is reminded at this point that all that is under discussion here is sexual morality. The morality (or lack thereof) of homosexual acts is our focus, not the place of homosexual persons in society or the moral treatment due to homosexual persons, but the Church's teaching on the Christian treatment of persons of homosexual orientation does command that they be treated with dignity and love.

Related to this, one must avoid the easy judgment of homosexual activity and its relationship to homosexual persons based on a too facile reading of Scripture. The Church's teaching wisely distinguishes between the categories of homosexual *orientation* and homosexual *activity*. It is clear from reading the isolated passages from Scripture mentioning homosexual activity, such as Genesis 19, Leviticus 18:22, Romans 1:24-28, or 1 Corinthians 6:9, that the authors did not make a distinction between the acts themselves and the people engaging in them. For we understand now that, though the situations may be exceptional, heterosexual persons sometimes engage in homosexual activity (such as in a prison situation or in pornography, for example) and homosexual persons engage in heterosexual activity (such as a homosexual person who marries someone of the opposite sex in order to hide his or her orientation). We must distinguish between the basic orientation of the person and the acts that he or she engages in.

But this is not to denigrate the insight that Scripture provides regarding homosexual activity. The immorality of homosexual activity is discerned from the Spirit's revelation of the nature and goodness of married sexual activity. The Scriptures reveal that the permanent relationship between a man and a woman, a covenant in which they offer their whole selves to the other, is not only "normative" in God's design, but is also a symbol for the covenantal love between God and His people, Christ and His Church. Marriage is a vivid symbol of the love story between God and ourselves. And this gives us the reason why homosexual activity is morally wrong.

Based on everything demonstrated thus far in the chapter, homosexual activity fails to actualize the meaning of the marital act. It fails to realize either the procreative possibility or the unitive possibility in the act. In fact, it is not appropriate to even call homosexual activity a "marital act." Instead, it is merely a use of one's sexual faculty for pleasure and to presumably express strong affection for another.

The failure to realize the procreative end should be self-evident. Simply put, there is no way that two men or two women can possibly bring about new life through their sexual activity. However, we have also seen that sexual activity is fundamentally oriented towards the possibility of new life. To blatantly ignore this intrinsic meaning is to be dishonest in our actions, to tell a lie with our bodies. Even if the homosexual partners wished to have a child naturally, their intention cannot be realized.

While the procreative dimension of our sexuality is obviously cut off in homosexual activity, one might make the case that the unitive dimension possibly remains. One must consider two counterpoints to this. The first point grants that this statement is true: that the love expressed between homosexual partners is a true, sincere gift of self to the other. Even if this is in fact the case, however, the very meaning of our sexuality is only truthfully expressed in its fullness, i.e., in the possibility of procreation as well. The unitive dimension alone is not enough.

The second point is whether or not unmarried persons of the same sex can in fact realize the unitive dimension of human sexuality in their activity. The unitive dimension encompasses a number of dimensions of sexual experience. Besides referring to the pleasure that the *spouses* give to one another, it can also refer to the expression of love one feels for another, and express the commitment to give one's life to another. Arguably, these last two aspects can exist in homosexual friendships as well. But the unitive dimension in marriage goes even further than all these characteristics. The unitive dimension differs in that it is also the understanding that the spouses have united their lives in Christ by the divine plan, that their *sexual* union is symbolic of the union between God and His people, and that this union is an expression of the divine plan of the Creator. These elements cannot exist in homosexual *sexual* activity because such activity is always going to remain an imperfect emulation of the marital act. God's design for our sexuality is bound up in the union of a man and a woman who have committed their lives to one another and who are open to the possibility of new life. The affective union of personhood represented by a deeply loving relationship in the homosexual context must express the true nature of that friendship in its personal interactions; it must neither usurp nor mimic genital activity that belongs only to marriage, the union of husband and wife.

Marriage, sex, and procreation: A fundamental connection necessarily exists between them. This has been obscured by the human impulse to create our own values, to define ourselves as we see fit, to create more comfortable lies for ourselves in order to avoid truths that challenge us to grow in holiness. This connection has been severed in humanity's understanding of itself. The result has been just as it was predicted almost 40 years ago: divorce is on the rise, marriage is held in low esteem, it is getting harder to instill moral values in the young, especially in regard to sexuality, women are increasingly objectified, even with some women going so far as to embrace their own objectification in a totally inverted sense of "empowerment."[50]

The truth of the love story is found first in understanding how God made us, and then understanding what that means. We are created as embodied creatures so that we can make love manifest in these same bodies. God has given us one unique way to do this in the permanent commitment of a man and a woman to one another: the marital act. In understanding the truth about ourselves as God made us, we open ourselves up to enter into honest relationships with one another, to develop strong character through the virtue of chastity, and in marriage, to live the love story more fully by entering into a covenantal relationship with one's spouse, just as God has done so with us.

Sexuality is not the only area in which the notion of human embodiment faces moral challenges in the modern world. Now more than ever, technological advances in the life sciences have made both miracles and nightmares possible. Medical ethics requires judicious application of the virtue of prudence. There are some key points of conflict between God's revelation of human personhood and the illusions of the same masked as truth in the name of medical science. This is our next consideration.

[50] These predictions were offered by Pope Paul VI in *Humanae Vitae*. See *HV* 17.

Chapter Six

The Beginning and the End of Life: The Modern Moral Battleground

Modern medicine has the capacity to work miracles in people's lives today, wonders inconceivable even 25 years ago. As we learn more about the human creature, we discover ways to live longer, healthier, and often more productive lives. Limits previously imposed on us by nature have been circumvented through technological advancement. What effect has this conquest of nature had on us, not simply as human creatures, but also as human *persons*? For all the good that medical science is able to bring about today in preserving and enhancing life, we must always keep in mind the more fundamental truth of what exactly life *means* for the person created in God's Image and called into loving relationship with Him. How do these wonders serve or deviate from those ends?

This continuous increase in technological advancement, in medicine as in most areas of human life, is a hallmark of the modern world. Through the ingenuity of brilliant people with creativity, vision, and intelligence, we now have better ways to provide food and shelter, faster methods of communication, more efficient ways to organize and disseminate information, and, as noted above, truly amazing ways to preserve life. Here it is vital to keep in mind that, in many ways, these new technologies reveal not merely the triumph of the human spirit, but in fact the gracious inspiration of the Holy Spirit in the world.[1]

For as many new developments revealing the efforts of men and women working in conjunction with the movement of God's grace, however consciously or unconsciously, there are just as many "advances" that demonstrate humankind's profound gravitation towards self. On the one hand, there is the very specific example evident in the proliferation of more efficient ways to kill one another in the name of ideology or nationalism. On the other, however, are the uses of otherwise beneficent technology for selfish ends. The use of mass media for ideological manipulation, for unbridled financial gain, for calculated consumerism in advertising as well as in the use of the Internet for the spread of pornography and hate-mongering is evidence of this.

This is true in the realm of medical technology as well. With such extraordinary ability to affect human beings, researchers in the medical field have devised means not only to improve our lives, but also unsettling ways to create, manipulate, and destroy it. Of course, in most of these cases, there is no deliberate malice on the part of doctors and researchers. Their intentions may often be quite the opposite: ostensibly to provide miracles for patients seemingly without hope, or to provide such persons an opportunity to live or (especially) die exactly according to a script of their own design.

But as has already been demonstrated, intention alone does not morally vindicate the choices that we make.[2] Moral decisions must also correspond to the truth of what it means to be human, not merely in the biological sense, but in the truth of being a unique person, called into personal relationship with God and utterly irreplaceable in creation. And many of the decisions that face doctors and medical researchers today have a direct effect on the status of human persons *as* persons.

---

[1] For a further explanation of this, as well as many examples, see *Gaudium et Spes*, 1-10, especially p. 5.

[2] See the consideration of intention above in Chapter Two.

This is why it is appropriate to refer to medical ethics as the modern moral battleground. Perhaps even more than in the field of sexual ethics, there is a profound tension between what seems to be subjectively good and what is in fact objectively true about the human person. In this chapter, certain fundamental principles are considered first, hinted at here already, and then some specific medical situations involving both the beginning and the end of life are examined, as a way of shedding light on some critical moral issues facing us today. In each of these two categories, the key meanings *behind* the issues are employed as a way to subsequently look at the issues themselves and the arguments that surround them.

Dignity and Utility Are Not the Same

One principle stands above all others when it comes to evaluating medical ethics, especially since this same principle is critical for morality in general: the inestimable value of human life. Human persons cannot be assigned a comparative value in relation to other human persons or to mere commodities or "goods."

The rationale for this fundamental understanding of the human person is the entire Christian ethic, explained succinctly by Pope John Paul II: "Man is called to a fullness of life which far exceeds the dimensions of his earthly existence, because it consists in sharing the very life of God. The loftiness of this supernatural vocation reveals the *greatness and the inestimable value* of human life even in its temporal phase.... [Life] is a process which... is enlightened by the promise and renewed by the gift of divine life, which will reach its full realization in eternity."[3] Thus, human life is valuable not just in itself or in its earthly existential phase, but because it orients us toward the true purpose

[3] *Evangelium Vitae*, 2. Emphasis in original.

of human life: eternal life. We are made by God, and our destiny is to return to God through Christ's life in us.

What this means, then, is each of us is extremely important! We *do* matter. This simple truth about our precious value, our irreplaceable uniqueness as individuals before God, is the antidote to the prevailing lack of self-worth in the developed world today. The modern world presents us with the possibility to choose a selfish version of ourselves without reference to God. Yet in doing so, we lose the very grounding that gives our lives any objective meaning. And still we wonder why we shake in existential terror about the "big questions" such as, What is the meaning of life? What is the meaning of death? What is our purpose here on earth?[4] The answers to these questions can only make sense when we understand the fact that we are infinitely valuable *because* we are created by the infinite God, created *for* God, created in His Image.

This fundamental primacy of the value of life must be the foundation for any authentic medical ethic. Building on this foundation, two other related issues come into focus: the notion of human dignity and the consideration of the idea of a "quality of life."

The value of human life means that there is an inherent dignity in being human. One can recognize this as a tenet of the natural law, inscribed upon human hearts, which makes it clear that the way a human is treated should be different than the way that a stereo is treated, or a car, or a tree, or even a dog.[5] It is easy to recognize that being human is different, that other humans are "people" capable of relationship, in a way unlike the relationship possible with any of the aforementioned items. One

---

[4] See *Gaudium et Spes*, 10.

[5] This point of view would perhaps be reprehensible to some, who would accuse the Christian of "speciesism" in his or her valuing of the human person over an animal. However, Judeo-Christian theology clearly prioritizes humanity above all other living things; see Gn 1:28. I assert furthermore that this truth is reasonable and self-evident apart from an appeal to Scripture.

might be hard-pressed to describe the possibilities of "relationship" that one can have with his or her stereo!

The dignity that human beings possess, just in being human, demands that the decisions that one makes in regard to human beings must pay respect to this value. One cannot simply dispose of another human being. One cannot simply create another human being in a manner of personal choosing. No one can simply decide that another human being has no right to live. No one can determine the comparative value of one person's life against another. These conclusions should be evident simply from the value of human life alone. The fact that these conclusions are not in fact readily apparent or a consensus without controversy leads to the rest of this chapter.

The above conclusions also lead to the second issue related to the fundamental value of human life: the consideration of a person's "quality of life." Both in medicine and in other areas of human life, sometimes this "quality of life" is invoked as a factor in decision-making. For instance, in another context, a person might choose one job opportunity over another because the quality of life offered by one job will be better than another. This might be based on any number of factors, such as salary, commute, job satisfaction, or opportunity for advancement. In any case, the evaluation of quality of life remains entirely subjective. The same method is sometimes used in making medical decisions, but here another type of evaluation is at work. A person might choose to forego, or a doctor may recommend foregoing, a particular procedure because the benefits may only come about through a significant diminishing of "quality of life." In the case of patient incompetence, his or her decision-makers would make these choices. In either case, the notion of quality of life remains subjective.

This is not problematic in itself. The problem arises when this category of moral evaluation is treated as if it were an objective truth: that "quality of life" could be standardized in such a way that it applies equally to all people. Is this, in fact, the case? Is there an objective standard by which the quality of life can be judged? Chapter Three established that one must consider the "manufacturer's design" in deducing the meaning and value of the human person. According to that design, the objective standard for human quality of life is determined by the simple fact that we exist; that God has made us and loves us. He is our Creator. His will for our lives determines "quality of life." Despite all human wants, desires, and so-called "needs," we live because God intends us to live. That intent has an inherent design which takes priority over all other subjective considerations.

Therefore, with respect for the Creator's design, Christians must assert several truths: the human person is important, infinitely valuable, possesses a special dignity which means that individuals cannot be treated as mere objects or as means to fulfill others' desires. The quality of life is determined first and foremost by the divine call to holiness,[6] a call for which we have been suitably empowered by God's Image. No other consideration, no matter how important, can violate, disregard, or minimize this value.

These principles, then, provide the basis for understanding medical ethics. Despite the complexity of modern medicine and the decisions that go along with it, a person can never be seen as less than a person. And yet that is exactly what some do in morally evaluating medical procedures. As the sections below will clarify, certain procedures *do* objectively treat human persons as if they were tools, rather than as persons. Dignity has been replaced with utility. *Products* are meant to be utilized. *Things* exist to be utilized. We cannot utilize *persons.* As soon as a procedure threatens to turn a person into a product, or otherwise treats the value of the person as if it were equally commensurate with other inferior values, one offends the dignity that is due to all people as creatures made in the Image of God. With these principles in mind, some specific issues within the realm of medical ethics can fruitfully be considered.

---

[6] See *LG* 40.

The Worst Kind of Industrial Espionage

The life of a human person begins with the conception of that person, when sperm and egg meet and form the beginning of life. The beginning of human life is also the beginning of human personhood, with all the consideration of value and dignity that "personhood" implies.

This relates importantly to medical moral issues involving the beginning of life. While abortion was considered separately, that procedure (which one can only call "medicine" by the loosest of definitions) is only one of a growing number of issues that involve the beginning of life. Doctors are now able to help people to have children of their own through various interventions in the reproductive process. New advances in science and technology have allowed an understanding of embryology of astounding proportions. This new understanding is part of the beneficial legacy of modern technology: the capacity to understand what it means to be human in all of its richness. Great light, however, also engenders deep shadows.

What we have done with this understanding is part of the problem in modern medical ethics. Discussions of the status of the embryo are at the center of the secular evaluation of the new technological options in genetic research, including the highly touted possibilities of stem cell therapy and cloning.

How must the Christian respond to these discussions and arguments? What is the true status of the human embryo? Christian anthropology clearly defines the embryo as a human person from the moment of conception. Is it not the same *kind* of human person unborn as "born"? Can it be treated as some variant of the human person instead?

This is, of course, a variant on the previous discussion of personhood in terms of abortion. In that sense, all that has been said about the embryo as a person remains true in these cases as well. Some might argue that the situation is significantly different than in the case of abortion. After all, it could be claimed, in the case of in vitro fertilization, there is a couple who desperately want a child to love. In the case of stem cell research or cloning, there is the vaunted possibility of many other peoples' lives being improved or saved. These are far more "noble" intentions. Therefore, one might subsequently argue, the situation is sufficiently different from abortion that it would be morally permissible to use embryos for these purposes.

Remember, human dignity cannot be at the service of mere utility! Human persons are never to be used. The "creation" of human embryos outside of the normal method of human reproduction, the disposal of unwanted embryos, the manufacturing and killing of embryos: all of these procedures demonstrate the power of human reason perverted by a profound disdain for God's design. This is the worst kind of "industrial espionage," the usurpation of God's authority as Creator or "manufacturer," all in an attempt to make the human "product" better according to merely human specifications.

The status of the embryo is at the heart of most contemporary beginning of life issues. In the remainder of this section, the most common forms of artificial reproductive technology and the basics of genetic research (including the debate over stem cell research and cloning) are examined.

In vitro fertilization and artificial insemination are the two most common forms of artificial reproductive technology. Artificial insemination (AI) is the older of the techniques; its use was employed in animals for decades before ever being applied to human procreation. In this procedure, sperm is both collected and inserted into the woman without normal intercourse, when the sperm is determined to need an "assist" because it is not strong enough to reach the egg for fertilization on its own.

In vitro fertilization (IVF), on the other hand, is a more difficult procedure, both morally and technically. Sperm and egg are collected from the man and woman independently and are united in a laboratory setting. Only after conception has occurred outside the uterus is the fertilized egg inserted into the woman, with the hope that it will be implanted in the uterine wall and thereby develop normally. This procedure was first used successfully in Great Britain in 1978, and its efficiency has only increased since then. The procedure is not a guarantee, nor is it inexpensive. IVF involves procedures that still often exceed a cost of $10,000 while generating roughly 30% effectiveness.[7]

Both of these procedures offer the possibility of a child to a married couple. Considering the relationship of marriage and children discussed last chapter, it could seem then that these forms of intervention are responsible uses of God's gift of human reason to find ways to make our lives better, to free some couples from the difficulties of a broken world and to help them fulfill God's will for their lives. When described in this biased way, it is very hard to understand how one could find either procedure morally problematic. Yet, the Church, as faithful interpreter of the teaching of Christ, has identified problems with both procedures which may not be readily apparent if one does not keep in mind the fundamental principles involved in medical ethics.[8]

As should be evident by now, the primary difficulty with both AI and IVF has to do with the dignity of the person. The 1987 document *Donum Vitae* by the Congregation for the Doctrine of the Faith explicates two related ideas in regard to a person's dignity and how he or she comes into the world: "The fundamental values connected with the techniques of artificial human procreation are two: the life of the human being called into existence and the special nature of the transmission of human life in marriage. The moral judgment on such methods of artificial procreation must therefore be formulated in reference to these values."[9] Human persons, created in the Image of God, have a right to be created according to God's design, not that of secular technology. Human beings participate in God's creative power through the marital act, a distinctly *human* action that can bring about the creation of a new *human person*.

---

7 The cost was derived from a survey of reproductive clinics in America in 2005.

8 The definitive statement on these issues is the 1987 CDF document *Donum Vitae*.

9 *DV* 4.

Such is not the case when artificial interventions are used in human reproduction. These procedures obviously do involve the actions of humans, but are not the same as human acts.[10] Human acts are actions that reveal the truth about what it means to be human. In this case, sexual intercourse accomplishes this. The creation of human life in a laboratory setting, or the specific interruption of the marital act with technology, does not.

Furthermore, the procreative aspect of the marital act also reveals that children are a gift. While a couple can certainly cooperate with God's design in increasing the chances of conception (for instance, by using Natural Family Planning), the actual creation of new life remains God's gift to the couple. This is vastly different from the experience of creating new life through the assistance of artificial interventions in the process! In this latter case, a couple (or even an unmarried woman) can decide to have a child on their (her) own terms, despite the difficulties imposed on them by nature or even by their own lifestyles (e.g., by waiting until they are significantly older and have "lived life" first before choosing to have children). Children cease to be a gift and instead become a commodity, based on the (no matter how elaborately justified) selfish desires of a couple or an individual.

This choice of our own will over God's will for us (the very heart of the definition of sin) demonstrates a correspondence between artificial interventions in reproduction and contraception very clearly. As noted in the last chapter, people want to be able to have sex without babies, and babies without sex. The human will can make this choice. Medicine can facilitate this choice. Note, however, the disconnection here between the two purposes of the marital act in these two technological possibilities.

That disconnection in turn speaks to the larger disconnection between the modern understanding of the human "self" in relation to its bodily component and the way in which we were

[10] This distinction between "human acts" and "acts of a human" is explained by St. Thomas Aquinas in *ST* I-II q.1 a.1.

lovingly created. As noted in Chapter Four, human bodies reveal profound truths about who human persons *are*. In contrast, what is revealed about this truth in cases of artificial intervention in reproduction? Many contrary possibilities suggest themselves: that our origins do not in fact make a difference in who we are, that the relationship of a man and woman who love one another and who have given themselves to one another fully is not necessary for the prospering of new life, that our bodies can in fact be viewed as products with no intrinsic connection to who we are as people, and that human beings can be created according to a time and manner of someone else's choosing. These ideas are an offense to the dignity we intrinsically possess as human beings.[11]

This is the principal reason why one cannot choose to treat a child as anything less than a gift from God. One cannot choose to "create" a child apart from God's design. However, this is not the only aspect of these procedures that is morally problematic. One must also consider the role of masturbation in the procedure, the question of marital fidelity in some procedures, the disparity in economic justice that the procedures support, and especially the dangers to frozen embryos created by in vitro fertilization.

In both AI and IVF, sperm needs to be collected for the procedure. The normal way by which this is acquired is masturbation.[12] The reasons why masturbation is not a proper use of the gift of sexuality were described last chapter. True, one can see a difference between a man pleasuring himself in order to have a child and a man simply pleasuring himself. But the intention of the act can never make an objectively immoral act moral. The ostensibly "procreative" ends cannot justify the means. Masturbation remains a deliberate misuse of our sexual

---

[11] For more on this, *DV* 3. For those seeking more on these issues, this relatively short document is an excellent, concise explanation of the Church's teaching on the issues of artificial interventions in reproduction.

[12] It is not the only way to collect it. For instance, a silastic sheath (basically a form of condom with a minute hole in it) could be used during intercourse. However, most secular fertility clinics find masturbation a more practical method.

faculties and, even for this arguably more "noble" purpose, the same mechanical "procedure" remains. Towards this end, the fantasy and objectification of others inherent in the act also likely remain. It is ironic that, in many instances, in the process of allowing a married couple to have a child of their own as an expression of their love for one another, there is a step that requires the husband to engage in a solo sexual act, perhaps while fantasizing about someone other than his wife.[13]

This act of objectification is not the only form of "marital infidelity" that is sometimes present in these procedures. If a man's sperm has been determined to be ineffective for fertilization, a couple may seek an outside donor. Thus, in some cases, the sperm to be used in the procedure does not belong to the wife's husband at all, or in fact there may not even be a man personally involved beyond the anonymous donation of sperm to a sperm bank. This is the distinction between *homologous* procedures (when the participants are married to one another) and *heterologous* procedures (when they are not).[14] Even an unmarried woman may use these procedures in order to have a child of her own by means of a sperm donor. While all participants involved may have given consent to the procedure, what does it say about the marital relationship when another person is involved, no matter how tangentially in the couple's or individual's perception? How is this involvement demonstrative of both the couple's total self-giving to one another and their acceptance of God's will for their lives? How does a single mother who wants a child in any way possible honor the truth that the birth of a child should be the result of a couple's self-gift to one another, guarded by

[13] Recognizing the "utility" of masturbation, some fertility clinics will even provide suggestive or even pornographic material to facilitate the process in an expedient fashion. It is a curiously modern idea that a single act of marital infidelity, even only within one's own mind, can contribute to marital happiness. As for those who would protest that a husband may in fact fantasize about his wife, the fact remains that he has objectified her in his mind; for one moment, she was not a person, but a means to an end.

[14] These are not moral categories. One is not more acceptable than the other! Both remain immoral choices.

the health of a spousal environment? Artificial interventions in reproduction, in some cases, damage the fidelity of the marital relationship or implicitly deny its value altogether.

These procedures also perpetuate economic injustices. Because of the advanced nature of the technology used in IVF, and the high cost charged for the process, those who can make use of it are restricted to comparatively wealthy people of the developed world. Thus, wealthy people in some countries, who have difficulty conceiving naturally, have an opportunity to have children of their own. Poor people or people in less developed nations with the same difficulties are deprived of the same opportunities. Despite the fact that the dignity of a human being is objectively offended by these artificial interventions, the fact also remains that wealthy people can use these immoral means to continue their families more easily than the poor can. Thus, there may be a racist or eugenic result, putting the poor at further disadvantage. The specific long-term effects of this disparity remain to be seen, but this is clearly the perpetuation of economic inequality in the world.

Finally, there is the matter of frozen embryos created in the process of in vitro fertilization. The procedure requires the woman to use fertility drugs to increase the number of eggs released during ovulation. These eggs are harvested in advance and then several of them are fertilized at once. Once fertilization occurs, these are new human persons. These persons are inserted into the woman one at a time, in the hope that one will implant in the uterine wall and then continue to develop normally.

What happens, then, to the remaining embryos that are not implanted? They are usually frozen until needed. Often, they will be "needed" if the inserted embryo fails to implant in the woman. If the procedure is instead successful, the remaining embryos will only be needed if the woman decides to have another child. Otherwise, the embryos may be stored until they are disposed of at the request of the "parents." The creation of these embryos is itself a grave offense to human dignity, setting in motion a sequence of further violations. The embryos are human persons, albeit tiny human persons. Their destruction is the deliberate killing of human life. The use of embryos for research reduces their dignity to that of a lab animal, crowned with the ignominy that this usually involves the inevitable death of the embryo in the process. If one understands what it means to be human, and when human personhood begins, the moral problem of IVF comes into sharp focus. Concealed behind the most sincere and loving intentions is a horror.

While AI and IVF are the most common artificial reproductive interventions, they are not the only ones. Complicated procedures like tubal ovum transfer (TOT) and gamete intrafallopian transfer (GIFT) have been developed in response to specific reproductive problems, but also in an attempt to develop procedures that respect the dignity of the human person.[15] After all, it is morally acceptable to use a procedure that *assists* the natural process, but does not replace it.[16] While the Church has reserved formal judgment on these new possibilities,[17] their advent reveals the distinction between using the gift of reason in an attempt to cooperate with God's will for our lives to live in love, rather than to circumvent that will.

The limits of genetic research comprise another set of critical moral issues regarding the beginning of life. Contemporary investigation into the very building blocks of our biological make-up has already revealed amazing things about our bodies and has offered the promise of even more. With advanced knowledge of the human genome, the genetic "blueprint" that deter-

---

[15] For more on this, see Peter J. Cataldo, "The Newest Reproductive Technologies: Applying Catholic Teaching," *The Gospel of Life and the Vision of Health Care*, Proceedings of the Fifteenth Workshop for Bishops, Dallas, Texas, ed. Russell E. Smith (Braintree: The Pope John XXIII Medical-Moral Research and Education Center, 1996), 61-94.

[16] See Pope Pius XII, "Discourse to those taking part in the 4th International Congress of Catholic Doctors," September 29, 1949.

[17] And one can make a solid case that these technologies do, in fact, replace the marital act rather than merely assist it, though many theologians accept these methods as morally licit.

mines our whole physical makeup, several possibilities present themselves. In the not-so-distant future, we can conceptualize medical procedures on the genetic level of persons, correcting genetic faults even before birth. But if genetic problems can be morally identified and corrected, so the argument goes, why not use gene manipulation to change undesirable genes to desirable ones? It is now in the realm of reasonable theory that a couple may eventually be able to decide what genetic characteristics they want their baby to have.[18]

If this technology does come into being, is this morally problematic?[19] If a medical procedure is able to correct genetic faults, even while the child is but an embryo, there is no moral difficulty with it, *provided that* the procedure is done with parental consent, with appropriate concern for the risks vs. benefits of the procedure, and that the procedure did not in any way offend the dignity of the child.[20]

There is clear distinction between legitimate medical *therapy* and genetic *manipulation*. It is one thing to use reason to create technology that can help heal some small part of the brokenness of fallen creation. This is one of the core principles behind the moral use of medicine in the first place.[21] However,

---

[18] This is the modern scientific equivalent of the older idea of *eugenics*. Various people throughout modern history have hypothesized that a group of people or the human race as a whole could benefit by the selective "breeding" of individuals to increase the chances of a child having desirable traits and/or lessening the chances of undesirable ones. The problem is that this idea has often been combined with elitist overtones in an attempt to destroy a group of people, as seen in the eugenic statements of people like Hitler and Margaret Sanger.

[19] To a limited degree, this technology already *does* exist, at least in terms of gender selection. Fertility specialists now have a few different procedures for vastly increasing the possibility of having a baby of the desired sex. They refer to this (ironically) as "family balancing."

[20] Consent is another central concept for *all* questions of medical ethics. A patient (or an appropriate proxy for the patient) must always consent to a medical procedure, because the autonomy of the human person must be respected. More on this can be seen in Kevin D. O'Rourke, O.P., J.C.D., and Dennis Brodeur, Ph.D., *Medical Ethics: Common Ground for Understanding* (St. Louis: The Catholic Health Association of the United States, 1986), 4.

[21] See Si 38:1-8.

when we instead use technology to manipulate God's creative action in us, to insist that our design is better than God's, we mistake ourselves for God. We cannot design human beings; we are not creators, but rather participants in God's creative power.

But not allowing genetic manipulation of this kind, by insisting on God's sole dominion over creation, even when the result may be debilitating illness, seems to suggest that God creates these illnesses. But this suggestion misses the point of the comparison. While it would be an act of charity to *heal* someone on the genetic level, it is not charity to actually *create* a person according to specifications. Even if technology allows us to create a human being, the human person's dignity exists because they are created in God's Image, in love, by love, and for love. How, then, can the creation of a human being through the deliberate thwarting of God's participation in the process be an act of charity? Charity responds to the genuine needs of another, not to one's own selfish desire to do as one wishes, even with the most noble of intentions. Thus, the "middle ground," as it were, between these two situations of genetic correction or genetic manipulation is to be born naturally, with all the good and bad genetic traits that includes, many of which we may not ever be able to correct. Thus, it might seem that God creates us with imperfections. This is not the case. As stated above, illness is not part of God's design, but rather a consequence of the sinfulness of the world. The healing of illness is an example of the in-breaking of the Kingdom of God into the world, and thus always good.[22] Genetic predetermination of a "perfect" child eliminates in advance the need for healing. To prevent the need for that healing, to prevent the opportunity for that healing, is not the same as saying illness is a good in itself. But *accepting* that there is a need for healing is also an acceptance of our need for God more broadly understood. Genetic manipulation according to our specifications asserts that

[22] This is demonstrated most strongly by the numerous examples of healing by Jesus in the Gospels. In fact, Jesus uses healing miracles more often than any other to demonstrate that the Kingdom of God is present.

our way is more important, that we can create a "perfection" that has no need for God.[23] Herein lies the heart of the moral issue, the same heart in all moral issues: do we use our freedom to do as we wish or do we instead freely choose to accept God's love and sovereignty in our lives? Do we choose to create our own world or do we choose to heroically work in love to transform the broken world around us? Do we act to benefit only ourselves or do we act in such a way that we manifest the Kingdom of God in our lives in the community around us? Does our *relationship* with God and others actually matter or are we simply concerned with our own desires?

To a certain degree, one can see the issue of the moral limits of genetic research displayed in the contemporary debates over stem cell research and cloning. Both of these technologies offer amazing possibilities for healing, but at what cost to the human person? Let's consider what is morally at stake in each of these situations.

Stem cells are a special kind of undifferentiated cell that has the capacity to become any other kind of cell in the body. An embryonic child possesses lots of these cells as its body develops and grows. As adults, some stem cells remain in us, but for the most part, by the time we are born, our cells perform the specific functions of the tissues and organs they belong to. But, through the use of stem cell therapy, it has been hypothesized that stem cells could be inserted and "trained" to replace cells in the body damaged by diseases such as Parkinson's. It is theoretically possible that any long-term tissue damage or nerve damage could be corrected through the use of stem cell therapy.[24]

---

[23] By way of example, there is a distinction between using therapy on the genetic level to correct Down's Syndrome before birth and manipulating an embryo on the genetic level to ensure that a baby has blue eyes.

[24] It is important to note that, at the time of this writing, very few *actual* applications of stem cell research exist. The research, while extraordinarily promising, remains largely theoretical. One example of recent application is in bypass surgery, using stem cells to speed recovery. See *Nature* 428 (April 29, 2004): 880. While the results of this application are contested, it is worthwhile to note that the stem cells used in this application are adult stem cells, not embryonic stem cells.

Like the theory of gene therapy, there is nothing morally challenging about this technique in its intention or outcome. It offers significant possibilities for healing, and thus is morally good in its object. However, the moral challenge comes about when one looks for a source of stem cells. As noted above, the adult body does possess stem cells, but not in great amounts. Embryos, on the other hand, have many. Therefore, embryos are usually considered the primary source for stem cells.[25] But attempting to harvest stem cells from an embryo also kills the embryo. Thus, a human person is killed in order to provide material for research and, in the hypothetical future, to help someone else. The moral conclusion then, based on the foundation established above, is self-evident: one may never accomplish a great good by evil means.

There are still possibilities for the moral use of stem cell therapy in the future. As mentioned previously, one can obtain stem cells from adults. Furthermore, there is also a rich supply of stem cells contained in the blood of a baby's umbilical cord. In the former case, an adult can give consent for these cells to be harvested without causing undue hardship or death to the person. In the latter, there is a source of stem cells that harvesting likewise harms no one. But some researchers attest that these stem cells are not as potent as embryonic stem cells.[26] Whether this is in fact the case or not will require further research actually using adult and cord blood stem cells. One cannot overlook a more selfish intention that may contribute to this claim: there is far more money to be made in producing embryos through in vitro fertilization and cloning than there is in harvesting from adults and cord blood. Furthermore, there are far more stem cells to be had, which in turn, increases research opportunities and the money available that funds those opportunities. One cannot

[25] Many researchers go so far as to say that embryonic stem cells are the only viable stem cells for research, though this is a contested idea.

[26] For example, see *Stem Cells: Scientific Progress and Future Research Directions*, Department of Health and Human Services, June 2001.

fault medical researchers from profiting by the discoveries they make that can help so many other peoples' lives; it is justice that they receive compensation for their work. But that compensation must never come at the expense of human lives.

The dignity of the human person and the value of human life place limits on the kinds of interventions we can make into reproduction and the manipulation of the embryonic child. But what about making human beings without normal reproduction? What about creating embryonic children without sexual intercourse? These are the questions which some would answer by the new technology of cloning.

The modern process of cloning achieved its first major success with the birth of Dolly, a sheep, in 1997 in Scotland. Dolly was "fertilized" by cloning, put back into her mother, and was born. This demonstrated that the process worked (although Dolly's premature death seems to suggest that the technology is far from perfect).

The same process can be done on human eggs, allowing eggs to become embryos without normal fertilization. Instead, cell manipulation and electrical current are applied to the egg and the egg becomes an embryo, a perfect genetic copy of the woman from whom the egg was derived.[27] The prospects for this technology are many. In the present, embryonic cloning offers a ready supply of embryos for both stem cell research and other forms of embryonic testing. In the future, it may be possible for humans to be cloned in order to provide perfect genetic matches for organ donation, or for humans to be cloned, implanted, and born as normal. The latter result would be identical twins, separated by the generation of maturity of the egg donor herself.

[27] Some scientists would rightfully point out that this is an oversimplification of the process. Some make the distinction between clones that have been developed from IVF embryos, and "nuclear transfer constructs" that are merely "human material" rather than actual persons. If stem cells can be obtained through the manipulation of human material that never has the potential to be a fully developed human person, the moral evaluation would be different. This distinction demonstrates the incredible complexity of these issues.

So far, there has been a widespread instinctual trepidation about the prospect of cloning, an echo of the natural law.[28] While some people see cloning of animals as a way to protect endangered species or increase food production, most seem to hesitate at the possibility of human cloning. There is the recognition that there is something different, something distinctive about human beings when compared to animals. But how long will modern society feel this way? Based on any number of other cultural examples, such as revisionist views on premarital sex, contraception, abortion, and homosexual activity, it seems quite plausible that eventually secular culture will "get over it," and consider the "benefits" of cloning, kept within what will be assumed are "reasonable limits," to far outweigh any other misgivings.

If artificial interventions into human reproduction offend the dignity of the human person, then the utter replacement of procreation with a technological procedure does so even more. It is a particular offense to men, who are not needed to "father" in the process (the manipulation performed on the egg does not require sperm). If both men and women are created equally in the Image of God, and a critical part of the meaning of being a man or a woman is the ability to give oneself to the other in love for the creation of new life, what does cloning attempt to "reveal" about us as human beings? Not just that we are animals, but rather that we are little more than biological machines, producing unique material to create a unique product: a human person.

And woman's role in cloning may not always remain either. While the present process of cloning would still require the cloned embryo to be implanted in a woman to "mother" it in order to actually develop and be born, what new technologies might supplant that? Already some scientists speculate about the possibility of artificial wombs in which children could be incubated.[29] As one ventures further into the realm of science fiction,

---

[28] Leon Kass has referred to this as "the wisdom of repugnance," the deep-seated trepidation against the idea of human cloning. See Leon R. Kass, "The Wisdom of Repugnance," in Leon R. Kass and James Q. Wilson, *The Ethics of Human Cloning* (Washington: The AEI Press, 1998): 17-19.

one can imagine worlds in which reproduction does not resemble anything that we know today.[30] And before one dismisses any of these ideas out of turn, it should be recalled that cloning itself was considered science fiction only a few short years ago.

Medical technology that impacts the beginning of life is not necessarily immoral in itself. But what is at stake are the fundamental principles articulated in the last chapter and at the beginning of this one: the value of life and the dignity of the human person, both objectively and specifically in the way in which a human person comes into being. Living the love story demands a loving response to God's gifts to us: the gift of life, the gift of love, the gift of children to a couple who have given themselves to one another, the gift of reason to allow us to help another who is in need. The challenge of the love story in regard to medical ethics at the beginning of life is recognizing the difference between who the human person actually is in God's Image and doing what we think best according to a flatly scientific understanding of that personhood, an understanding darkened by wills turned toward self rather than God. The challenge of evangelization on these subjects rests in the unique pain of those who suffer in these areas. From the married couple who desperately want to be parents, to the parents of an unborn child diagnosed with a debilitating illness, to the patients who suffer from conditions that could benefit from new genetic therapies, it is easy to understand why they might believe that the Church has simply said "no" to the perceived answer to their pain. Their pain is so great that it can conceal the truth.

If we are to evangelize, then, to invite others to live the love story in communion with us, we need to adequately convey the truth about the human person. We need to be able to explain the extraordinary value of human life and the unique dignity that

---

[29] Research and experimentation with such an idea occurred under Dr. Hung-Ching Liu at the Cornell University Center for Reproductive Medicine, beginning in 2002.

[30] The best example of this, of course, is the incredibly prophetic work of Aldous Huxley in his 1932 (!) work *Brave New World*.

we possess as creatures made in the very Image of God Himself. But more than that, we need to let people know about God's love amid suffering. We need to let them know of God's immense desire to love them, to encourage them in freedom to actually accept God's love, and to be receptive to that conversion that can only happen because of that love. This is the only context, the only answer to the pain that can possibly hope to provide a strong enough "voice" for the moral principles articulated here. Let's keep this "good news" of God's love in mind as we turn to the other locus of controversial issues in medical ethics: the end of life.

Death: The Price for Everlasting Life

Much of what has been said so far in this chapter has had an underlying theme regarding the meaning of suffering. When looking at the existentially heavy question of human suffering, it seems too easy for the Christian to conclude that suffering in the world is simply the result of disorder in creation, brought about by sin. This answer not only seems too easy, but is of no consolation either. Where is an all-loving, all-powerful God in our suffering? Why doesn't He act? Trying to understand God's actions in a fallen world without recourse to revelation leads to *theodicy*. But such comprehension goes beyond the capacity of mere human reason.[31] In the context of medical ethics, however, one can deduce some meaning to both suffering and death, at least in the abstract, in order to further deduce appropriate moral principles for issues pertaining to the end of life.

In all the various ways of human suffering in this world, we seek to find solace. In the realm of physical suffering, we turn to medicine to ease our pain. This technological response corresponds to a spiritual reality mentioned in the last section:

[31] One could do no better than to look at the Scriptural meditation on this question: the Book of Job.

the in-breaking of the power of God's Kingdom, the action of the Holy Spirit in our lives. Herein lies a clue to the answer to the question regarding the meaning of suffering for medical ethics.

The life, passion, death, and resurrection of Christ is the consummate divine action by which He ransomed all of humanity from sin and death. This gives power to the truth most relevant to moral theology: Christ's action is a model for our own lives and, in Christ, it is possible for us to follow His example. As Christ lived and gave up His life for others, so we are called to do the same. We have seen this already in the definition of marriage in Chapter Five. We are challenged to give up our life in many other ways. Some of the more common ways seem mundane, such as the myriad, apparently small, ways one person can help another, even when it is an inconvenience.

But sometimes how one's life is offered for others does not appear to have any *direct* effect on another. For example, among these might be the soldier who fights for his country, or the law enforcement official who stops a criminal before a crime is committed, or even a researcher who invents better safety features for cars. These individuals sacrifice their time, their energy, sometimes even their lives, not for someone else specifically, but to help others in a more universal way. Other people experience trials in their lives that again have no tangible effect on a particular person necessarily, but which may in turn affect and inspire millions. When thinking of people such as these, their efforts cannot be discounted because they did not do them for us individually. And, oftentimes, they themselves would rather have not had to endure these trials. The soldier does not want to die in a war; the law enforcement official would rather that there be no crime; the researcher wishes that there were no need for automobile safety. The inspiring "hero" does not wish his or her life and its trials on anyone else, yet their suffering has a positive effect on many.

In a similar fashion, the suffering we experience toward the end of life can have a positive effect on us and especially on others close to us. By accepting physical suffering and infirmity with faith, we conform ourselves more fully to the sacrifice of Christ.[32] This pain is not a "good" in itself, but for the individual who accepts it, it is a reminder of his or her need for God's love in human life. It is an invitation to conversion and a sharing in being Christ for others. As others witness this suffering, and especially the individual's response to it, they too can experience these same insights. The suffering itself never becomes a good, but it is a great mystery by which God can conform us more fully to Christ, to make us holy, to make us truly human.[33] Thus, a great good can come from the trusting acceptance of this suffering or the faith-filled endurance of this evil.

Suffering thus makes some kind of sense. Only then is it also possible to more fully explore the meaning of death. There is no objective evil in this world that human beings fear more than death. Much of this fear is appropriate; death appears to be the final separation from loved ones, the end to all of our activities, the final cessation of one's growth as an individual. And this fear is exacerbated by the fact that death is not God's idea, but the crowning result of human alienation from the living God. But through the truth revealed in Christianity, all of these "ends" really only apply to the qualitative way in which we understand our lives here and now. The Christian has faith that death is *not* the end of existence. We are painfully aware that fullness of meaning in one's life is unattainable in this present life, which is a "proof" that we have a destiny beyond the world as we understand it.[34] Death is not an end, but a transition. Understanding this truth will not necessarily remove the fear of death, but it does give death meaning. It gives meaning to the individual who experiences it, for it is the illumination, as well as the culmination, of one's whole life. It is not unreasonable to say that dying is the most significant action that will occur in

---

[32] Col 1:24.

[33] See CCC 1508 and 1521.

[34] See Rom 8:18-25.

any human life. Every moment of human existence on earth is preparation for death. The covenant of Word and Sacrament is the impulse to welcome the transition to everlasting life that faith promises, not without fear, but especially with hope.[35] For one who experiences the death of a loved one, the experience can serve as a powerful encounter of what has been revealed to us by faith. Everybody likes the idea of life after death, of heaven, of life everlasting. But it has a price: death. We must recognize death for what it is and realize first that death has been conquered in Christ, and then, more importantly, that human immortality is the promise sealed by His cross.[36]

So what does the meaning of death reveal about medical ethics? On the one hand, death can be treated similarly to an illness. It is acceptable to want to fight off death just as one fights off disease. The difference between death and sickness, however, is that, sooner or later, death will succeed. We are called to everlasting life, but our present bodies are not immortal.[37] And thus, in considering forms of treatment for terminally ill patients, it is not morally necessary, or sometimes even desirable, to treat death as if there were a cure for it. On the other hand, even though death is a necessary transition for all human beings, the inestimable value of life reveals that we cannot entirely be masters of our own fates. Though we are given life as a gift, it is a gift containing a responsibility to the Giver; we cannot dispose of it as we see fit. These two ends of the spectrum, preserving life at all costs and disposing of life as one wishes, provide the framework for discussing the key issues of medical ethics at the end of life. It is worthwhile to note here that the Catholic moral teaching on these issues is among the least understood.

One must make the distinction between what are normally referred to as *ordinary* and *extraordinary* means of preserving life.[38] Due to the dignity possessed by the human person, the

[35] See CCC 1817-1821.

[36] See 1 Cor 15:54-58.

[37] See 1 Cor 15:35-44.

Church teaches that one must always use all ordinary means of preserving life. If a physician has the capacity to heal a patient, and the patient has a reasonable chance of recovery according to the present state of medicine, and the method used to heal the patient is not excessive, burdensome, or so costly as to deprive basic medical care to another, then the physician must do so. This constitutes the ordinary means of preserving life. "Ordinary means" adapts its meaning to technological advances in the sense that what was "extraordinary" in the past becomes ordinary as it becomes commonplace and more readily available.

"Extraordinary means of preserving life" has a more complex definition. It can encompass methods that cause serious burden or risk to the patient or his or her family. That is, if a procedure does little more than keep a body alive that would otherwise die without it, or if a procedure is experimental and has a serious risk of negative side effects, even death, or if it is so costly as to deprive the patient or the family of their ability to sustain themselves financially, or if it will cause excessive pain to a patient with little guarantee of benefit, then it can be deemed an extraordinary means. Because death is ultimately unavoidable, and is in fact not an end but a transition, it is not morally necessary to use any or all extraordinary means of preserving life. However, it is not morally *un*acceptable to make use of those means, provided the patient (or an appropriate proxy) gives consent to them.

The distinction between ordinary and extraordinary means is useful for analyzing most medical procedures that may be considered for a seriously or terminally ill patient. If a person gets into a car accident and needs to be put on a respirator until his or her normal lung functioning returns, this would be an example of ordinary means of preserving life. The patient will recover, but requires this machine in order to do so. But suppose the same car accident created much more serious trauma to the

---

[38] For more on these terms and their application one could consult the CDF's 1980 *Declaration on Euthanasia.*

body. Suppose the patient's brain, and thus his or her lungs also, were no longer functioning at all, and a respirator was the only thing keeping him or her alive. The *person* has basically died, but a machine can keep the *body* functioning. The use of the respirator in this case would be an extraordinary means of preserving life. It could be morally permissible to use it, but it would not be immoral to discontinue its use. Letting the patient die in this case would *not* be the moral equivalent of killing him or her, but rather a recognition of the limits of both our present bodies and medicine. Furthermore, given the limits of medicine and our ability to regulate pain, it is even morally permissible for a patient to request appropriately high doses of pain medication for extraordinarily painful conditions, even when there is the risk that such high dosages of pain reliever (such as morphine) will unintentionally end the life of the patient.

Is providing food and water (nutrition and hydration) to a patient an example of ordinary medical care? Or are there cases in which it too would be considered an extraordinary means of preserving life? Let's consider this from the example of our normal, everyday lives. Is eating and drinking an "extra" for us? Is it something that we choose to do only when we wish to? Or is it rather something that is necessary for us in order to keep functioning? Obviously, food and drink are necessary, not just an extra. A simple application of this same principle determines the place of nutrition and hydration in medical care. These are aspects of basic medical care; there is nothing extraordinary about them.

But some people view the situation of a patient who is unable to feed him- or herself, such as in the case of a comatose patient or a patient who is in a vegetative state (such as the case of Terry Schiavo here in America), in a different way. Some would argue that if a person cannot eat or drink on his or her own, then nutrition and hydration becomes a form of medical treatment. Even as a medical treatment, it would seem to fit the category of ordinary means of preserving life. However, if a patient has little or no chance of recovering (e.g., a persistent vegetative state), and food and drink is all that is keeping the person alive, couldn't a case be made that this is instead an extraordinary means of preserving life, and therefore not morally necessary?

Answering this question requires an accurate assessment of what nutrition and hydration actually are. Above, it was noted that some would consider nutrition and hydration to be a form of medical treatment in certain cases, but is this in fact accurate? Can providing something that is essential to all people at all times become medical treatment simply because the person in question can't provide it for themselves? By that standard, feeding a quadriplegic or an infant would also constitute medical treatment! This particular issue in medical ethics has been debated for quite a while, even in Catholic circles. However, Pope John Paul II provided guidance on the issue in a statement made in 2004. The Holy Father stated: "I should like particularly to underline how the administration of water and food, even when provided by artificial means, always represents a *natural means* of preserving life, not a *medical act*. Its use, furthermore, should be considered, in principle, *ordinary* and *proportionate*, and as such morally obligatory, insofar as and until it is seen to have attained its proper finality, which in the present case consists in providing nourishment to the patient and alleviation of his suffering."[39] Nutrition and hydration of a patient is not medical treatment, regardless of the circumstances of the patient. Therefore, care providers must respect the dignity of their patients as human beings made in the image and likeness of God by providing this natural means of preserving life.

The issues that have been considered so far in this section have dealt with the necessary treatment due to a person on account of their being human. We have examined what kinds of procedures are morally necessary to honor the dignity of the

[39] *Address of John Paul II to the Participants in the International Congress on "Life-Sustaining Treatments and Vegetative State: Scientific Advances and Ethical Dilemmas,"* March 20, 2004, 4.

human person, and which ones are optional in maintaining life. Now let's look at the other side of the spectrum. Are there any conditions in which it is morally permissible to terminate the life of a patient?

Euthanasia constitutes those actions or omissions that have as a result the death of a patient. Thus, one can make a distinction between *active* euthanasia and *passive* euthanasia. Active euthanasia is when one takes actions that deliberately end a patient's life. Examples of active euthanasia would include administering an overdose calculated to kill a patient, turning off a life-supporting machine, or even something as vulgar as smothering the patient. By contrast, passive euthanasia is when one kills a patient by the omission of an action. For example, failing to provide medication to a patient who needs it to live would constitute passive euthanasia.

While these distinctions are useful for describing means which could be employed to kill another, the differences between them remain relevant only to those who wish to make the case that one form of euthanasia is morally superior to another. Some might make the case, for instance, that it is wrong to actually kill another person directly, but if they wish to die, it is permissible to refuse to treat them.

However, given the value of human life, and the simple truth that this life is a gift, it can never be morally permissible to end or hasten to end a patient's life. To claim such authority, a physician puts him- or herself in the role of God, deciding who deserves to live or die. While the notion is increasingly contested, society in general so far has balked at the idea that a physician could have the right or the legal authority to kill.[40] Contained within these laws is the intuition from natural law that we cannot kill another. Based on the value of life, then, one

---

[40] In countries that permit euthanasia, such as the Netherlands, it ends up being practiced frequently, even without the patient's consent! See the report "Euthanasia in the Netherlands," from the International Task Force on Euthanasia and Assisted Suicide.

must conclude that euthanasia is never morally permissible. Killing another can never be an accurate response to the call to love one another.[41]

But the fact of the matter remains that few people today are concerned about giving doctors the authority to make judgment calls on their own about whether another lives or dies. Rather, the heart of the issue in contemporary consciousness is in the *patient* who desires to end his or her own life. Based on the category of "quality of life" (or perceived lack thereof), some people advocate the notion of "death with dignity," that one should die in the way one chooses, rather than at the mercy of the inevitable failure of drugs and technology. The intentions of the many who hold this view are understandable and even noble to a point. The desire to die in a dignified manner inherently speaks to the goodness of human life, but suicide is an affront to the sovereignty of God, the master of human life.

Despite the intention of those who seek death with dignity, however, they suffer from a fundamental error in their reasoning. As noted in the beginning of this chapter, it is true that we possess a special dignity on account of being human. It is also true that long illness and the threat of death could seem to threaten that dignity in our understanding. The terminally ill patient, suffering from the ravages of whatever ails him or her, may sincerely feel that there is nothing worth living for anymore. However, our dignity finds its source in the Creator whose Image we possess, and no circumstances can ever destroy that Image in us. Because we were created in love, no matter how we die or how much we may suffer beforehand, it is impossible for us to *not* "die with dignity." We cannot define human dignity for ourselves, nor can we assign for ourselves or for another a "quality of life." This has already been done for us by God when we were created. One must decide whether one is going to accept being human in the face of life's biggest transition or give death

[41] See *EV* 64-67.

a finality it does not deserve.

Even more so than beginning of life issues, medical ethical issues at the end of life are especially prone to raise feelings that in turn give rise to such statements as, "You can't possibly know what I'm going through," or "You can't understand the thoughts that go into making decisions like these." And this is true; it is always easier to make moral evaluations divorced from the concrete circumstances of our sometimes tragically difficult lives. But while we may not be able to fully empathize or understand the experiences of those who suffer, we can take confidence in the fact that our God does. Christ entered into suffering, took it upon Himself, so that it could be transformed into the gateway to everlasting life.[42] Whether we are the ones experiencing suffering, or are compassionately (literally, "suffering with") giving ourselves to the one experiencing suffering, this foundational truth of human experience must be borne in mind and heart.

The same challenge for evangelization noted earlier in the chapter applies here as well: trying to concentrate on fundamental truths about what it means to be human, even in the light of difficult circumstances. People who are suffering are in special need of knowing that God loves them and that opening oneself up to that love is the surest way to come to know meaning in one's suffering.

The difficult and controversial issues considered in the field of medical ethics highlight in a special way some of the most obscure parts of the love story between God and His people. In particular, these issues highlight the pain that we experience in fallen creation. It can serve to remind us of our need for God. It also highlights what God has done for us, not just in loving us, but also in His embrace of human suffering Himself in order that we might be saved from its emptiness, from its apparent lack of meaning.[43] Prior to the Parousia, the return of Christ at the end

---

[42] See Servais Pinckaers, *The Pursuit of Happiness – God's Way: Living the Beatitudes* (New York: Alba House, 1998), 84-87.

of time, we will never be free of suffering and hardship in our lives, and for many of us, we will experience that difficulty most poignantly through the physical suffering of injury and illness. The love story reminds us of the liberation and wholeness that God offers to us in the suffering, death, and resurrection of His Son. This suffuses our trials with meaning.

Moral choices in medical ethics require us to act rightly in regard to the truth of what it means to be human. Those actions enable us to subsequently *become* more human. And the more human that we are, the better we are able to give ourselves in relationship to one another. Medical ethics provides us with a unique way of contributing to the human community, not only in reminding us of our relationships, but more importantly by providing the opportunity to care for the "little ones" of the Gospel.[44] The ways in which we can evangelize by our actions in this regard are many; we simply need to have the courage to respond to the call to love.

Sexual ethics provides a way of understanding how we are to live in intimate relationship with one another. Medical ethics goes beyond the bounds of the intimate communion of the two in marriage and calls us to love those members of the community whose physical well-being is in danger. However, morality is about more than just relationships with those close to us. It is not merely a private affair. Morality is the sure guide for the structuring of the entire human community. Therefore, we can now turn our focus on how our actions form our characters into being people who can enter into loving, fulfilling relationships with all others, for the betterment of all God's people.

---

[43] Ibid., 44-47.

[44] See Mt 19:13-15.

Chapter Seven

The Soul of the World: Moral Theology in Social Issues

Everything that has been considered so far in this book is a testimonial to the complexity of the modern world. This complexity continues to flourish as years go by. And it inevitably infects the way in which we structure our interpersonal relationships. While it might seem like sexual ethics and medical ethics are more relevant to the personal scope of one's individual life, the Christian cannot overlook the proverbial big picture. Living the love story is a clarion call to nothing less than the transformation of society. This is a big picture indeed, for it far surpasses the simple concern for one's own choices. We must come to understand that living in society requires us to work toward making the diverse communities of the human social framework correspond more fully to the truth revealed about us by God. An essential component of that truth is that we must live in love with one another.

This seems, certainly, like an insurmountable task. How are we as individuals supposed to affect society on a grand scale? How can we as individuals hope to have a lasting effect on the world around us? For most of us, we can't make pervasive changes or have lasting influence over culture itself. But for the Christian, this apparent impossibility is mitigated by one overriding factor; we are members of a covenant community. We are called and empowered by God (for whom "nothing is impossible")[1] to live and love and work with one another according to this covenant promise. Without that divine impulse, our efforts as a community will ultimately yield nothing. It is always the action of the Holy Spirit operating in those united in baptism that effects good in the world.

This may still be too abstract, so it will help to clarify and establish some premises regarding the discussion at hand. If one asked a group of people to create a list of contemporary moral issues, a number of prominent issues would most probably be identified that could, broadly, be placed under the headings of "sexual ethics" and "medical ethics." There may also be a smaller number of issues that do not fit into those two categories, issues such as war and capital punishment. These latter issues can be categorized under the heading of social ethics.

Social ethics certainly seems to receive less popular attention than the ethical issues considered in the last two chapters. Part of the reason is that these issues don't affect most of us in a pointed way. While war is still devastatingly frequent in the modern world, many people are content to evaluate war as a political issue rather than a moral issue (aside from the banal observation that it would be "nice" if there were no war). The same could be said about capital punishment, except that people's politics in this regard might not even permit considering an ideal world without capital punishment. Other issues can be analyzed similarly: issues like the question of homosexual marriage, or how to deal with poverty and homelessness, or the relationship between Church and State, all seem to be largely matters of politics, not morality.[2]

This is unfortunate. While it would be a huge mistake to

---

[1] Lk 1:37.

[2] It is particularly unfortunate when people who consider their political views to be "conservative" or "liberal" too easily equate their theological views likewise. Such terminology is not really appropriate for discussing theology and creates a situation where some people subsequently equate their political opinions with their theological opinions. The result is that the view of a particular political platform becomes a theological view as well.

say that matters of human sexuality and modern medicine are not important for people trying to construct and maintain loving relationships with one another, the fact of the matter is that the Christian message is about a personal transformation ordained to a greater end: the transformation of the world itself. Why do we strive to make Christ present in our own lives? So that Christ can be present to others we meet. In the Gospels, Christ Himself spoke clearly and authoritatively about social ethics more than all other moral issues combined. Therefore, we cannot minimize the importance of critical social issues simply for the selfish reason that they seem less personal to us. A Gospel approach to issues of social ethics is the highest calling followers of Christ have received from Him.

By its very nature, social ethics encompasses a wide range of issues. And the details and approaches to *these* issues change even more rapidly than advancing technology changes medical ethics. This chapter will consider some critical contemporary social issues. More importantly, the Christian principles necessary to properly understand these issues must be unambiguous. In order to accomplish this, an overview of these critical concerns as they are commonly understood in the world today is a good place to begin. With this picture of the world as background, key principles of Catholic social ethics will be explained and applied to some specific issues.

It's All About Me

No one who has reached adulthood could doubt that there is a crisis of meaning in contemporary culture. As our world gets more and more complicated, louder, more impersonal, colder, we all strive to find our way, to find meaning in our lives. We all want to believe that there is a point, a reason why things are the way they are. While people are seeking these answers, they are pulled in multiple directions by dozens of voices telling them who they should be, how they should live, how the world should be, and a whole litany of other "shoulds" ad infinitum. Given this list, perhaps the cruelest irony of all is a message that accompanies all of these other "sales pitches" thrown our way: Be yourself. Be an individual. Do it your way. Make your own path. We must be a perfect society of self-defined individuals, each marching to the beat of his or her own drummer, yet suspiciously alike in the way that all agree about how things are and/or should be.

Reference has been made to this fundamental selfishness throughout this text. It underlies the symptoms of why we are the way we are and not how we might be. But this selfishness is more than just an effect on our personal understanding and the quality of interpersonal relationships in our life. A world of people who are both fundamentally selfish and who furthermore are constantly being told that this is in fact the way one needs to be has provided a self-fulfilling prophecy, a necessarily defining character on society as a whole. Herein lies the foundation for examining some key issues pertaining to social ethics.

An overarching obsession of the modern world is the acquisition of money and material goods. Those who have money want more, and those who don't have it want it and are willing to do most anything to get it. Political philosophers and economic theorists can argue about whether the principle of capitalism is a good thing for the world or not. But capitalism and the profit motive is undeniably the engine for the entire world, regardless of political ideology to the contrary.[3] This has created great incidences of injustice in the world based on the vast differences between wealth and poverty among various people.

But is this a matter of injustice? Some might facetiously seek

[3] For the political philosopher or the economist, this is obviously a huge oversimplification of incredibly complicated factors that create the political and economic climates of the world. However, I think that the simplification is both fundamentally accurate and demonstrative of the "core situation," as it were, that demands a Christian response. The same methodological principle undergirds this whole chapter.

to deny that. For instance: If some person or group of people lack means, isn't it simply because they haven't made use of the tools at their disposal? If one lives in a highly developed country, one might accuse that individual of being lazy or at least not working hard enough. If he or she is from a less developed nation, the answer is that the person should perhaps seek to live elsewhere in order to create better opportunities for him- or herself ("as long as its not in my backyard," the speaker might add).[4] Sometimes, it's simply a matter of looking at the destitute and proclaiming it "too bad" that they don't have more, as if cruel circumstances, impersonal fate, or implacable forces were to blame.

At this point, someone might claim that this is unreasonable, that most people are not so cold as to say that "the poor"[5] just aren't trying hard enough or that they are doomed to remain poor. However, by action, or perhaps more accurately by omission, this attitude is in fact clearly demonstrated. When "getting stuff" becomes something that one feels one "deserves" as a reward for hard work, when money is something that is hoarded "just in case" a massive crisis occurs in one's life, when sharing our means with those who have less seems at best like a necessary concession (being a "good person") or, worse still, as a cruel imposition forced upon us by an abstract sense of obligation fueled by the superego, one does in fact say: "The poor are not my problem."

Economic injustice is not the particular form many people first think of when they hear the word "justice." Justice, in its truncated common usage, is a word that relates to crime and due punishment. In this vein, many people today not only support the idea of capital punishment but, in fact, also think that there

[4] This language of self-sufficiency is also a key component of the radical individualism referred to above. The modern world may permit God to "help" us, but we are all too convinced that our successes are our own, while our failures are often someone else's fault.

[5] There is a reason for demarcating "the poor" as a type in quotes. It will be explained in the next section.

is even more need for it in light of the increasing villainy of modern times. All crimes against another human being scream out for justice, but it seems indisputable that sometimes the call for "justice" is instead a call for vengeance. For the worst crimes committed, it seems to make sense to solve the problem in society by removing the problem altogether. While we are all concerned with the ideal that people should get along, we also readily admit that some people don't seem to fit in. The answer, for some people, is to kill those problematic members of society.

The way that society deals with the challenge of poverty or the way it deals with criminals is a matter of politics. We are all familiar with politics and how it affects our lives. We may not so readily understand just what politics is, however. Aristotle defined politics as the way that people of a community agree with one another in order to work towards the good of all.[6] In order for this definition to be applicable to particular situations, there has to be some consensus regarding just what constitutes the "good." Aristotle would answer that the good to which all people strive is happiness. This too is a term most people would be inclined to agree on. But what *is* happiness?

This is a more complicated question. In a world in which "it's all about me," such as our contemporary culture, happiness has as many definitions as there are people. So too in the realm of politics, there are necessarily disagreements between people. Some of these disagreements are means to a better end. For example, deciding how to construct a law that will contribute to the economic well-being of all people in society will likely involve disagreement depending on whose wallet is at stake. But the interplay of those disagreements can result in the good of all people. However, if happiness is subject to a relative definition, politics will also foster numerous disagreements that are seemingly irreconcilable.

---

[6] See Aristotle, *Politics* I.1.

The current debate over homosexual marriage is an example that fits well into this latter category. Respectful consideration of the rights due to a homosexual person is fair and a necessary component of political discourse. Competing definitions of happiness have recently made the question of homosexual "marriage" — and the re-definition of that institution — possible. If each individual is allowed to define for oneself what "happy" means, it is then impossible to deny that homosexual persons should have the same rights to marry as heterosexual persons. Furthermore, because of the same relative definitions of happiness, if a person in society suggests that homosexual marriage may not in fact be good for society or even for homosexual persons, that individual may be deemed a problem: either a threat to good order and good politics, or else at least a reactionary thinker without the community's best interests at heart. After all, who can reasonably deny another person their "happiness" when our very definition of happiness necessarily differs from person to person with no objective referent either to higher truth or the "happiness" of others?

The same questions regarding the good of society and the happiness of its members also relate to issues that seem to have nothing to do with happiness. War is such an issue. On the one hand, when war is defined as a matter of politics rather than ethics, it is all too easy to adopt a tribal mentality: a conflict between "us and them," in which the "us" must invariably be right. Here, rational thinking and conscientious principles are suspended in the name of loyalty to the clan. This kind of rationale is easy to witness in national halls of power, as the powers that be justify armed conflict in the name of one ideal or another depending on the ruling agenda. Yet one can easily perceive other, less noble motives. On the other hand, it would also be an easy mistake to say that a misbegotten notion of war is only held by those with the supposed authority to wage it, especially when the violence and mayhem does not occur on one's own soil.

War affects all members of a society so engaged.[7] Some will too readily identify with the motives of the ruling body, unable or unwilling to question the reason for war. Conversely, some will also too readily criticize the decision to wage war, denouncing it in the name of higher ideals, simultaneously marginalizing the efforts of those called to fight in a war, people bound by circumstance. The critic of war will retort that he or she supports the soldiers while denouncing the conflict, but this support ultimately seems superficial. What can it mean to say that I support your efforts towards a purpose with which I fundamentally disagree?

Not everyone falls distinctly into one of these two camps regarding war, however. For many, it's a matter of conditional acceptance, marginal support, or unacknowledged apathy. While the two extremes of support and protest might each have moral difficulties associated with them, what about those who choose not to have a well-formed opinion at all? While perhaps not as obnoxious as some other forms of self-expression in modern culture, this desire to be free of an opinion is another manifestation of selfishness, of self-absolution from responsibility, an apathy that is itself murderous.

Issues of politics, morality, and the relationship between them are not only present in secular society. They are also very much a matter of church society. This is especially so in the relationship between "church and state." This problem is experienced more pointedly in the United States than in many other countries, specifically due to the First Amendment of the

---

[7] The comments that follow about war are specifically aimed at those parts of the developed world that have not seen conflict on their own soil in decades. This perspective on war does not really apply when battles rage outside one's own door. In that case, the perspective for a detached evaluation of the morality of war is non-existent. In that case, one is faced not only with the decision to agree or disagree with the politics of the war, but also how one will act in order to survive. While these are relevant and heart-wrenching issues, the focus on evaluation and evangelization in this text precludes a specific consideration of the actions one may take as a soldier or as a non-combatant forced into combat by circumstance.

U.S. Constitution, wherein a "separation of church and state" in American society is supposed.[8] This phrase is invoked quite readily against religious leaders, especially Christian leaders, and most especially Catholic ones, when they speak out publicly on matters of morality. "Separation of church and state" is used as a muzzle in order to keep "religious" matters out of what are perceived to be solely matters of politics.

The inevitable result of this interpretation of separation of church and state is the privatization of religion, a concept alien to Catholic tradition and its mission to build the Kingdom of God here "on earth as it is in heaven." Religious experience in America early on became a relative and unassailably private matter of the individual conscience. While it may be one of many voices that influences one's political sense, it can never be invoked specifically in political matters, because there is a separation between church and state. Thus, what should be a fundamentally relevant factor in creating a more humane culture, our covenant relationship with God, becomes officially marginalized to the point of uselessness.

Aristotle's definition of politics also applies to the Church itself. It too is a community of people working together for the common good. In some cases, approaches to politics adopted in the secular world also affect Church government. Such an approach refuses to know the Church for what it is: an organization of human beings formed by God, ultimately governed only by God and His revealed Word, enabled to lead people to an end beyond this present world. The Church is often regarded merely

---

[8] While more will be said about this below, it is important to remind the reader here that this is *not* the intention intended by the separation of Church and State in the 1st Amendment. On the contrary, the 1st Amendment was written in defense of religious freedom. The founders recognized the critical influence of faith in framing a just society and wished to protect religion so that it may continue to be a positive influence on the machinations of sinful human beings. Unfortunately, the wording of the amendment, along with a self-inflicted blindness on the part of society, have sadly reversed the amendment's meaning in the minds of many.

as a generally noble human institution, a great charitable organization made up of broken people and managed by broken people. This is the truth about *who* makes up the Church. However, the Church is not simply a "noble human institution."[9] But if it is perceived as such, it is reasonable to assume that the Church should be treated like any other human organization. This is the basis for those who wish to see the Church invent more "inclusive" or "democratic" structures, or who wish the Church to change to match the cultural fashion around it. Some people holding these views do not have any rancor against the Church, but there are also some who wish to have the comfort of the Church as an organization, as a community, while still wishing to define membership in that community on their own terms.

By examining these prevalent attitudes towards the modern world, several common themes emerge: a desire for autonomy and self-definition and a desire for community without concern for all of the corresponding responsibilities that come with being a member of the community. Catholic social ethics offers a response to this perspective, as well as an alternative that is instead true to the covenant call to love instilled in us by our Creator.

Separating the Sheep From the Goats

As mentioned earlier, Jesus' moral teaching is more concerned with what we would now call social ethics than any other ethical question. Jesus offers us many more warnings by far about the dangers of wealth than about sexual misconduct. Two examples of Jesus' specific teaching on social ethics highlight these priorities.

[9] For readers interested in more about the divine constitution of the Church, see the entirety of the Dogmatic Constitution on the Church from Vatican II, *Lumen Gentium*.

The Beatitudes from the Sermon on the Mount are rich in social implication.[10] In each of the conditions of blessedness Jesus proclaims, the reader or listener notes that people whom no one would think of as "blessed" are nonetheless affirmed in this way. What's so "blessed" about being poor or meek or persecuted? Contained within this paradox is a key truth of Christian social ethics. Jesus overturns expectations about just who is the object of God's passionate concern. The rich and the powerful don't need special protection, the poor do. In contemporary theology, this is referred to as the Lord's (and so the Church's) *preferential option for the poor.* God's concern is for the *anawim* (the poor, the oppressed, the marginalized of society, those disenfranchised by misfortune). Jesus makes this crystal clear in His Sermon.

But there is still more for us to learn in the Beatitudes. When we recognize ourselves in our creatureliness in contrast to our Creator, are we not also poor and powerless? Yet God loves us rather than abuses us. All people who recognize their dependence, then, are *anawim* before God, blessed in the recognition of the need for God. This observation does not eliminate the preferential option for the poor. Rather, it serves as a teaching example: if God is so good as to take care of us in all our needs, then as we are created in His Image and Likeness, we must do the same for others.

A second example of Jesus' social teaching is one of His parables of the Last Judgment.[11] In this parable, God separates the sheep from the goats. The sheep are those "blessed" who are welcomed into God's Kingdom. And God tells them *why*: "For I was hungry and you gave me food, I was thirsty and you gave me drink. I was a stranger and you welcomed me, naked and you clothed me. I was ill and you comforted me, in prison

---

[10] See Mt 5. For an excellent readable explication of this idea at length, see Servais Pinckaers, *The Pursuit of Happiness – God's Way: Living the Beatitudes* (New York: Alba House, 1998).

[11] See Mt 25.

and you came to visit me."[12] When the sheep asked when they did this for Him, Jesus responds: "As often as you did it for one of my least ones, you did it for me."[13] The Lord then turns to the goats, who failed on every count in which the "sheep" succeeded. The sheep are welcomed into the Kingdom, while the goats are cast out, to live forever apart from the love that their selfish choices denied.

There is little room for ambiguity here. Jesus is teaching His disciples that caring for one another, responding to the needs of one another, is the loving response demanded by God's covenant call. Failing to care for others is a failure to recognize God's image in those around us. While the examples in the parable seem to correspond more readily to interpersonal relationships, clearly a wider framework of "social ethics" is revealed here. In fact, by the very words of Christ in the broader context of the Gospel, these examples speak to more than just our call to aid those close to us.[14] To serve *all* others in the human community is the inescapable mandate of the Gospel, the terms of salvation itself. These two examples drawn from Jesus' announcement of the Kingdom provide us with the key principle to guide us: because we are created in God's Image, we have a calling, not merely a duty, to care meticulously for one another, to love one another as He has loved us.

As the earliest Christian communities adopted Jesus' teaching and began to strive to be Christ for the world, they encountered persecution. In fact, the early Christians experienced persecution to such a degree that their ability to affect the social conditions around them was understandably rather minimal, despite a desperate need for that prophetic witness. Yet as Tertullian framed it: "The blood of the martyrs is the seed of the Church." The situation changed for the young Church with

---

[12] Mt 25:35-36.

[13] Ibid.

[14] See Mt 5:46: "If you love those who love you, what merit is there in that?"

the Edict of Milan in 313, by which the emperor Constantine legalized Christianity as a religion. While this was by no means the end of persecution (which continues even in the present day), for the most part, Christianity was able to serve as the prophetic voice that it is called to be. But this freedom was not an unmixed blessing. The secular needs of the imperial state increasingly became the standard of what was "good" for Christianity. Continual social compromise of the Gospel began a steady erosion of radical Christian ethics concerning politics, economics, power, and especially, non-violence. This practice continued until the Church arguably reached its height of social power and authority in the Middle Ages. With the increase in ecclesiastical influence also came an increase in the possibility of abuse. Individuals used the name of Christianity and the authority afforded by their positions to abuse others rather than to shepherd them.

The world continued to expand and become more complicated as the centuries passed, and to a large extent the Church eventually lost the prophetic voice that had once been its hallmark. But there always were those who refused to relinquish the radical values of the Gospel in the Church. These holy men and women separated themselves from the secular deviations and formed Gospel communities of monks and nuns and, later, friars. By the time of the Protestant Reformation, the Church had in too many ways become part of the power system it was always intended to challenge. Ironically, the Reformers conformed religion even further to secular, individualist, pragmatic values. Their vaunted "return to the Gospel" did not include renunciation of war, unbridled greed, or oppression of the poor. And as entrenched as it had become, institutional Catholicism was in no position to counter the Enlightenment and the political violence that came with it. As a result, the Church suffered great violence at the hands of supposedly "enlightened" men.

This shock to the system was not the end of the story, however. As the partially misplaced enthusiasm of the burgeoning modern age began to wane under the realities of human selfishness, the Church spoke up and asserted the counter-cultural values of the Gospel, denouncing slavery in the 16th century, the violence of colonizers in the 17th century, and the alignment of the Church with political aims in both these centuries.[15] Another example is Pope Leo XIII's encyclical *Rerum Novarum* (1891). This document addresses the conditions of the working class in the new age of industrialization. It is a firm reminder to the secular sphere that workers are not mere resources to be used, but persons to be respected.[16] What has come to be known as the Catholic Church's modern social tradition had begun. It is hard now to appreciate how revolutionary this courageous teaching was at the time.

The momentum generated at the end of the 19th century continued throughout the 20th and into the 21st centuries. Dozens of Church documents have been written to address numerous social issues of the day, commenting on war, economic injustice, the dignity of all people, and authentic civil rights. As it was in the early Church, the Church has once again become a challenging prophetic voice in the world, and she suffers the same calumny that the prophets experienced in the Scriptures. But even in the light of persecution, the Christian maintains hope in the power of God to transform human hearts and with it, human society. Servais Pinckaers writes, "Without this hope, so vigorously affirmed in the beatitudes and in numerous other Gospel texts, as well as in the acts of the martyrs, Christianity would be simply one more mystical or social utopia among other human doctrines, the teaching of a banal, watered down idealism."[17] The Church's voice is not predicated on "good ideas," but rather on the power of God and the saving message of Christ crucified,[18] made vibrant and vital by the Covenant in Word and Sacrament.

---

[15] For more on this, see Vincent Carroll and David Shiflett, *Christianity on Trial: Arguments Against Anti-Religious Bigotry* (San Francisco: Encounter Books, 2002).

[16] To this day, the term "human resources" fails to do justice to the reality that an employee should always be valued more than a corporate profit motive.

[17] Pinckaers, 186.

[18] See 1 Cor 2:2-5.

The Church's wisdom on matters of social ethics is vast and covers a lot of material indeed. Rather than a cursory summary of principal texts, a look at one specific text in more detail is more illustrative. Vatican II gave us this document to provide a set of principles for the Church in the modern world. By examining it, counterpoints to the various arguments put forth in the beginning of this chapter are better illuminated.

Joy and Hope vs. Sadness and Despair

One of the most significant documents of the Second Vatican Council is *Gaudium et Spes*, sometimes referred to by its much-longer title in translation, "The Pastoral Constitution on the Church in the Modern World."[19] This document proposed not to describe the Church in itself (that was the goal of the document *Lumen Gentium*), but rather to describe the unique place of the Church in the modern world. In describing its role, specific and certain principles of social ethics emerge.

After a brief introduction, the document describes the situation of the modern world. Though composed in the mid-1960s, almost all of what is contained in this description is still relevant to the 21st century. Attitudes towards politics, religion, morality, economics, and the social order are always changing. There is still great economic inequality among the people of the world.[20] At the same time, never has the prospect of human advancement been greater. While some might say that the heady idealism of the '60s has passed, it is safe to say that, for many people, our confidence in democracy endures and technology keeps alive the hope of a "better world." Yet at the same time as people cling to these hopes, humankind cannot escape the big-

[19] The Latin titles of Church documents are often baffling to readers, as the translations at first seem to have little to do with the contents. In fact, the titles are simply derived from the first words of the document in Latin.

[20] *GS* 5-8.

ger question behind all this effort: What is the point of making a better world? Isn't all happiness in life ultimately transitory in the face of inevitable death?[21]

This is where the Church comes in. The next section of the document describes who the human person is,[22] how and why human beings form relationships with one another,[23] the nature of human activity,[24] and how the Church animates all of this.[25] In summary, the Church dispels any doubt that we are created in the Image of God, which gives us an intrinsic freedom and dignity. In our relationships with one another, which are God's design, we must honor, love, and respect one another. This is made manifest on an individual level, but also on a social level in structuring a society according to the common good. Furthermore, people everywhere have an obligation to participate in the process of making society good for *all* people. This is brought about through our actions, which are always threatened by the contagion of sin. Finally, the Church recognizes that different social entities have responsibility for that in which they are competent. For example, politicians should be competent in running government, business persons should be competent in running corporations, doctors and other health professionals should be competent in providing medical care, and teachers should be competent in providing education for the members of society. So what is the Church's special competency? The Church teaches us the truth about ourselves, revealed by God, without which all the above is dismally finite. It is this truth that must inspire all of our social efforts in the world.

After presenting this view of society in general, the remainder of *Gaudium et Spes* addresses specific issues *within* society, such as marriage and family, popular culture, economics, and

---

[21] Ibid., 9-10.

[22] Ibid., 12-22.

[23] Ibid., 23-32.

[24] Ibid., 33-39.

[25] Ibid., 40-45.

war. The document is an excellent, concise treatment of many issues, and is certainly worthwhile reading for anyone who wants to temper the method of evangelization by their very lives with a solid grounding in principle, backed by many examples. Three principles of social ethics that the document provides for us deserve some elucidation.

The first important principle expounded by the document is the common good. The Council Fathers define this as "the sum total of social conditions which allow people, either as groups or as individuals, to reach their fulfillment more fully and more easily."[26] This can be contrasted with the utilitarian approach often advocated in modern political discourse, which instead seeks the greatest good for the greatest number. With the complexity of the modern world, a utilitarian approach could seem like the only reasonable approach, and with it, inevitably some person or group will suffer as a result. Striving for the common good, the sincere person recognizes that a political principle or law that fails to take care of all persons in society, or at least fails to protect them from avoidable hardship, is not an ideal principle or law. This is a difficult principle to aspire to, yet we are given the command, "You must be made perfect as your heavenly Father is perfect,"[27] and "For God, all things are possible."[28]

Two other broad principles can also be derived from the same chapter of the text. The first of these is the fundamental equality of all persons, which thus requires a corresponding respect for all persons, even our enemies.[29] The Church wisely warns us against the "us vs. them" mentality that too easily afflicts us as human beings. This mentality can be seen in all forms of human conflict in the world today, from derisive political debate to marginally justifiable acts of war. The principle here is not an idealistic plea for us all to "just get along"; rather,

---

[26] Ibid., 26.

[27] Mt 5:48.

[28] Mt 19:26.

[29] *GS* 27-29.

it is a reminder that there are persons and there are ideas. Ideas may be wrong and require correction for the good of all. Persons may be wrong for holding certain ideas, but all persons always deserve to be loved (especially when they are in error).

The last principle can be simplified in the cliché that "We are all in this together." While so much of moral evaluation may have to do with individual actions, one cannot maintain a purely individualistic morality. As must be clear at this point, each person must keep in mind that what he or she does affects more than just him- or herself. This is easy to see in some cases. One's decision to drive while intoxicated can clearly affect other people's lives adversely. As the leader of a nation, one's decision to send people off to war clearly affects other people's lives. But even "private" actions, or "personal" moral choices, affect others, because they imprint on the actor's character. Do our actions show us to possess characters that contribute to the building up of loving relationships with others? If the individuals within a nation cannot form good relationships with their neighbors around them, how can one reasonably expect that nation to form good relationships with other nations? There is an unbreakable connection between our individual morality and our social ethics. And because, indeed, "we are all in this together," we must also participate in "this." That means that one has an obligation to participate in society's system of governance, and to work towards making sure that that system strives for the common good of all.

These three principles, concern for the common good, the fundamental equality of all persons, and an emphasis on the community, can be applied to more specific categories within social ethics. Let's begin with economic justice. Concern for the common good demands that we think of others carefully in our economic policies. Laws that ignore the poor, or worse, that increase their hardship, can never be good laws, regardless of how much such legislation may appear to benefit society "as a whole." This is grounded in the fundamental equality of all persons. As we are all human persons, we have a mutual responsibility to make sure that all people are taken care of.

This is not intended as an indictment against any political or economic ideology specifically. It is simply the recognition that a corporate mentality can too easily assume that what's good for the group as a whole must thereby be good for every individual in that group. This can readily be assessed in the way that a nation chooses to prioritize categories of spending such as the military, education, and health. The argument can be made, for instance, that defense spending keeps citizens safe. But is that security so important when they lack the means to live decently in the first place?

Concern for the community in terms of economic justice is made manifest in personal choices about material goods. To hoard personal finances beyond the need to live in reasonable comfort probably doesn't send up a moral red flag for most people. The Gospel says that it should. Reticence to give away surplus resources, whether to keep it for oneself or to deliberately deny it to another as "undeserving" is a wake-up call to the state of one's soul. The simple fact that some people have means and some people lack them is an invitation to show love. How often does the temptation to cling to what we have win out instead? Perhaps we fear becoming those we are called to help.

The rationale behind the application of social ethical principles to questions of economic justice also applies more broadly to wider questions of social justice. Concern for the common good necessarily means that different groups of people, however defined, whether by race, nationality, gender, or religion, cannot be deprived of their dignity or their rights as human beings for the benefit of society as a whole. Because all people are made in the image of God, we are equal in our status as individual creatures. Additionally, concern for the community in this case means that one group or representative of one group in society cannot vilify another person or group without ultimately doing damage to everyone in the long run.

In the 21st century, this selective application of these principles is largely taken for granted in the Western world. After all, everyone knows that everyone else has to be treated as an equal. Nonetheless, there are three points that need to be clarified in terms of social justice. First, humankind must always remember that the "modern, enlightened world" of the 20th century saw the concerted effort of one group of people working vigorously for the total extermination of another group of people (and Nazi Germany is not the only example of an attempt at genocide in that century). In other words, we as the human race can never assume that we are so enlightened that we forget that we are also sinful human beings, not benevolent gods.

The second point is a corollary to the first. Genocide is not the only enemy of social justice. We must not be blind to other less egregious forms of "social violence" that we perpetuate on others. Examples of this can be seen in the racial inequality that still exists in many parts of the world, ethnic disparity in many cultures, religious intolerance, and the cultural marginalization of whole groups of people based on their identity or point of view. Social and political discourse often contains statements with an underlying theme of, "Of course, my group is equal with your group, but if your group no longer existed, things would surely be even better!" Seeing that enlightened moderns can never be as blunt as that, it is made manifest in more subtle, insidious ways.

The third point is the most significant. It is easy to tout the equality of all people and the availability of rights for all. But what do these concepts mean? We are fond of claiming "rights for this" and "rights for that," but where do these rights originate? For an American, he or she often believes that these rights "come from" the Constitution. In many situations, a case can be made for this, though certainly the claims on some rights (such as a woman's decision to abort her child as somehow corresponding to her right to privacy, a right explicitly mentioned nowhere in the Constitution) seem to stretch the understanding of those rights beyond reasonable bounds. But even so, how can a nation's constitution make claim to rights? These rights must have a source, after all. Therefore, the origin of these rights is either human or else they transcend human reason alone.

If we state that human rights have been defined by human beings, how can the authority of these rights be maintained? Beyond a mutual agreement to not kill and dominate one another, what force do these rights have? Only as much as the power of any such group of people have to enforce them. This seems dangerous in light of human selfishness and history attests to that danger. Furthermore, many people are more comfortable with the notion that human rights transcend the rational process of any group of human beings from any period of history, no matter how exalted in nobility or intellect.

This leaves the alternative: that human rights transcend human reason alone. This does not eliminate a need for an author for human rights. Even from a purely abstract philosophical point of view, then, God can be identified as the author of human rights. If this is the case (as it certainly is in Christian social ethics), then one must be careful about too readily claiming rights that simply do not exist. The abortion example above is but one example of this. Simply put, merely making a claim to rights and then backing those claims up with some sort of reasonable argumentation is not sufficient. Rights must protect authentic human values and build up the good of the community.

Furthermore, while human beings possess a *fundamental* equality on account of being created in God's Image, we are *not*, in fact, equal on all counts! This truth also tends to fly in the face of contemporary ideals. Nonetheless, the objective truth is that some people are more capable in some areas than others. Some people are smarter than others. Some people are stronger than others. Some people are more responsive to God's covenant call to love than others. But rather than hold these differences up as a means of manipulation or abuse of others, these differences are a treasure to be honored and to be used to build up the whole human community.

These differences correspond to another related concept that is held up as critical for the modern world: diversity. In fact, diversity — properly understood — is a specifically Christian value. Diversity demonstrates the wondrousness of God's creation. Authentic diversity demonstrates the varied gifts that different people can bring for the mutual building up of the Kingdom of God.[30] However, there is another version of diversity more commonly understood in which the very notion of "diversity" is held up as a social ideal in itself. The pursuit of representation of this kind of diversity in the political system or the workplace or the classroom *simply because* diversity is held up as an abstract good fosters an illusion: the lie that a wide cross-section of people selected according to principles of "diversity" will somehow perform a task better than simply the *right* people, objectively qualified.

The principles of equality and diversity also provide the grounding for the principle of tolerance. Tolerance is often presented as a specifically Christian virtue, and rightfully so. A central truth of the Gospel message is the fact that all persons have been redeemed in Christ. There is no condemnation for anyone in Christ.[31] Because of this, we who are in Christ must also not condemn another. Some people will instead preach intolerance in the name of Christianity as a way to absolve themselves of the moral injunction to love one another. A specific misreading of the Scriptures seems to offer ample ground for such an interpretation. For example, Jesus says, "Do not suppose that my mission on earth is to spread peace. My mission is to spread, not peace, but division."[32] Earlier, He says, referring to the work of evangelization, "Do not give what is holy to dogs or toss your pearls before swine."[33] And when a non-Israelite woman asks for healing, Jesus' first response is, "It is not right to take the food of sons and daughters and throw it to the dogs."[34] These

---

[30] See 1 Cor 12.

[31] See Rom 8:1.

[32] Mt 10:34. Perhaps for theological reasons based on his Jewish-Christian community, several of these passages are found in the Gospel of Matthew.

[33] Mt 7:6.

[34] Mt 15:26.

do not appear to be the words of a teacher advocating absolute tolerance! In each of these cases, however, Christ is not advocating intolerance. These are examples of proof-texting: reading a passage of Scripture according to an interpretation one brings to the text beforehand, rather than letting the text speak for itself.[35] Such proof-texting has been responsible for many decidedly un-Christian attitudes and actions throughout history, while completely denying the very truth contained in the Name invoked.

On the other hand, the authentic sense of tolerance taught by Jesus in His life and teachings has also been altered in contemporary usage. Tolerance is a social value inasmuch as it applies to treating other human beings as human beings. In other words, another person should never be marginalized for any reason, including holding particular beliefs or ideas. However, "tolerance" is sometimes invoked in such a way that all points of view are to be considered intrinsically valid and completely equal to one another. Authentic Christian tolerance does not hold all ideas to be merely "different, but equal." When a person lives his or her life in contrast with the objective truth of the human person, or worse, when that person's decisions based on erroneous ideas about the human person directly affect others, fraternal correction is necessary. Allowing someone to persist in error in the name of tolerance is morally irresponsible. It is not a loving disposition towards that person, nor does it reflect the teaching or ministry of Jesus.

The modern emphasis on equality, diversity, and tolerance is ultimately grounded in the notion of the pursuit of happiness. As noted above, people pursue competing definitions of happiness, rather than seeking after a happiness in objective terms that answers human longing. St. Thomas Aquinas ("baptizing" the

---

[35] This process is also known as *eisegesis*. While discerning spiritual truths in prayer relevant to one's particular situation, one may read a passage in a different way than its "objective" meaning in context. This is not the same, however, as deciding on a point of view in advance and then trying to make the Scripture conform to it.

philosophy of Aristotle) said that the good to which all human beings aspire is *this* happiness, an answer to all human longing. More importantly, this applies not just to the present topic, but also to all of morality: living the love story is about being happy.[36] Genuinely good relationships will lead us to happiness.

In order to find an objective definition of happiness then, one could consider all the items, concepts, and ideas that make people happy. Some of these are petty and/or selfish, such as money and power, while others seem rather noble, like virtue and friendship. True happiness, then, would have to be something that nothing else could supersede, that nothing else could surpass. When examined in this way, one must logically conclude that our true happiness lies in God and God alone. He is the only answer to all human longing, and the only sure guarantor of a happiness that will never fail.[37] It is *this* understanding of happiness that must undergird our consequent understanding of concepts such as diversity and tolerance.

The application of moral principles found in *Gaudium et Spes* to the categories of justice has yielded economic and social conclusions in the abstract. But the document also addresses some ideas particular to the Church. The document attends to the Church's role in political discourse, a topic that is important for contemporary discussions of social and political issues. As noted above, the Church's divinely defined gift to society is as expert on the human condition. As politics attends to the secular organization of the human community, it logically follows that the Church must comment on politics.[38] This is not the same as saying that the Church should define politics or that it should

---

[36] The word "blessed" used in many English translations of the Beatitudes can also be correctly translated as "happy": "Happy are the poor in spirit: the reign of God is theirs." Reflecting on the Beatitudes in this way gives us important clues to the answer to the question of all human longing.

[37] A more detailed presentation of this argument can be found in Kreeft's *Making Choices: Finding Black and White in a World of Grays* (Ann Arbor: Servant Books, 1990), 73-91.

[38] See *GS* 42.

be a governing body for the civil order. History has shown that such attempts tend to go rather poorly! Then again, to say that the Church should not "run" society does not mean that there should be an absolute separation between Church and State.[39] Rather, politicians are responsible for structuring society according to the common good, and the Church should maintain a prophetic stance of evaluating the work of politicians by Gospel standards. This is not an imposition of religion into the realm of politics, but rather a safeguarding of the authentic rights of all people. If one were to say that the Church's involvement is still predicated on a specific philosophical or theological vision of reality, one that everyone might not agree on, the onus of responsibility falls back upon the critic to demonstrate how the historical precedent of concern for the rights of all people is somehow exclusively "religious" or not universally applicable.

The Church itself is also a political organization, albeit a differently constituted organization based on its divine origin.[40] This means that the same principles required for a just and fair society also apply to the Church as a society. The Church is therefore fundamentally concerned about the common good regarding its members and their awareness of the Gospel values of justice. Every member of the Church is equal in the order of grace, meaning that all people are called to the same holiness and all have equal "access" to the Spirit.[41] Concern for the community should be paramount; all members of the Church must seek to make the needs of others their own.[42] Unfortunately, these principles have not always prevailed and are not always

---

[39] The modern world curiously wishes to drive wedges between dyads (two units regarded as a pair) that should in fact exist and/or work together. We see this in the desire for absolute separation between Church and State, and also in the separation between body and soul, or between the Law and the Spirit. All of these pairs work together, yet so often, contemporary thought seeks to separate them. The result, an attempt at codification and control, instead yields confusion.

[40] See *LG*, especially Chapter 1.

[41] See *LG* 39-42.

[42] See Rom 12.

manifest in the Church today. People in authority too often lord that authority over others in direct violation of Christ's command,[43] rather than acting as servants and shepherds. Christ gave us an example of servant leadership,[44] yet too often people are consumed with the maintenance of power instead. While the Church is indeed a nuptial covenant established by God, the institution is necessarily made up of sinful human beings. After all, there is no other kind! This humble observation is a cogent reminder of the limits of human authority and must foster a gracious appeal for God's love and mercy.

Gaudium et Spes literally translates as "joy and hope." This is the promise that Christianity offers to society. And our society certainly seems to be in need of joy and hope! Around the world, there is sadness and despair. Can Christians change the world? We must believe this. We must believe that our lives can be witness to joy and hope as an antidote to the poison that has seeped into our social and political discourse. But this will require our efforts, inspired and directed always by God's grace, grounded in His promise. The foundational principles articulated here certainly and obviously do not exhaust the richness of Christian social ethics. They are only intended as a beginning. Some people may even find these principles to be so cliché as to question their usefulness in an immensely complicated world. However, these principles do actually speak deeply and hopefully to the controversies that exist in contemporary social ethics. They are the tools for allowing the Spirit to give joy and hope to the human race through the medium of Christians living the Gospel sincerely: living the love story.

---

[43] See Mt 20:25-28.

[44] See Jn 13:1-17.

YOU GOTTA HAVE SOUL... YOU GOTTA *BE* SOUL

As has been emphasized throughout this text, the cause of evangelization in the modern world needs both the power of reason and more importantly the witness of lives lived with the "mind of Christ."[45] Such lives will speak to others more profoundly than the best argument ever will, but words help to explain, to help others to make sense of why we do what we do and why we live the way that we do.[46] Given the complexity of some modern issues, understanding them is key to resisting the easy critique against believers that we are simply applying facile principles to difficult situations. However, our progressive understanding needs a starting point: applying the principles articulated herein to the issues considered at the beginning of the chapter.

Many social ethical issues relate to wealth and materialism. Far more than lust, there is no more perennial human example of selfishness than greed, the aggressive desire to acquire more and more. As a result, people are abused on all levels. On the personal level, some are willing to cheat, steal, or just use others in relentless pursuit of acquisition. On the corporate level, companies will often use every means available to them to bend and stretch the civil law in order to protect what they have and to consistently acquire more. On the international level, countries abuse other countries in usurping their resources or even their lands, even waging war to force this injustice. This conflict is invariably given a noble spin in order to mask what is nothing more than an act of armed robbery.

What must be the Christian response? If indeed such oppression "cries to heaven for vengeance,"[47] we must be pre-

[45] See 1 Cor 1:16.

[46] The quote attributed to St. Francis comes to mind here: "Preach the Gospel at all times. Use words if necessary."

[47] See CCC 1867. The new catechism removes the phrase "for vengeance" from the older catechetical tradition.

pared to address this problem of greed and materialism on all levels. On the national level, the Church teaches that faithful Catholics need to use their abilities as participatory citizens to question the motives of those who manipulate other people in the name of national gain. While it may seem to have the least direct effect, this is likely to effect the greatest changes against economic inequality. In a similar vein, we need to be aware of the business practices of the companies we work with, even on a directly personal level (e.g., the places we choose to shop). While it is exceedingly difficult for an outsider to be able to know the whole story behind a company, well-educated consumers and marketplace participants are in the best place to implement Christian justice.

This does not exhaust our personal engagement with issues of economic injustice. To contribute to one's community, financially or otherwise, is merely doing our part for the common good, especially regarding our church communities. Mindfulness of the needs of the others who people our daily lives is itself the spur to aid those whom we have the ability to help. The resources we have are God's gifts of health and wealth to enable us to live our lives in the best possible alignment with the divine call to love. Everything else we have beyond what we need is a reminder of the responsibility we have towards others. Even more so, our own attitude towards our possessions is subject to moral evaluation. To strive to have more at the expense of our obligations to others, including our relationship with God, is gravely sinful and disordered. This is a question that must be answered by all people, and the answer becomes increasingly more difficult when one has more.[48]

The death penalty speaks to humankind's need for justice: there is a certain inherent (if primitive) logic in the notion that if someone kills someone else, the killer's own life is forfeit. Even

---

[48] One need only recall the story of Jesus and the rich young man in Mt 19.

Moses in the Old Testament taught Israel the idea of an "eye for an eye." There is somewhat debatable evidence that suggests that the death penalty may be a deterrent against violent crime. This thinly veils a blood-thirst for revenge. Less hypocritical, perhaps, is the "pocketbook argument": that the death penalty encourages economic justice because it is cheaper to kill a prisoner than to house one for his or her natural lifespan. Even the Church in the Dark Ages conceded a philosophical construct in defense of the death penalty based on a social conception of the moral principle of totality. The argument stated that if a person represented a threat to the common good of society, that person thereby forfeited his or her rights to live in society, and therefore just authority could kill that person.[49]

The counterpoints to these arguments are many, but the Christian can focus on one in particular: how does exercising the authority to kill someone, no matter how heinous their actions, demonstrate our own commitment to the sacredness of human life, let alone the call to love one another? What authority can "authorize" so direct a violation of God's sovereign rights? "Even in the murderer, the image of God cannot be effaced."[50] Based on all that has been said regarding medical ethics and the inestimable value of life and the incomparable dignity of the human person, how can one possibly consent to the deliberate killing of another?[51] This is the most important question that must be answered before someone could ever consent to the execution of another. After this, other counterpoints can be made. How should one determine whether "just authority" exists? How can one conclude that God grants human beings authority over the

---

[49] Compare this to Jesus' response to capital punishment in Jn 8:1-11.

[50] John Jacob Raub, *Who Told You That You Were Naked?* (New York: Crossroad, 1992).

[51] Many people in the Church presently refer to this as the consistent ethic of life, the idea that life should be protected from conception until natural death, thus encompassing the issues of abortion, euthanasia, and capital punishment.

life and death of other human beings? Can merely economic considerations determine the value of a human person's life? While there is — as mentioned above — evidence within the Church's own moral tradition in support of capital punishment, a broader investigation of the issue from the point of view of the sanctity of all life supercedes abstract logical argumentation.

The issue of having the authority to kill one another also brings up the issue of war. The Christian tradition has had a curious relationship with war and the military. From the beginning, we see both Jesus and John the Baptist specifically not criticizing the military life, even though both Jesus' and Paul's teaching emphasized love of enemies.[52] In the early Church, due to the connection with paganism and murder in war, Christians were forbidden to participate in the military. Then with Constantine's baptism of secular imperial values in the 4th century, the notion of a Christian soldier became acceptable, even common. Up until that time, the universal motto for those seeking baptism was invariably *Christianus sum, non possum militare*, "I am a Christian, I cannot fight." But from Constantine forward, the notion of Christian soldiers and Christians waging war continued for a long time, spawning the so-called "just war" theory and the idea of using armed force to serve the cause of "evangelization." While pacifist ideals (e.g., monasticism, the Quakers, etc.) always existed alongside these views throughout the centuries, it was arguably not until the advent of the massive destructive power of late 20th century weaponry that Christian tradition more adamantly re-emphasized its pacifist stance.[53]

What is the appropriate Christian assessment of war in the modern world then? Does one ignore the tradition of Christian philosophy in support of armed conflict in some circumstances, given its theoretical "last resort" status? Or does one instead

---

[52] See Lk 3:14 and Mt 8:4-13.

[53] This is especially so in the writings of John Paul II. See, for example, *Evangelium Vitae*.

embrace a pacifist stance, which some would accuse of ignoring the complexity of military violence in the 21st century?

The first approach makes an appeal to the *just war theory*. This set of principles suggests that, while war is always a social evil, there may be very specific circumstances in which the defense of the common good can permit war as a means. On the personal level, this is justification for self-defense (of one's person or of those for whom he or she is responsible), never aggression. In the wider sphere, specific principles are invoked to first determine whether it is morally permissible for a government to declare war. These principles are particularly stringent and hold war to always be a last resort. There is also a second set of principles invoked that determines "moral conduct" in the course of warfare.[54] Regarding the specific action of soldiers killing one another, which on the surface seems to so directly violate the fundamental principle of moral law, "Do not kill," a distinction is made according to this theory. Soldiers serving in an official capacity for their government who kill other soldiers (not civilians or non-combatants) are theoretically engaging in a qualitatively different action than, for example, murder. The soldiers are representatives of the governments at war, "extensions" of their influence, if you will.

Of course, the pacifist counterpoint to this is that a human person can never be merely an extension of an abstract body. Furthermore, critics of the just war theory point out that this aspect of tradition does not coincide with what has been revealed in Scripture. Those critics also accuse the theory of being a philosophical defense for the selfish desires of nation states.

---

[54] Details of these principles can be found in *CCC* 2307-2317. These principles have also become part of the lexicon of secular moral philosophy regarding war. Other sources for description and commentary are readily available. Modern thinkers reflecting on just war theory are now also considering a third set of principles articulating how a victorious nation is to act justly towards the defeated after the war is over. See Kenneth R. Himes, O.F.M., "Intervention, Just War, and U.S. National Security," *Theological Studies* 65:1 (March 2004), 141-157. See especially pp. 154-156 for a survey of thought over the past 10 years.

How should one determine a Christian approach to issues of war? Due to human sinfulness, both approaches must be considered. War can never be deemed a good, nor can it be used as a legitimate means of improving social conditions on its own. The ends can never justify the means in even valid moral aims. Furthermore, it must always be considered a last resort when all other alternatives have been tried and failed. All that being said, however, "As long as the danger of war persists and there is no international authority with the necessary competence and power, governments cannot be denied the right of lawful self-defense, once all peace efforts have failed."[55] Soldiers in these situations should see themselves as "custodians of the security and freedom of their fellow countrymen."[56] Unavoidable war can seem to be a regrettable aspect of the human condition. Christians, for their part, must try to minimize the evil as much as they are able to do according to their lot in life. But more importantly, Christ leaves us no alternative but to strive heroically for a world without war. This is more than empty idealism; this is confidence in the power of God's grace to bring about His Kingdom in our midst.

Turning to a different matter, there is also a loud political battle going on in developed Western society: the debate over whether homosexual persons should be allowed to marry. Addressing this issue requires us to recall what was said about both marriage and the morality of homosexual acts in Chapter Five. These observations must be combined with the principles articulated in this chapter in order to arrive at appropriate conclusions to this question.

Marriage as a concept serves the common good of society. At its most basic level, it contributes to society on account of providing society with new members. However, while this may be

[55] *GS* 79.

[56] Ibid.

marriage's fundamental function, it is easily demonstrable that, technically speaking, marriage is not necessary in the modern world for new people to be born into it. Thus, while marriage is intrinsically tied to the concept of children, marriage is also about more than just children. It is also about the relationship of two people giving their lives to one another and creating an environment that is best suited for the upbringing and education of children. Because of this, society has a vested interest in protecting valid marriage, as it ultimately protects the health and well-being of society as a whole.

As noted in the beginning of this chapter, this is not the concept of marriage that prevails in the developed West today. Marriage has become little more than a public (and ultimately temporary) commitment of one's sexual rights to another, more or less bound up in an affective commitment of greater or lesser depth. Understood in this way, it makes perfect sense to allow anyone to "marry," whether heterosexual or homosexual. In fact, with so loose a definition of marriage, there are really no rational grounds to forbid "marriage" between more than two people, or between family members, or between a person and an animal, or even a person and an inanimate object.

Marriage is either an objective reality or it is not. Society has been successfully structured on a standard and traditional definition of marriage. To disrupt this definition is to invite catastrophic disruption into society as a whole. As noted in Chapter Four, the understanding of what it means to be man and woman is necessarily complementary. Evidence of this is borne out by biology, psychology, anecdote, and social mores throughout history. The inevitable consequences of re-defining marriage, of eliminating the intrinsic primacy of this complementary relationship, will include a weakening of all human relationships, not just marital unions. How will society, either on the level of law or simply on the level of interpersonal relationship, understand its priorities? Who will have the moral right to bear and raise children? How could a state fairly decide who possesses this right? If this right is open to all, how will the proper education and rearing of children be secured?[57]

Even the compromise of recognizing such relationships as civil unions rather than as marriages fails to adequately address these concerns. If a civil union provides all the social benefits of marriage, maintaining the term "marriage" solely as a mark of honor for couples able to have children, how is this any more than a semantic difference? Homosexual persons seeking marriage likewise have reason to be unsatisfied with civil unions, as it ultimately fails to provide the complete social equality they seek, even though this social equality is based on disordered presuppositions about happiness.

In a similar way, heterosexual married couples have particular reason to be concerned about the prospect of homosexual marriage becoming an equivalent relationship under law. What reason would heterosexual persons have to marry? The law would no longer respect their unique contribution to society: children. Society would no longer respect their unique witness to love in complementary relationship. Homosexual "marriage" is an anomaly and would inevitably undermine the contribution and witness of heterosexual married love.

Despite the grave threats to society that an open redefinition of marriage poses, this cannot be an excuse to ignore the pain experienced by homosexual persons in their desire for social recognition of their love. Even less can their desire for full social equality ever be grounds for oppression and discrimination. But marriage is neither possible nor a valid vehicle to attain these just goals. The nature of committed love and marriage is fundamentally important to humankind and to the realization of true humanity. It is a great gift that God has provided, an

---

[57] Proponents of recognizing civil marriage or civil unions might accuse their opponents of being "chicken little," hypothesizing worst-case scenarios that may or will never come to pass. However, preliminary evidence to the contrary can already be seen in countries in which homosexual "marriage" has been permitted for some time, such as in Sweden and Norway. See Stanley Kurtz, "The End of Marriage in Scandinavia," *Weekly Standard* 9:20 (February 2, 2004).

image of the Covenant love He has for us. It is intrinsic to us as persons made in God's Image to want to share our lives with one another. Therefore, any discussion about the re-definition of marriage cannot remain solely a matter of politics and/or intellectual debate. It is not an abstract hypothetical, but rather an issue impinging ultimately on the life of every member of society.

The seriousness of this leads to the necessary approach one must take on this issue in order to promote the cause of evangelization. First, we must love one another. We must recognize the pain suffered by the homosexual person and by others incapable of marital union for any other physical or emotional reason. It is our duty to share their suffering with them. Only in a context of relationship ordered to human nature, in which genuine charity and sincere respect for persons made in God's image is operative, can a rational appeal to the truth have any hope to make sense. In this loving appeal, society can be improved and the authentic rights of all members of the community can be respected.

So many of the questions addressed in this chapter run into the broad — even if contrived — controversy over the relationship between Church and State, a very popular argument. Some would say that the role of politics in the modern era (and the post-modern era) is not to legislate morality, that the role of the Church in society must be limited to an expression that is no more valid than any other opinion. In fact, "church" opinion does not even enjoy this diminutive acceptance. It is held as even less valuable, even contemptible by some, as it is disdained for its basis in the "irrationality" of faith.

In terms of evangelization, this is an instance where an appeal to transcendent truth, while ultimately critical for a proper understanding of ourselves, must yield to the more common ground of an appeal to reason. Catholic thought has always been a matter of *fides et ratio*, of both faith and reason. Therefore, in explaining the prophetic role of the Church in society, one need not appeal directly to Scripture or Tradition. Rather, one needs to demonstrate that the social critique offered by the Church is grounded in a reasonable understanding of history and human experience. Reflection on both of these concepts demonstrates the grounding of Christian social ethics and is the heart of evangelization.

In the inevitable conflict with the post-modern obsession with radical subjectivity, however, more will be needed. Someone will say that just because things were thus and so in the past, or just because many people are so oriented, why should that be grounding for future societies? Where is the room for evolution in thought that could hypothetically yield an even better society? A full response to this requires an appeal against relativism in particular and subjectivism overall; this goes well beyond what can be covered here.[58] However, a beginning of a response can be found in charitable dialogue between disparate schools of thought: *Why* is a more "traditional" view no longer valid? *Why* does a "new" view, contrary to Christian revelation, better reflect the truth of the human person? The purpose of this dialogue is to strip away arguments over particulars in order to arrive at the core of the truth as revealed by God in Christ. When these truths come to light, the possibility of a more direct evangelization is revealed.

Unfortunately, circumstances and events within the Church sometimes do tremendous damage to its ability to function as a prophetic voice. The controversy in the United States over clergy sexual abuse is such an event. Many people point to this perceived rampant sexual abuse as an indicator that the Church's voice is compromised at best, completely irrelevant at worst. Unfortunately, the facts overall do not permit the possibility of a triumphalistic defense of the Church. Persons responsible as shepherds of God's people were guilty of perpetuating patterns

---

[58] The struggle against relativism in particular is a key aspect of the contemporary work of Pope Benedict XVI. This can be noted, for example, in his homily for Pope John Paul II's funeral.

of abuse by men who themselves were supposed to be acting as servants to the Church community.[59] Attempts to address the problem were done in a manner that was often too little, too late, or too enthusiastic about the wrong elements of the situation, such as removing accused priests from ministry without due process. Maintenance of power and control trumped the responsibility Christ gave the shepherds to care for His people.

Admitting the failings of the Church in this regard, however, is not to say that the Church has lost its right to serve in a prophetic capacity. The Church remains a divine institution, the Body of Christ, guided by the Spirit. The actions of any members of the Church, no matter how heinous, do not invalidate the value of the Church itself. Human sin cannot silence the voice of God present in the hearts of the faithful. Nor can media hype make any dereliction greater than God's power to heal it and set it right.

Furthermore, an honest evaluation of the facts is needed: for every member of the clergy trumpeted in the media as a sexual predator, there are literally thousands of clerics heroically living out their vocation with no more fanfare than the occasional recognition by their own congregations for their service to God and His people.[60] To say that the Church can no longer function as a critic of modern society because of the failings of some of its members reveals an agenda of hypocrisy. It was in *disobedience* to Christ and His Church that these crimes were committed.

All the challenges presented by the complexity of the modern world are ultimately little more than an echo of the ancient love story still being told throughout human history. God continues to relentlessly extend His Heart and calls to us in deepest love. His boundless desire is to give Himself to us, if we would

---

[59] For a fair and balanced account of the scandal, see Mark S. Massa, S.J., *Anti-Catholicism in America: The Last Acceptable Prejudice* (New York: Crossroad Publishing Company, 2003), 165-192.

[60] See "Ten Myths About Priestly Pedophilia," *Crisis* Magazine E-Letter, 2002.

but let Him. And our response is far too often to define ourselves apart from Him, to continue to remain trapped in the illusion of our false selves, our comfort zones that demand nothing of us. These false selves are introduced into our relationships, replacing true love, a free gift of the self to the other, with a mutual self-absorption masked as trust, respect, or affection for another.

This failure in our interpersonal relationships can't help but finally have an effect on society. If we are trapped in the illusion of our false selves, this composite of comfortable lies abdicates our responsibility to be transformed in Christ. We bring this false self into the public arena with inevitable results. A society that protests that it is "seeking the common good," that it seeks to maintain the dignity and human rights of all its members, but which in fact acts from self-interest and self-preservation, is nothing more than a series of power plays in polite tension. The love story demands more from us.

Christians have a unique role to play in this context, more than simply active, participatory members of society, more than merely sophisticates thoughtfully engaged with the issues of our time. We are called to be the very soul of the world, its vivifying presence. An anonymous early Christian document, a letter to one Diognetus, explains it this way: "To put it simply: What the soul is in the body, that Christians are in the world. The soul is dispersed through all the members of the body, and Christians are scattered through all the cities of the world. The soul dwells in the body, but does not belong to the body, and Christians dwell in the world, but do not belong to the world."[61] While we must always rest in hope that our final destination, our eternal destiny, exists beyond the limitations of this world, we can never forsake the truth that the Kingdom of God is here among us.[62] As subjects of so great a King, we must work to build up that kingdom here and now.[63]

---

[61] *Letter to Diognetus* 6:1-3.

[62] See Mk 1:15.

Perhaps even more than the circumstances presented in the previous two chapters, the issues raised by questions of social ethics have the greatest effect on the greatest number of people. In the most serious of circumstances, these issues literally mean life and death for some people. With such high stakes, and with so great a calling in Christ to bring about the transformation of the world, evangelization in this broad area of morality is critical. The avenues of evangelization are many. First and foremost, there is "grassroots" cultural transformation which occurs by the witness of our lives, to the faith, hope and love brought about by God's grace. Second, our active participation as citizens through the political process furthers the Gospel message through the secular "process." Third, we can appeal to the truth revealed in love through rational explanation, both with explicit reference to the divine origin of this truth, and by appeals to a purely "natural" reason. Our efforts may seem to have little effect, but our trust in the power of the Holy Spirit will not go unrewarded.

Throughout this book, we have considered circumstances in the modern world, as well as some philosophical and ideological underpinnings of those circumstances which spawn our contemporary moral confusion. In each chapter, the context has broadened and the effect on our relationships and the number of relationships affected has increased. At many times, living the love story seems to be a daunting task. How can one find the strength to participate in not only the transformation of self in Christ, but also the transformation of the whole world? Where can one find the confidence to trust that our best efforts are not still hindered by the rationalized self-interest of our false selves? How do we prevent our desire to live the love story from becoming little more than a righteous crusade, fueled by lofty ideals,

---

[63] Augustine's seminal work, *The City of God,* posits two co-existing cities: the City of God and the City of Man. All belong to the worldly City of Man, but Christians are also citizens of the City of God.

but lacking in love? We must constantly return to the Source. We need to be fed by the One who empowers our actions with His grace, who molds our characters to be like His own, who provides His Spirit to lead us into happy and healthy relationships. We will conclude our reflections with food for the journey.

...And I Will Go to the Altar of God: Ritual, Worship, and Morality

We have come to the end of our exploration of the relationship between moral theology and evangelization, probing the implications of living the love story in a variety of situations. Yet, just as with the Gospel itself, the "ending" is really a beginning of a living out of the vision made clearer and more compelling by the teaching contained therein. Were this simply a denominational perspective, it would have to take its place among other philosophies. However, this vision engenders a way of thinking the Church has always understood as having a different origin than other perspectives: the Heart of God who has written human fulfillment into the hearts of His people. Hence there is no attempt here to cover every moral possibility in human society, still less an attempt to command the reader *what* to think (as though that were possible) but to share the living experience of God's mind in the Christian tradition for those who sincerely seek to live His will. Basic to every idea discussed herein is that there must always be a relationship, not just between persons, but also between rational explanation of the Christian ethos and the example of lives lived consistently and concretely according to the fundamental call to love and be loved. Only this potent union can serve to navigate the complex intellectual and affective climate of the modern (and post-modern) world. Indeed, no one would deny that the demands this places on the individual believer are occasionally extraordinary. While "the times are never so bad that a good man cannot live in them,"[1] human society in general and the Church in particular has always felt the need for the support of a community in order to persevere in our task. We need to be wildly dependent on God's grace, which is, of course, the only possible impetus to success in the building up of the Kingdom Jesus died and rose to establish and which He animates still by that same grace. The Christian instinctively recognizes, therefore, the necessary relationship between morality and liturgy.

In order to better understand this relationship, we need to consider the more abstract categories of ritual and worship and how they relate to Liturgy properly so-called, in order to consider the effect of liturgy on the moral growth of those who actively participate in it. Armed with this boundless source of grace in the Liturgy, the constant presence of God dwelling in our midst, all the principles, arguments, and concepts contained throughout this text find their true meaning: living the love story.

Looking Behind the Curtain

While this book does not purport to be a work on scientific anthropology, it is important to explain the meaning of two related categories of human activity: ritual and worship. Each in their own way constitutes a series of actions in which all humans engage, because of universal human need, albeit often in vastly different formats. The core meaning behind these actions, however, is a conscious or unconscious quest to plumb the deepest questions of human existence for possible answers. What is the meaning of life? What is the meaning of death? Why am I here? How should I live my life? All human beings seek the answers to these questions and, in one way or another, all human beings use ritual and worship in order to reach that goal.

[1] Attributed to St. Thomas More.

Let's consider ritual activity first. By "ritual," one refers to the decision to engage in specific actions consistently in order to provide structure to one's life, a specific part of one's life, or access to an intuited presence or value. Furthermore, there is usually (though not always) a community dimension to ritual. A group of people share some form of self-identification as a community and therefore enact the same actions over and over again as an affirmation of their identity.

Ritual, by this definition, can be seen clearly in the lives of adolescents and young adults. Through common interests, social cliques, and especially sports teams and the sub-cultures that accompany certain lifestyles and musical styles, ritual activities are enacted. These activities serve to strengthen common identity and the bonds that exist between the members of the group. This can be a two-edged sword; ritual connections can lead some young people to identify with authentically human values, or conversely, they can lead other young people to identify instead with criminal activity through gangs or even cultic activity in fringe religion.

Other forms of ritual activity are evident in the lives of adults. Many of these ritual activities can seem superfluous at first, such as the dedication shown to particular professional sports teams in the form of styles of dress, chants, and even superstitious behavior aimed at providing the team with "luck." Some adult ritual activities also demonstrate a more "mature" solemnity: the signs of commitment made to various charitable and fraternal organizations, or the attitude one takes towards national symbols such as the flag, or actions taken, for instance, during the performance of a national anthem.

What is the importance of these rituals? On the surface, even those practiced with the greatest reverence often seem to be of little practical importance for day-to-day life. But that is part of the very nature of ritual, its practical "uselessness," and this conclusion belies the subtle significance of the rituals. Ritual action does more than simply provide structure to one's life. It also provides structure and access to the *meaning* of one's life. Ritual activity speaks to who we are as individuals, how we identify ourselves, and what we consider to be important. Add to this the unique character of ritual as somehow originating outside of oneself from a "higher plane." Furthermore, as noted above, there is often an explicit community element to ritual. This leads one to ritual self-identification as a member of a specific community. The ritual activity provides a social necessity, a meaning for our lives because through it we know that we *belong*. Even a ritual activity that does not have a specifically communitarian aspect to it, or that might even be enacted specifically as "anti-community" in some way, provides important meaning by its iconoclasm. Thus, the importance of ritual is in how it provides tools for self-identification, and then serves to reinforce that identity.

On the other hand, some might say that they personally do not engage in any ritual activity of the type described here. While it seems that it would be the rare individual who does not at least indirectly identify him- or herself with some particular group of persons (family, club membership, etc.) or ideas (political, religious, ethical) which provoke a ritual response, such a person does in fact exist. But even in these situations, ritual remains in the patterns of behavior found in everyday actions as mundane as hygiene, household chores, recreation, and seasonal activities. If one were to doubt the value of these patterns as formal ritual activity, one simply needs to observe what happens when one attempts to abandon them. Inevitably, new rituals will take their place.

Worship, another specific category of human action, sets itself apart by being even more distinctive from other categories of action. Here, I am appealing to a very broad, very abstract definition of "worship": an individual or community's conscious reflection on and affirmation of the transcendent character of reality. Ritual is necessary to worship because this reality exists beyond our "everyday" perceptions. Worship focuses on how those reflections and affirmations impact how we understand ourselves and others.

Using this definition of worship, anytime an individual raises his or her thoughts to the notion that there must be something "more" to human life and then concludes that that something "more" demands a response, he or she has engaged in an act of worship broadly understood. By the same definition, when a person prays to a God of their own understanding in the privacy of their room, or when a person muses that the universe may be a benevolent place after all, or when a community gathers in a church to sing their praises to God, these are all acts of worship. Worship is the perceptible act which responds to the unseen "sacred." Even the misguided belief that the endless acquisition of material possessions can produce lasting happiness is a form of worship.

Like ritual activity, then, all human beings engage in some act of worship. It is in the very nature of the human person to do so.[2] The value of ritual activity is to express the meaning of human action and to strengthen bonds of community. Worship serves a similar purpose. Through acts of worship, the individual acknowledges the presence of something beyond him- or herself; one recognizes that, no matter how radically self-centered one is, the universe is a bigger place than the person alone.[3] Furthermore, this conclusion demands a response. How one worships, what one worships, whom one worships, will determine how one lives his or her life. Thus, there is a more direct corollary between the triad of ritual, worship, and action, or more clearly stated, worship and morality.[4]

This connection between worship and morality is some-

---

[2] The Church even affirms this very fact in *GS* 21.

[3] This does not rule out the possibility of a sincere attempt to literally worship one's self. In such a case, one makes one's self the god of their own universe and acts accordingly. While we have rightfully reflected on the "worship of self" as a lasting problem contributing to our modern crisis in morality, a radical self-worship according to the terms being discussed here would be nothing less than a psychosis, an utter breaking from reality. After all, such an individual would be positing nothing less than the fact that the universe is literally all about him or her, and that he or she was the cause of all that is.

[4] Jesus says, "Where your treasure is, there also will your heart be" (Mt 6:21).

times subtle and sometimes explicit. For example, reflecting on the beauty and wonder of the natural world can be an act of worship, but how does that affect one's morality? One can speculate that this act of worship translates into a respect for nature, a concern for ecology and responsible stewardship, and perhaps even a respect for other people as a part of nature. On the other hand, Christian worship (in whatever form one wishes to consider it: personal or communal) has at its core a more direct connection to morality. By recognizing the dominion of Christ, by recognizing the presence of Christ active in one's life, specific moral conclusions present themselves.

These two special categories of human activity, ritual and worship, provide similar but distinct benefits to human beings. Each of them provides a glimpse behind the curtain of our everyday lives, providing meaning for our actions and a sense of value in what we believe to be most important. Of course, in order for ritual and worship to be most effective in forming us as human persons, these actions need to correspond to the truth about the human person as revealed by God, an objective truth. Hence, this is not an appeal to a subjective sense of God, but rather to an encounter with the "really real." This unique opportunity is identified by Catholics in the Covenant of Word and Sacrament, the very identity of the Church.

Returning Home to Find Yourself

Many Catholics remain unaware of the tremendous gift we have in the Liturgy, which provides for us the best elements of ritual action and worship, but with critical differences that surpass the limitations of these concepts in the abstract. Before considering why the Liturgy is so important for the topic of this book, we need to understand what the Liturgy is. The perspective of the categories discussed above is a good place to start, enhanced then with the wisdom of the Church to which this great gift has been entrusted. Liturgy consists of the celebration of all the Sacraments, the sanctification of time in the Liturgy of the Hours, and those celebrations of human events we cherish in the light of God's love. Most Catholics find their most common experience of Liturgy in the Mass, the source and summit of the Church's life.[5]

The Mass is obviously a ritual action to anyone who has ever witnessed or participated in it, whether in a solemn "High Mass" or in the informality of an intimate Eucharist offered for a local prayer group gathered in someone's home. This ritual provides consistency with the worship of all those who have gone before us throughout 2,000 years of the Church gathered at prayer everywhere in the world. We are confident that we share one experience, the one Sacrifice of Christ forever and everywhere saving His people. Furthermore, this ritual strengthens the bond of community that we share with one another. In both of the above examples of the Mass, despite being very different, the Church makes the Eucharist and the Eucharist makes the Church. It is not inappropriate to say that no aspect of the Church's whole tradition unites us in the way that the Liturgy does.

The Mass, as an act of worship, centers the whole ritual action, constitutes our reflection on God's love for us, and is particularly centered on the Eucharist. In the experience of the Eucharist, the gathered community not only shares a sense of the presence of God, which springs from a common identity in Baptism, a communal solidarity. It also actually experiences God Himself, literally taking in and being taken into the Divine in order to effect a transformation in each member of the community, receiving Sacrament to become Sacrament to the world.[6] This transformation serves two purposes: first, it empowers each individual member of the community, now "become Christ," to go and *be* Christ for all those whom he or she encounters. Secondly, it unites the community as literally one body, the one Body of

---

[5] See *Sacrosanctum Concilium* 10.

[6] See *SC* 59.

Christ. So the Liturgy as an act of worship broadly understood not only gives one a sense of the divine with an invitation to respond. It actually brings one into the presence of the living God and, as the roots of the word "Mass" (*missa*) imply, sends him or her away to mirror that Presence in daily life.

The Council Fathers at Vatican II wrote, "The Liturgy is... the outstanding means by which the faithful can express in their lives, and manifest to others, the mystery of Christ and the real nature of the true Church."[7] This definition affirms what was said above about the communitarian nature and value of the Liturgy as a ritual act of worship. However, the Liturgy clearly is about more than just ritual or worship. Rather than being a mere reflection on the transcendent God, the Liturgy is a movement beyond the here and now. It is "making way" here and now for the presence of eternity. In the Liturgy, our prayers are joined to all those who have gone before us who worship still and we realize (i.e., make real) the very act that we celebrate.[8]

This means that the Mass is more than just a "commemoration" of the Last Supper, and it is certainly more than just a memorial of Christ's saving action for us. Instead, "Christian liturgy not only recalls the events that saved us but actualizes them, makes them present. The Paschal mystery of Christ is celebrated, not repeated. It is the celebrations that are repeated, and in each celebration there is an outpouring of the Holy Spirit that makes the unique mystery present."[9] Thus, the Mass is a ritual act of worship that transcends our own limitations of time. It is not the "re-sacrifice" of Christ on the Cross,[10] but the eternal saving power and reality of that act made present for the community at that very moment of worship. It is through "conscious, active,

---

[7] *SC* 2.

[8] This makes sense through the Church's teaching on the communion of saints. The Church at prayer involves the action not just of the local community, or even of the whole Church on earth, but rather the prayers of the whole Church that has preceded us, i.e., those who even now are enjoying the presence of God.

[9] *CCC* 1104.

[10] This is a commonly held misconception by non-Catholic Christians.

and fruitful"[11] participation in the Liturgy that the faithful "can express in their lives, and manifest to others, the mystery of Christ and the real nature of the true Church."[12]

Before more clearly establishing the link between Liturgy and morality, it is important to be very clear what is occurring in the Liturgy. More than just ritual, more than just well-intentioned worship, the Liturgy is a participation in the priestly action of Christ Himself.[13] In the community's participation as the one Body of Christ, they make real the saving action of Christ for the world. Their specific communion with Christ in the Eucharist divinizes them, transforms them. The members of the community are now empowered to be Christ for others, not in some purely metaphorical sense of bringing Christ to others or being Christ-like for others, but in the sacramental sense of actually *being* Christ for others. What an awesome gift! What an awesome responsibility!

It is this gift and responsibility that brings these reflections on the Liturgy back to the realm of morality. It is all too common in the modern world for well-meaning but ill-informed Christians to make a dichotomy between superficial worship on Sunday, and their behavior the rest of the week. This sharp distinction is often highlighted by admonition in theology classes and homilies, often enough to prove that some people fail to understand this problem. Others do acknowledge this dichotomy and compensate, re-committing themselves to doing "more" during the week to express their faith, often in the form of trying to be nicer to other people, praying a little more often, and thinking more about the people in the world less fortunate than themselves. There is absolutely nothing wrong with any of this. Yet clearly one must admit that even all this put together is a far cry from the divine transformation described above! Surely,

---

[11] See *SC* 11 and *CCC* 1071.

[12] *SC* 2.

[13] See *SC* 7.

we know that Christ incarnate in the hungry, sick, and poor demands more of *us* as Christ incarnate in the modern world than to be "nice people" who think positive thoughts about those who are suffering!

Perhaps, then, we need other language to understand this transformation, to clarify the link between Liturgy and morality. The interpersonal relationship that is the Trinity is a perfect community of love. There exists an eternal love story between the Father and the Son and the Holy Spirit, between God and His Word in the perfect Energy of Love. As the Father loves the Son, the Son loves the Father and the love that the Father and the Son have for one another is the third Person, the Holy Spirit. Therefore, their love is made manifest in a living, real way.

In the fullness of time, the Word of the Father became incarnate among us by the power of the Holy Spirit.[14] In becoming one of us, He gave us the possibility to become children of God, through the power of that same Holy Spirit.[15] As we are God's children now through the Eucharist, we also participate in that same love story in an infinite and perfect way, even though our human capacity to understand this is limited. It is exciting and empowering that, even given this limited understanding, we are in some vital and personal way part of the love story that is the Most Holy Trinity! However, what we do understand gives us a certain "response-ability." In the transformation we undergo incorporating us into the Body of Christ, Son of the Father, we experience the power of the Holy Spirit to "make all things new."[16] This wisdom helps us realize that we must try to love as the Father and the Son love, such that those we come in contact with must realize the love of the Holy Spirit present in us, present *for* them. To be saved is to take this transformation seriously and act accordingly.

---

[14] See Heb 1 and Jn 1.

[15] Jn 1:12-13.

[16] See Ps 104, especially 104:30, and Rv 21:5.

Is this too remote or too abstract to integrate into our lives? The Church's tradition has a principle that can help us understand the link between Liturgy and morality. From ancient times, the Church has always insisted *lex orandi, lex credendi*: "As the Church prays, so she also believes." This means that the prayer of the Church reflects what the Church believes.[17] In fact, the adage puts a primacy on the role of worship in helping to define what we believe as Christians. So how does this translate into the relationship between Liturgy and morality? The same principle can be applied to each of us as individual believers. Do our actions reflect the way that we pray? Do our actions reflect the fact that we pray at all?

Simply put, those who participate more actively and more often in liturgy also have an easier time understanding morality, as well as greater ease in living the love story out in their own lives as a result. On the other hand, those who do not participate actively in the Liturgy, or worse, do not participate often or at all, have a harder time witnessing to the truth of the Christian moral tradition and a harder time integrating it into their own lives. How can one expect to make sense of the moral teaching of the Church if one lacks the relationship with God that liturgy engenders and sustains?

For those who would claim that the Mass is not necessary for worship, that one can worship Christ just as well in the privacy of one's home or one's heart, one must wrestle with the words of Christ in this regard. At the Last Supper, in the institution of the Eucharist, He said, "Do this as a remembrance of me."[18] In the Bread of Life discourse, He said, "If you do not eat the flesh of the Son of Man and drink His blood, you have no life in you."[19] While it is true that one can worship God outside

---

[17] This can even be seen in Paul's letter to the Colossians. After explaining how they are to live, he tells them to worship. See Col 3:5-17.

[18] Lk 22:19.

[19] Jn 6:53.

the confines of the Mass, such worship is additional, as there can be no substitute for the effect of the Mass on the way that we live our lives.

Our moral lives are contingent on our lives of worship. The action of worship itself demonstrates our desire to celebrate our love for God, our desire to affirm one another as a community of believers, and a desire to make God's love present in the world around us. The decision to participate in Liturgy reflects on our characters, demonstrating what kind of people we are and especially what kind of people we wish to become. And most importantly, the Liturgy is the most intimate expression of our relationship with God, the place in which our union with God is realized and deepened. As a result of all these truths, the person actively engaged in the Liturgy is better prepared for good actions, to demonstrate good character, and to form good relationships with others. To fail to take the Liturgy seriously is to fail in our attempts to live good moral lives. We will also fail in our task of evangelization.

Based on these implications, some ideas readily suggest themselves for improvement in living the love story, first and foremost, to improve participation in the Liturgy. At its most basic, this means attendance! But merely coming to Mass and going through the motions (quite literally) will have little lasting effect on us. Christians must come to understand the Church's prayer as our prayer. We must listen attentively to God speaking to us through the Scriptures, and we must engage the homilist in his attempt to impart some practical wisdom to us.

The entire Mass is one act of worship, not merely a collection of parts,[20] which comes to its climax in the Eucharistic sacrifice and communion. In this prayer, the mystery of our redemption is made real before us — not in signs or memorial only, but vividly real before us. In our celebrity-drenched culture, it is startling to note how few people rush to kneel before the

[20] See CCC 136.

very presence of God among us, present in the Eucharist![21] It is here, then, that we can be especially active in the action of the Liturgy. We are called to worship, offering our prayers, our very lives, to Christ.[22] Our attentiveness to prayer here is especially important. And with Christ's presence among us, we receive Him into ourselves, becoming one Body of Christ in unity. The line to receive communion should be approached with the reverent solemnity it deserves, yet so rarely receives. Some gesture of this reverence and adoration before taking communion reminds us of the majesty of the King before us.

The action of the Mass also does not end with the final dismissal. Fortified by the Holy Spirit in Word and Sacrament, the members of the Body of Christ are sent out into the world to be Christ for others. The Mass as an action must continue beyond the doors of the Church, to impact our lives until the next time we participate in the Mass. And we should certainly participate as often as we are able! What possible reason could we have to not be in the presence of our Beloved? We need to always return home to the Liturgy, where we ultimately find ourselves, a people who image the One present there.

Today is the Day

In concluding our reflections on living the love story, let's summarize the lessons learned along the way. We began with two stories: the story of the modern world and the love story. Both of these stories are familiar to us, but oftentimes the story of the modern world, the very origin of the pernicious illusions that we surround ourselves with, seems more "real" to us than the true story of God's love for us. We have to know both stories because, for better or worse, both of them define who we are as

[21] See *CCC* 1373-1381.

[22] See *LG* 10.

people. The goal of evangelization, then, in terms of these two stories, is to minimize the damage caused by one, and bring forth the healing and happiness promised in the other. In order to effect this, we make an appeal to both mind and heart.

The appeal to the mind began in the abstract with three foundational principles for moral theology: action, character, and relationship. Action and character are related concepts. Our actions demonstrate what kind of character we have, and in turn, our character should determine what kind of actions we take. The two exist in relationship with one another, each influencing the other. The interplay between these two concepts produces an effect on the third principle, the most important of the three. The actions that we take, the character that we demonstrate, reveal the quality of the relationships that we have with others, with ourselves, and most importantly, with God. God initiates the relationship with us; we are called to respond to His love in the many relationships of our lives.

The chapters of this text record many ways in which we respond to His love for us in the myriad circumstances of our lives. In order to respond authentically, we have to know what it means to be a person created in the Image of God, even though as human persons, this also means that we are created with male bodies and female bodies. Being in the Image of God provides an irreducible dignity to us from the very moment of our coming into existence. Being male and female reveals that we are called to live in right relationship with one another. Being a body means that we experience the whole of the love story through the medium of that body; *What we do in our bodies matters!* It does have an effect on us as persons. Because of all of these truths, we realize that no human being can ever be thrown away or treated as an object or mere resource, but rather each must be treated as a person created in love and for love.

More specific ramifications of this principle were highlighted in the areas of sexual ethics, medical ethics, and social ethics. Within the intimate interpersonal relationships covered by sexual ethics, respect for persons was made manifest most specifically in an understanding of the unique form of human relationship called marriage. While marriage encompasses the raising of a family and the sharing of love and self-donation between two people, it also specifically images the love of Christ for His Church. As married people make this love known to the world, the relationships of unmarried people, and the relationships of married people with anyone else, reflect God's love in other ways that also do justice to it. The world loves more truly, more really, because of the good example of faithful married persons.

Our unique nature as body-persons engenders special concerns in the realm of medical ethics. We can never lose sight of respect for life and the dignity of the person in questions of medicine, even when other strong motives vie for our attention. Therefore, a person can never be reduced to their perceived value in someone else's eyes, or their usefulness to society, or even to the individual's own definition of "quality of life." It is the Creator who establishes our inestimable value as persons made in His Image, and decisions about the beginning, maintenance, and end of life must be evaluated according to that dignity.

The principles and conclusions articulated in terms of both sexual ethics and medical ethics have special resonance in the field of social ethics. Social ethics, while often deemed less interesting or less provocative than the other two categories, is actually most important of all. Aside from personal issues such as the way we must treat one another in our day-to-day lives, social ethics encompasses nothing less than the principles that guide the community towards building up the Kingdom of God. Whether in politics, economic policy, concern for justice for all, or the relationship between nation-states, our ability to recognize that we have been called to love as a community, that no one stands alone, will make the difference between the ultimate success or failure of the project of civilization.

Before entering the Promised Land, Moses spoke to the

nation of Israel at great length. He was trying to impart to them the critical importance of fidelity to the covenant between Yahweh and the people. Fidelity is not about following a set of rules because God ordained them from on high as an abstract set of prescriptions, but rather about the people experiencing the fullness of life as God intends. Moses says to them, "I set before you here, this day, a blessing and a curse: a blessing for obeying the commandments of the Lord, your God, which I enjoin on you today; a curse if you do not obey the commandments of the Lord, your God, but turn aside from the way I ordain for you today, to follow other gods, whom you have not known."[23] Three times in these verses, Moses explains that *today* is the day to turn away from our other gods and *today* is the day to obey the commandments. And the purpose of following the commandments is not a slavish adherence to rules, but rather in order to participate in a blessing. We now understand that that blessing is participation in the love story, a participation that will never end. This passage demands a response from us just as it did for the Israelites on the border of Canaan: today each of us is offered the opportunity to live in relationship with God, as He desires to live with each of us. Or we can continue to be enslaved by "other gods," those illusions that tell us that we don't need God, that the world will get by without Him, that His values are somehow obsolete. A brief look at the track record of history demonstrates what our answer must be as believers.

All of the reflections on the lived experience of the love story throughout this book lead to the concluding theme offered in this chapter: our love must lead to reverence and worship. Our love should lead us to offer some token that demonstrates our response to God's call, albeit infinitely insufficient in comparison to His gift to us. In this, we recognize the critical relationship between our active, involved participation in the Liturgy and our moral development as people in love with the God who has saved us.

---

[23] Dt 11:26-28.

At this point, let's return to the love story as described in Chapter Two. There is a fulfillment to the story (not an end) that hasn't yet been described. In the fullness of time, God came among us as one of us, in order that we might learn how to live. When the Son returned to the Father, He sent us a Gift that would enable us to actually put into practice that which He taught us: the Holy Spirit, the very living and active presence of God among us.[24] So then where is this story leading? What happens next? At the end of time, Christ will return to us in the same way that He left,[25] to fulfill His promise of eternal life for all those who have lived the love story. He will judge the nations and the thoughts of all will be made clear.[26] Isn't talk of judgment and revelation contrary to a "love story," like the story of a wedding that ends with one of the spouses saying, "Now, for the rest of our lives together, I'm going to judge the quality of your love for me"? Many Christians who are living loving, holy, human lives live in fear of death and/or the end of time (whichever comes first!). But this is based on a mistaken notion of judgment as "unloving."

Let's continue using the example of the spouses mentioned above. There is a natural, reasonable expectation that spouses will love one another and, in various ways, that they will demonstrate that love for one another. However, suppose this were not the case. Suppose one of the spouses did something that distinctly demonstrated a lack of love for the other. This could be as grievous and explicit as adultery or as simply insidious as one spouse taking the other for granted and never really showing love and affection for the other. In either case, shouldn't the offended spouse have recourse to call on the beloved to explain him- or herself? Isn't an explanation the very least that the offending spouse owes the other? And if love is to survive and

[24] See Jn 16:5-14.

[25] Ac 1:11.

[26] See Mt 25:31-46 and Lk 8:17. See also Lk 2:35.

thrive, if the offender seeks sincere forgiveness, shouldn't the spouse thereby extend mercy? Such is the case also with our divine Beloved. God's judgment is not about punishing wrongdoing, but rather calling us to account for what we do love. In His boundless love, God will permit us to love what we wish, even if it's not Him. And in His mercy, He will extend mercy to us when we ask for forgiveness for the ways in which we have failed in our relationship with Him.[27] But that same love does not impose upon God to ignore justice. The covenant relationship is a reciprocal relationship. This also means that those who actively strive to live out the love story should strive to love even more, so as to avoid fear of judgment, for perfect love casts out all fear.[28]

In Chapter Two, the love story was also described in terms of the Covenant. By its very nature, covenant requires a relationship. Our covenant relationship with God then becomes the model for all other relationships, with loved ones and family, with friends, and even just with people we meet. The call to love knows no exceptions. Even our relationship with ourselves requires us to love ourselves. The primacy of love in Christian morality is a foundational principle for all questions of morality.[29] The complexity of many moral situations in the modern world, however, can cause us to distrust this extremely general principle. So we invoke additional avenues of wisdom to arrive at Truth. The call to love remains. The call to be for others remains. The call to be one Body of Christ remains. For all these reasons, the emphasis favors relationships as a principle, while not ignoring action and character. As the love story leads us to encounter God in worship, that encounter must then lead us back out to continue to love in all of our relationships.

---

[27] And God's mercy far surpasses all human mercies. See Lk 11:11-13.

[28] 1 Jn 4:18.

[29] Mt 22:37-40.

PERFECTED IN FIRE

One last element of Jesus' teaching deserves consideration at the end of these reflections. In the Sermon on the Mount, Jesus announces, "In a word, you must be made perfect as your heavenly Father is perfect."[30] What a tall order! God calls us to holiness, to be nothing less than perfect as He is Himself! An honest appraisal of our lives even at the best of times would reveal that this is nigh impossible. But note that Jesus says that we must be *made* perfect. This is not something that we can do on our own. Fortunately, Jesus also tells us how we might be made perfect: "If you seek perfection, go, sell your possessions, and give to the poor. You will then have treasure in heaven. Afterward, come back and follow me."[31] Many of us might empathize with the response of the rich young man with whom Jesus was speaking: he went away sad because of his many possessions.

Given Jesus' concern over the dangers of greed in general and the context of the conversation specifically, there can be no doubt that Jesus meant the words exactly as He said them: to divest ourselves of those things that we don't need and give to the poor, as discussed in Chapter Seven. Perhaps we can apply an additional layer of meaning to this statement of Christ's. What else besides material things constitutes our possessions? Does it not also include our false images of ourselves, our selfish attitudes, our opinions that we hold so highly as to pretend that they are objectively true? Does it not also include our selfish use of time, our reservation of warmth and affection only for those we like, our prejudices about those we've never even met? Jesus is demanding that if we would be perfect that we must get rid of all of these "possessions" as well.

Jesus then says that we must give to the poor. Obviously, we can and should give of our material goods, but does true love end there? Is not Christian love, *agape*, about the gift of self to another? Therefore, we must give to the poor of our time, our

---

[30] Mt 5:48.

[31] Mt 19:21.

attention, our prayers, our love. And who are the poor? Considering sinful humanity in the sight of a just God, are we not all poor before Him? Jesus is then demanding that if we would be perfect, fulfilled, complete, then we must give of ourselves in love to others. In doing this, He promises us treasure in heaven.

To turn from our self-will and follow the example of Christ's love in all of our relationships is the key to the promised treasure. In turn, the surety of having "treasure in heaven" will effect a clear transformation in us here on earth. This transformation goes beyond our thoughts, beyond our direction in life, beyond the things we hold to be important; it is more than all of these. This transformation is *theosis*, divinization, becoming God-like. The Holy Spirit, the passionate fire of God's love remains operative in the world, especially through the love we share with one another. With the Spirit active within us, that same fire burns away all that keeps us from loving others and provides light and life for the whole world. In the sayings of the desert fathers, Abba Joseph told one of his young charges, "If you will, you can become all flame."[32] This wisdom coincides well with Jesus' fervent prayer, "I have come to light a fire on the earth. How I wish the blaze were ignited!"[33] We have all been baptized to be that blaze of fire on the earth!

Jesus concludes his answer to the rich young man by telling him to come back and follow Him. When we turn away from our old lives, we find new life in Jesus. The joy of this new life is more than can be contained within ourselves; it must be shared with others. This is the impulse to evangelize. But the process of evangelization will never succeed if it remains merely a matter of the mind, of theological speculation. It must be a vital matter of the heart, and others must witness the love that is in us, to evangelize with our very lives. And this is why it is important to not just read the love story, not just study the love story, not just talk about the love story: we must *live* the love story.

---

[32] Quoted in *The Sayings of the Desert Fathers*, trans. Benedicta Ward (Kalamazoo: Cistercian Publications, 1975), 103.

[33] Lk 12:49.

Selected Readings

The following is a small selection of suggested readings for those who would like to learn more about some of the subjects discussed in this text. This is not at all exhaustive; rather, these texts represent a very small selection that I find particularly helpful for a general audience. Additional suggestions for reading can be found in the footnotes throughout the text.

Documents of Vatican II

It is unfortunate that more people don't take the opportunity to read these texts directly. Daunted by the idea that the texts are too dense, Catholics miss the opportunity to really appreciate the meaning of the Church and its place in the complicated modern world. In particular, I would recommend the two constitutions on the Church: *Lumen Gentium* and *Gaudium et Spes*. If you can only read one, read the latter.

The Writings of Pope John Paul II

There is much profit to be gained from reading this pope's voluminous writings. In terms of the subject matter of this book, I would recommend the encyclicals *Veritatis Splendor* and *Evangelium Vitae*. It is also worthwhile to consider the entirety of his *Theology of the Body* (Boston: Pauline Books and Media, 1997). Many people find the style of John Paul II's writing to be challenging. In regard to the *Theology of the Body*, a number of readable summaries are available, such as Christopher West's *Good News About Sex and Marriage* (Cincinnati: Servant Books, 2000).

The Writings of Benedict XVI

At the time of this writing, Pope Benedict XVI has not written nearly as many encyclicals as his predecessor. However, his first, *Deus Caritas Est,* is especially applicable to the themes of this book. Furthermore, Benedict XVI has an extensive body of work as a theologian prior to his election as pontiff. Much of it deals with the relationship of Christianity to the modern world, often in a far more lucid style than the writing of Pope John Paul II.

Other Documents of the Church

There are too many documents worth reading just from the past forty years alone. I will highlight two particular ones here. The first is the *Catechism of the Catholic Church.* This invaluable resource is always an excellent first place to seek an answer to a theological question. Of the dozens of other documents available, I would like to highlight Pope Paul VI's encyclical *Humanae Vitae.* While generally known as the encyclical forbidding "birth control," its vision of married love provides remarkable food for reflection on the Love Story. For additional material, I would recommend the topical essays edited by Janet E. Smith in *Why Humanae Vitae Was Right: A Reader* (San Francisco: Ignatius Press, 1993). I would also recommend Janet E. Smith's excellent book *Humanae Vitae: A Generation Later* (Washington: Catholic University of America Press, 1991), though some might find that text to be confusing in its depth of detail.

Theological Texts

Once again, there are far too many theological texts worth reading, from both contemporary and classical sources. I wish to highlight a few here. I highly recommend a small text, F.J. Sheed's *Theology for Beginners* (Ann Arbor: Servant Books, 1981) for anyone who wishes a simple, elegant primer on Catholic systematic thought. In the field of moral theology, a number of general texts are available, some of which are referenced in the footnotes of the text. For those seeking a more advanced course, one might decide to consider the classical authors of the Church, such as Thomas Aquinas and Augustine, or any of the Fathers of the Church.

Contacting the Author

The author can also be contacted directly through his website, www.ChristopherKlofft.com

Index

This book was produced by ST PAULS/Alba House, the Society of St. Paul, an international religious congregation of priests and brothers dedicated to serving the Church through the communications media.

For information regarding this and associated ministries of the Pauline Family of Congregations, write to the Vocation Director, Society of St. Paul, 2187 Victory Blvd., Staten Island, New York 10314-6603. Phone (718) 982-5709; or E-mail: vocation@stpauls.us or check our internet site, www.vocationoffice.org